AF479385

HE SEN

DAMIANI

Damiani editore
via Zanardi, 376
40131 Bologna
t. +39 051 63 50 805
f. +39 051 63 47 188
www.damianieditore.com

CONCEPT
Primo Giovanni Marella

EDITORIAL COORDINATION
Elisa Tumminello

GRAPHIC DESIGN
Lorenzo Tugnoli

ISBN 978-88-6208-137-5

Printed in March 2010 by Grafiche Damiani, Bologna.

HE SEN
PAINTINGS

DAMIANI

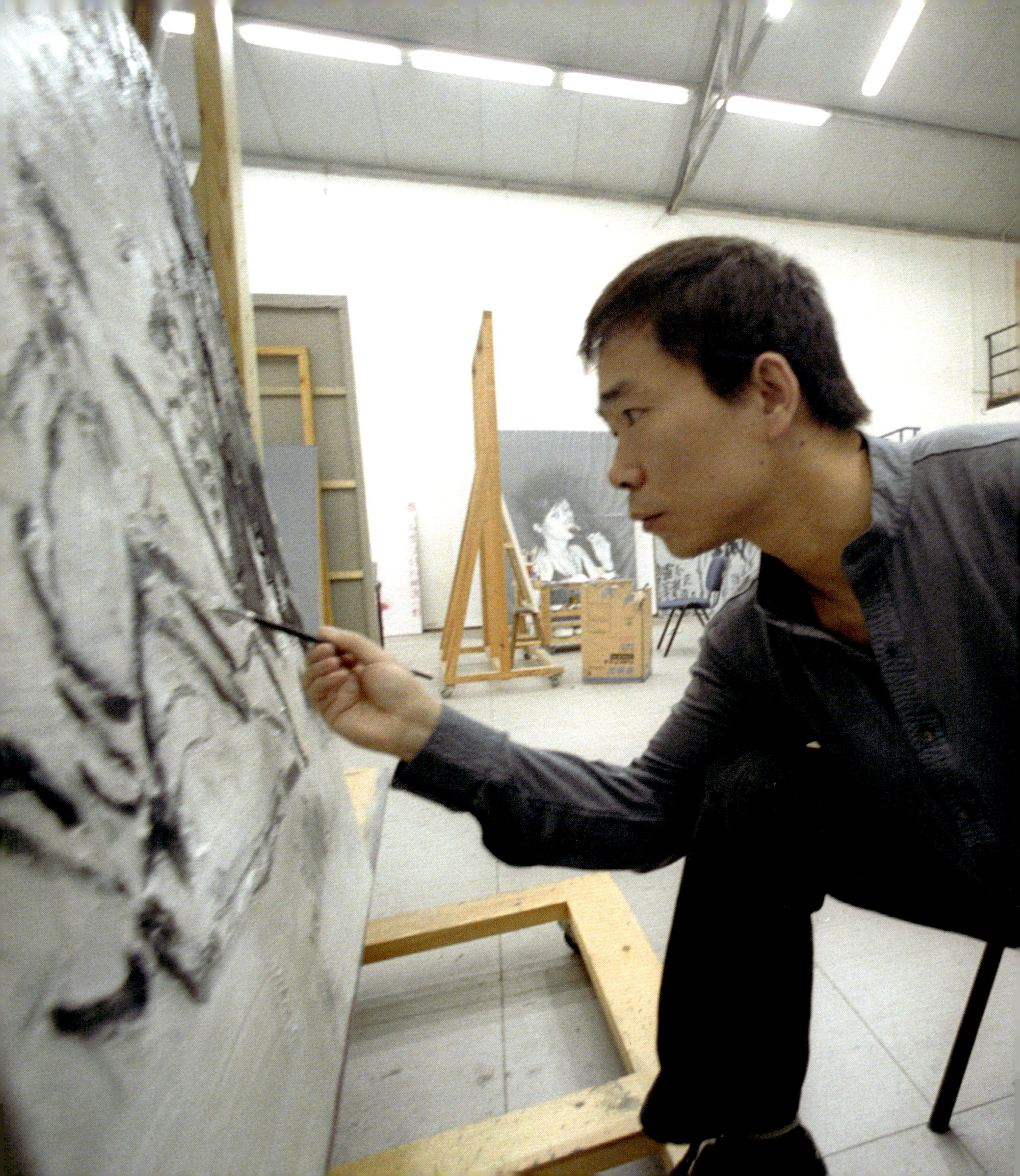

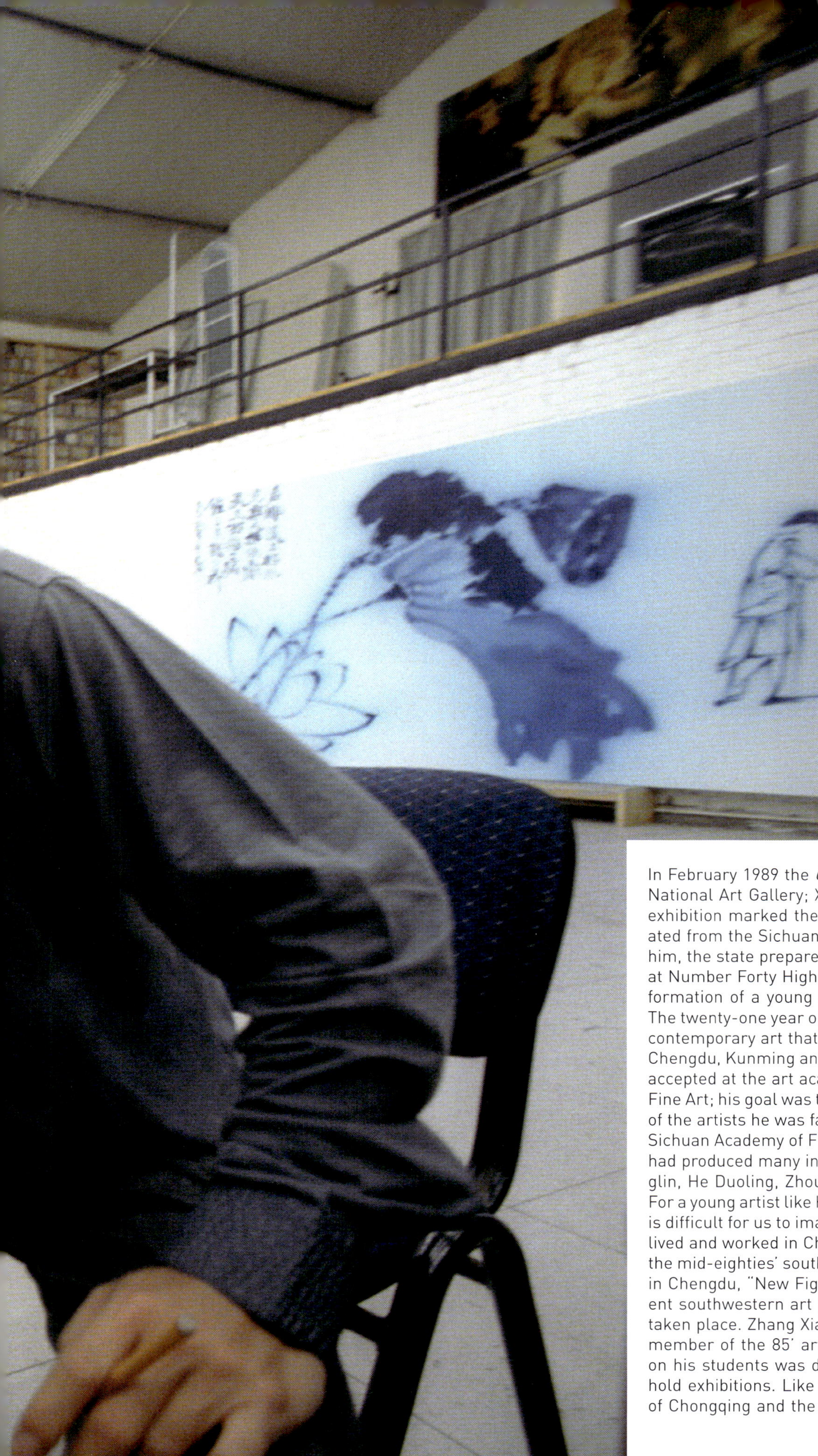

SYMBOLIZING SADNESS AND ISSUES. ON HE SEN'S PAINTING

Lu Peng

In February 1989 the *Chinese Contemporary Art* exhibition opened at the National Art Gallery; Xiao Lu's two gunshots at the chaotic yet energetic exhibition marked the end of art of the eighties. In June, He Sen graduated from the Sichuan Academy of Fine Arts. Like most graduates before him, the state prepared and allocated a position for him as an art teacher at Number Forty High School in Chongqing. It was a crucial period in the formation of a young person's memory and in his ability to understand. The twenty-one year old graduate already had a good understanding of the contemporary art that he had been exposed to in his school, as well as in Chengdu, Kunming and other cities. He now recalls that even before being accepted at the art academy he would often visit the Sichuan Academy of Fine Art; his goal was to acquire exciting information and look at the works of the artists he was familiar with. As he put it, "My reason for applying to Sichuan Academy of Fine Arts was that the graduating class of 77' and 78' had produced many influential artists in China—Luo Zhongli, Cheng Conglin, He Duoling, Zhou Chunya, Zhang Xiaogang—who I respected a lot." For a young artist like He Sen, this background was almost deterministic; it is difficult for us to imagine how He Sen would have turned out if he hadn't lived and worked in Chongqing and Chengdu, or if the 1979's scar art and the mid-eighties' southwestern art activities (The "Red Yellow Blue" group in Chengdu, "New Figurative" group in Kunming, as well as other different southwestern art groups' activities and exhibitions thereafter) hadn't taken place. Zhang Xiaogang was He Sen's professor. As a representative member of the 85' art movement in southwest China, Zhang's influence on his students was direct: he encouraged students to create freely and hold exhibitions. Like the atmosphere resulting from the unique climate of Chongqing and the specific environment provided by the art academy, from the end of the seventies' until the mid to late eighties, contemporary art produced in the southwest region showed great complexity. For example, the re-examination of history began with students of Sichuan Academy of Fine arts – Gao Xiaohua, Cheng Conglin, Luo Zhongli; and direct reflection on the reality of art came from the sensitive artists Zhou Chunya, Zhang Xiaogang, and Ye Yongqing; the understanding of a person's internal loneliness started with Mao Xuhui who had read Sartre, Saul Bellow, Jose. If they weren't classmates, they were friends; because of their understanding of the freedom of art, they became inseparable comrades. For those who long to understand contemporary art, they form an actual and indispensable spiritual resource.

Coming to 1988, the air of reform had been seeping into the streets and alleys for almost ten years, there has no other time as filled with instability and potential as 1988. The contradictions between rapid economic growth and slow change in the reform system became more apparent. The development of market mechanisms in the economy over the previous few years had further destabilized the once established social order. All kinds of disturbing phenomena accompanying the reforms began to emerge: tens of thousands of people from rural areas began to abandon agricultural production and flowed into the large metropolises to pursue their dreams; bankruptcy in some factories, insufficient work and rumors of the possibility of massive and imminent unemployment created fear; incompetent management in the railway system led to a seemingly incessant string of accidents; on university campuses, a spirit of absurdity, indifference, superficiality, dispiritedness, and chaos filled the air; this was accompanied by inflation, a fervor for "toppling officials", and nepotism among officials. All of this caused an unbearable mental burden and psychological pressure. Artists began to focus on the individual, focusing on issues brought about by small changes. In May of 1989, the clash between society and politics came to a boiling point, the reaction of the soul became even more complex.

He Sen's graduation paintings showed a heaviness of visual habit. He maintained the depth and strangeness of space in his *Shattered World*. Obviously, he had been affected by ideas of surrealism; however, in terms of its construction, the strangeness shared similarities with earlier scar art – for instance, the obscurity seems to have been absorbed from Cheng Conglin's *Guards' Morning of Excecution*, and the fear seems to have come from representational paintings such as Zhang Xiaogang's *Sick Bed*. Such influences were certainly subtle and unconscious, yet also natural. The 1985 Movement provided all the resources of modernism; any young individual could have adopted them. These graduation pieces were completed between April and May of 1989, a chaotic and anxious time. However, the sensitivity and focus paid to the state and problems of the individual allowed the artist to control such anxiety within an environment of neglect and exhaustion. The artist offered us a conjectural setting, a space that was perhaps close to his own living environment and habits. However, this space appeared only on "paper", which proves that the artist was unwilling to consider it an actual reality, but rather thought of it as a type of conjecture. In this period (until 1991), another classmate, Shen Xiaotong, was also interested on the effects of "paper", and Guo Wei had also presented similar surreal environments. There was certainly a psychological contradiction, a questioning of one's own living environment. Having left school and stepped into society, He Sen completed many works that revealed similar sentiments: in works like *Still life and People* (1990), he incorporated into his compositions objects that he himself used or was fa-

miliar with in everyday—bags, clothes, cups, ashtrays and cigarette butts of various length. These objects symbolized the chaos of his personal life, having left school and entered into society. In fact, their existence also became evidence for the artist's attention to his personal life and his break away from the pursuit of the essential principles of the 1985 Movement. Until the end of 1991, He Sen used his friends and classmates as objects of representation; but, unlike the scar tradition, these people did not revolve around a problem or goal—even though the compositions are the same, there is no relationship between their facial expressions and actions (*Two on a Chair*, *Joyful Years*, 1991). That is, the psychological details of essentialism were neglected, even though the artist's application of complex brush strokes were a trace of the profound nostalgia for his professor – a nostalgia that couldn't be quickly severed. Whether it was his sentiments that brought forth a new consciousness, or whether it was the effect of a new generation of art, in either case, He Sen's feelings for the reality of this period must have **shared** some similarities with artists in Beijing. In 1996, He Sen told the editor of *Gallery* magazine,

"The series of works between 1991 to 1992 are basically a compilation of personal experience, an accumulation of culture, and a synthesis of many years of undefined urges. I endowed familiar people, friends and personal belongings with sacred meanings. The representational language that I made my own naturally became my spokesperson. In those images, the "close distance" in the unlimited expansion of personal sentiment matches up perfectly with the methods of the "new generation" of artists in Beijing – subsequently categorized as "Pop art" in the Post-89 exhibition. However, in my opinion, the heroic impression and representational language is in contradiction with the attitudes of "Cynical realism". But, apart from a release of personal emotions, these works lack broader social meanings. Thus, in 1993 the only adjustments I made were in my subject matter – for instance, marches presenting a social scene and a symbolic copper bird.

He Sen's self-description reveals similarities with the new generation of artists, he even admits, "apart from a release of personal emotions, these works lack broader social meanings". However, his emphasis on "heroic impressions" demonstrates a preservation of his unique sentiments; and he believed deeply that these sentiments would gain the approval of professors in the southwestern region. In 1992, He Sen painted *Two Artists* based on a photograph of Zhang Xiaogang and Chen Weimin. He Sen applied his brushstrokes with anxiety and used a grayish tone to comprehend his two professors. In the top corner of the work, He Sen wrote, "Setting up a stele and establishing a record of the venerable Zhang and Chen". This shows his respect for professors who disagreed with an attitude of "non-seriousness". Indeed, in *Life Triptych* (1992), even though the subjects have upturned lips, their smiles are forced; in *Centered Landscapes* (1992) the females' smiles are not enough to alleviate the heavy hearts or even anxiety of the men. The artist loves music, he even says that music is "more enriching and energetic than paintings". However, even in his compositions related to music, the "music" we feel is very heavy – this is the soul in the tradition of southwestern artists. Rough and repetitive brushstrokes, towering compositions, as well as the grayish tone mark an obvious distance with the "new generation". This situation is related to the artist's understanding of his experience; an expressionist vocabulary often appears in the painting of artists who feel suppressed or are in actual difficulty. Indeed, in the works of his close friends of this period—Zhang Nengzhi, Yin Ruilin, and Du Xia—anxiety, anonymous violence, and oppression comprise the basic tone of the artworks, even though each applies his own method. Such a phenomenon also explains what led the artist to portray the highly symbolic "copper bird": the chained up bird expressed the artist's helplessness. The reason for the artist's selection of this particular bird is in fact unclear, however, since the he uses heavy strokes and colors, and since he piles a thick layer of material on the image, it would be best to view the bird he painted as a convenient conjecture, it is not a conjecture regarding the ill omens of western mysticism, even less an orientalist auspiciousness, rather, it is merely a record of the state in his life, a kind of diary that when recalled many years later would bring forth sadness and sorrow. After this work, He Sen rediscovered his hope and imagined himself breaking away from the chains and flying away, consciously or not, he created a relationship with society. In his own words:

Thereafter, the experience of being a guest host at a TV station in Chongqing allowed me to personally sense the power of media, adding to this my exaggerated ideals from an earlier period, my rebellion against –isms, in 1994, I painted the *Stage* series. This series was intended to unveil the social reality of contemporary people's conscious or unconscious "acting", as well as the mutual influence of media. At the time, I over emphasized the artist's reaction to his immediate environment. However, just as one's choices become limited when one enters a certain setting, the overly direct and determined model, along with my relatively introverted character, formed a serious contradiction. (*Gallery* Magazine, combined issues of 5, 6, 1996)

Here, the artist has touched on the popular cynical realism and Pop art of this period, as well as the kitsch art that branched off from these two. He Sen's description is real, his introspection makes him accustomed to and interested in flavors of expressionism, but the immediate environment is telling him that the society is undergoing obvious change. *Stage* series is He Sen's break away from an overemphasis on the self, and entry into a period in which he paid greater attention to social change and hoped to more accurately express his feelings. He recognized the problems stemming from "exaggerated idealism" and "ideology", he noticed the endless "sighs" of souls that appeared in the late eighties, he no longer believed that a clamoring for idealism was appropriate or meaningful. On the basis of memories, reality and his particular environment, he built a new stage, microphone, television, media studio as well as memories and street banners. However, no matter how much the artist attempted to present a relaxed and dissipate guise, traces of expressionism and complex composition led viewers to make a connection with recent history – the contemporary nature of "scars" and romanticism. As the new generation's clean and neat compositions became popular, He Sen, living in the city of Chongqing and working in the gray smog and greasy corners of Huangjiaoping, could not truly be involved. This unique environment prevented He Sen and his other friends from using the flat smearing and commercial like manipulation used by artists from the north.

In December 1994, He Sen collaborated with his friends and classmates Yin Ruilin, Chen Wenbo, Du Xia, and Zhao Nengzhi on the exhibition *Slice*. This took place during a particularly difficult time in the lives and work of He Sen and his friends. They put together a very simple exhibition catalogue, not only was the printing of the photographs in black and white, but they were also rather unclear. Yet, in this exhibition catalogue they expressed a sharp and opinionated understanding: in the section entitled "slice selection" they expressed their opinions on art. Yin Ruilin warned, "the colors in our paintings are becoming brighter… it is not a direct re-

lease of emotions and personal sentiments, but being outside the works and narrating in a relatively objective fashion a shared and common inheritance"; Zhao Nengzhi noticed that, "most of our works have elements of documenting and reporting, we are careless and unwilling to clearly show overt criticism or other attitudes"; Chen Wenbo noticed the influence of Pop, although he subtly despised the direct expression in Pop works such as "Mao Amin's Songs". When faced with the influence of popular mass culture, He Sen expressed his an inner complexity, "Everyone knows that what's most contemporary is most direct, for instance popular films all make use of direct and shocking modes of expression. However, the more contemporary people become, the more complex is their psychology; this contrast will certainly become greater, and the inner complexity will become impossible to discard. As we put it into the form of art, we can express such complexity, but the directness will naturally be diminished. This is a contradiction."

Therefore, the rather 'hesitant' psychological state that became dominant in the mid-1990s did not lead toward memorable images and symbols. As the northern painters directly spoke of their boredom and helplessness, He Sen used popular images to warn people that neither stage or actual life were any more real; fabrication itself should be pointed out, however, He Sen seems also to have expressed his attachment to reality:

The amusement of the stage: people can see truth through fabrication.
The danger of the stage: people can see fabrication through truth.
The seriousness of the stage: people can see invincible strength through concise logic.
The safety of the stage: what's played is all unreal.

He Sen's way of thinking came from his professor's tradition, this tradition began with scar art's questioning of history, and later was affected by principles of western essentialist philosophy; up until the first half of the nineties, artists working and living in the southwest maintained their understanding of issues related to reality.

In fact, after 1989, the logic of essentialism had lost its existential reason, people no longer agreed that there existed actual collective issues. A social life produced from unique political events had clearly warned people: there is no actual meaning in the pursuit of truth. Not only can exciting events happen naturally, people can set up a stage at any time and in any place, and act out a moving performance. It is not a matter of being willing or not, if each person does not take on a role and participate in it, it would become worthless. Therefore, the knots and pains in one's heart become insignificant. In the eighties, pain and loneliness became the artists' resource, they became evidence of the necessity of resistance in preserving one's life – this was the common subject expressed by Mao Xuhui and Zhang Xiaogang in the ten years prior to 1992. But, at this moment, such a mental state was being questioned, the relationship between the individual and society was once again being taken seriously. In 1994, Zhang Xiaogang had already painted the mature *Family* series. Mao Xuhui's *Parents* had already evolved into a scissor that moved from dissatisfaction to ease; Ye Yongqing had begun the "graffiti" that brought together a literati attitude; Zhou Chunya, inspired by the ancients, was enamored with studies of the *Rock*… this was an overall change, although compared to the phenomenon in the north, it was a change that had not derailed from its essential track. Nonetheless, He Sen accepted the influence of Pop-art, yet, red flags, merit certificates, red scarf, and all these images are not only borrowed, at the same time is also a documentation of memories and reality. As the artist combined symbolic meanings of politics, history and society, when the artist freely combined different sections, he in fact was involved in resolving historical and actual issues with the "new generation", "cynical realism" and "pop-art". Having been washed by modernism, He Sen's composition is expressive, surreal, collaged, advertising as well as photographic. Naturally, like most southwestern artists, He has kept a vigilant stance toward the entrance of modernism.

The relationship between emotions and rationality is difficult to explain. At the same time, the influence of a region on the artist is not limited to matters of style, the style brought forth by "internality" and "caution." To what extent is it appropriate in terms of the trend? For He Sen this is an issue. Clarity and simplicity allows these images to be distinguished and remembered, even though they're common "kitsch" paintings, they became popular. Such a situation made He Sen anxious, therefore until 1996, He Sen wandered between his expressionism and his hesitant complex world. He focuses on the inside, but he realizes that one's heart is not everything; he is concerned with reality, but he realizes art is not reality; he longs to be acknowledged, but he realizes this is not a genuine artistic problem; how should one deal with all this?

In 1996, Huang Zhuan asked, "since the mid-1990s there has been a trend toward conceptualization in Chinese visual art; what is your opinion of this trend? Do your works have this sort of character or pursuit?"
He Sen answered, "This conceptual tendency provided a new point of entry for figurative artists in their search for a new field after Pop-art and cynical realism. It also benefited from the impact of the stimulating and vibrant installation and performance art movement. If paintings no longer serve as bearers of meaning, they could not stand along side installation art, performance art and video art as authentic media of contemporary art. Such a change reflects a disconnection with the old reaction model. Buy this is only a premise; that is to say, it has already become another beginning, and it is only on this basis that the artist can begin to re-explore and reconsider issues of interest, enabling artistic method and cultural direction to be further emboldened, in which case new artistic strength can be born. Do we still have imagination? That is the premise for an artistic dead-end. I continue to have a lot of work to do on this.

By re-organizing the compositional structure and basic language, I am hoping that painting will no longer remain a simple reaction to the outside world. In my basic language, it is necessary to sort out the more expressionist language from the danger of simply venting my enjoyment, and then setting this into a rational structure, getting rid of visual chaos, not adding meaning through the process of painting and the brushstrokes themselves, or else the origin of the concept would be squandered completely. Here, the presence, typicality and plot have no function; the question is how to minimize relations of inheritance, and make it picturesque. Using expressionist methods to multiply an object several times, reaching a level of refinement at which there will be contradictions with the meaning of this body of language, contradictions with unique spiritual meaning; making ambiguous that which is signified. In the end, that which stands out is the effect, the images; it's no longer simply the dregs of emotional release, rather, meaning is brought under historical observation.

In his answer to this question, He Sen is obviously quite clear about his future work, he genuinely began to interrogate the dangers of accustomed

methods of expression in forming contemporary artworks. He thus entered a new artistic period.

Perhaps there is no great significance to an individual's psychological uniqueness; however, once this uniqueness is transformed into a language, there is the possibility of producing meaning. As early as the 1990 work *Space Inside*, He Sen began placing some ambiguous spots on the upper corner of the background, there is no particular meaning to these spots, rather, they are an effect of the artist's treatment of the piece. Looking at these in terms of psychological exploration, they perhaps could be taken as a display of "complete ignorance". In 1991's *Still life* series and his work on figures, the indistinct clumps produce a tone of melancholy expressionism. What is interesting is that other artists of the same period—Shen Xiaotong, Xin Haizhou, Guo Wei and others—also presented these floating clumps in different forms. Under what kind of circumstances would these ambiguous feelings become a type of language instead of being merely self-initiated presentations? We don't know the particular circumstances, but one day in 1996 He Sen transposed these indistinct masses onto figures; to a certain extent, he kept their "form", however, these masses started to become apparent and rigid, the forms were fossilized, they began to take on the appearance of stone. As the artist became more enamored with this effect, even heads could be seen as a fake stone. Works completed in 1996 are uniformly allusive: they reveal internal contradictions, a realization of the heaviness and necessary response demanded by reality. Among these fossilized works, the subject's daily life is fixed, they might lead us to make a connection with the history of Pompeii, but the stones under He Sen's brushes remind us more easily of Chinese stones. No matter how much effort the artist has made in style or linguistic level, his stylistic tone still leans towards expressionism: complexity, incomprehensibility, serious reasoning. Such a style has clearly extended the distance between He Sen and other artists. Yet, the effect achieved only with special techniques has prevented the artist from clearly conveying his attitude: is it a reliance on modernism, or is it an attempt to truly break away from the entanglement of psychological details? To a great extent, this was a mark of distinction, a watershed pointed to by critics – between modernism and post-modernism – letting the metaphysical individual attitude to be effaced.

On the basis of a "fossilized" aesthetic, the artist began to relax his mood, the complexity of his thoughts gave way to a probing of imagery and interest. Among works done in 1997, rigid objects (including people's heads) suddenly emitted light, in sharp contrast with the lifeless rocks from the past. Who or what was the reason allowing "fossilized" objects to emit light?

What He Sen was truly focusing on were not the rubbish-like "adhesive things", an image that appeared to be carved by a knife was not necessarily what he wished for. What kind of miracle could be created with the techniques and enlightenment accumulated over the years – this question could only be clarified through constant experimentation. If this sort of repetitive manipulation still couldn't make him break away from the details of the past, then perhaps completely discarding this could lead to a new direction. He began to subtract the complexity and the layers of his images; it is unclear which source of light gave the artist a clue, if soft lighting could diminish the complexity of the image and bring forth other possibilities, the artist would have found an effective path for discarding the detail of expressionism. He Sen began to recall his own artistic history, he even returned to the experimentalism of 1990; in works completed in 1998, *Girl biting hands, Wandering, Scream, Self-portrait – Hiding face*, we see a summary of his previous works: a return to "paper", the cleanliness of realism as well as expressive brushwork. However, the artist began to calmly study his compositions, he courageously gave up complex and un-clear content, and reduced his expressive brushwork to a minimum. Light has become a crucial element influencing his composition – especially the abrupt light that made people's eye disappear. This was an era in which digital photography replaced film, free and careless use of the camera be-came possible. It is not important when He Sen began to pay attention to the special effects of lights on images and photographs, especially in situations without specific manipulation, but this provided the artist with important clues. We also are unclear on when He Sen began paying atten-tion to Ritcher's work, but he mentioned that he really enjoyed the art of this German artist. Obviously, the Western artist's experience also served to provide encouragement and inspiration for He Sen's experiments. Over-all, among all the possibilities, He Sen chose the effects of photography, just as Richter once said, "photography once attempted to achieve the effects of paintings, today, works on canvas are beginning to learn from photography." Such an opinion is also supported by Duchamp's observa-tions, images painted in the form of photographs can also be productive of new conceptual compositions. *The girl lying on a sofa* became the earliest bold trial in using photographic effects – completed in 1998, it was a shot without planning, it was a spontaneous flash. Up to 1999, this sort of coin-cidence was of great assistance to He Sen; he completed a large number of works of this type. He completely abandoned expressive methods, and seemed to think that adding coincidental factors onto the canvas directly would be sufficient – this was He Sen's new turning point.

Certainly, unlike other artists who use photographs in their painting, He Sen remains cautious; he has noticed the effects of light, however, by highlighting those effects, and especially highlighting the simplification of forms caused by the flash, he creates a unique mood. Therefore, if we check the photographs He Sen refers to, we discover that the artist relies on the visual inertia led to by the simplification of form to purposefully wipe off the eyes of the human subjects. He Sen once said, "the previ-ous *Accumulation* series took "stone sculpture" as the original inspiration, and stone sculptures have no eyes; thus, when I switched to girls, they also had no eyes". However, in the actual situation, this is not necessarily because when "the flash goes on, people's eyes become undefined", the artist has only appropriated people's visual understanding of the flash's effect – intentionally erasing the eyes. Such manipulation is very impor-tant, because through it He Sen has an opportunity to underscore the fear that has always be present in his heart – this kind of mental state has been directly revealed in expressionism. Now, the artist has added another thought to the images, "the girls in my paintings don't have eyes because I believe there is an unreachable distance between people, making them unable to clearly recognize reality. They are confused, cold, and see reality without actual attention." (*Female Portraits, Social Projection?* Ke Ning, June, 2006)

He Sen has finally discovered an experimental path that he feels comfort-able with, the concept of painting photographs allows him to apply his solid realist techniques and abilities without any obstacles, the subject matter and its content allow him to distance himself from the endless caricatur-ing of "beautiful" subjects. With such conceptual support he has begun an endless representation of girls: their poses are listless and uninter-

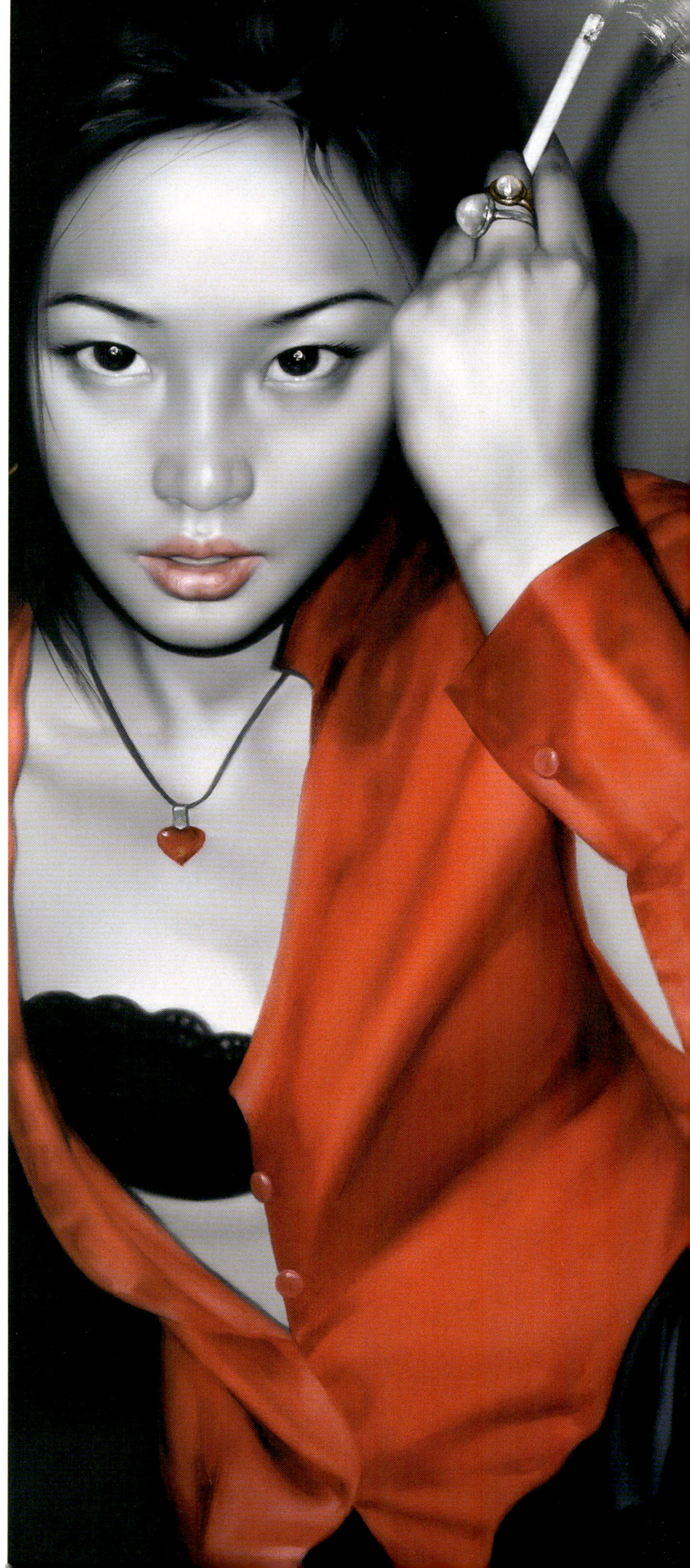

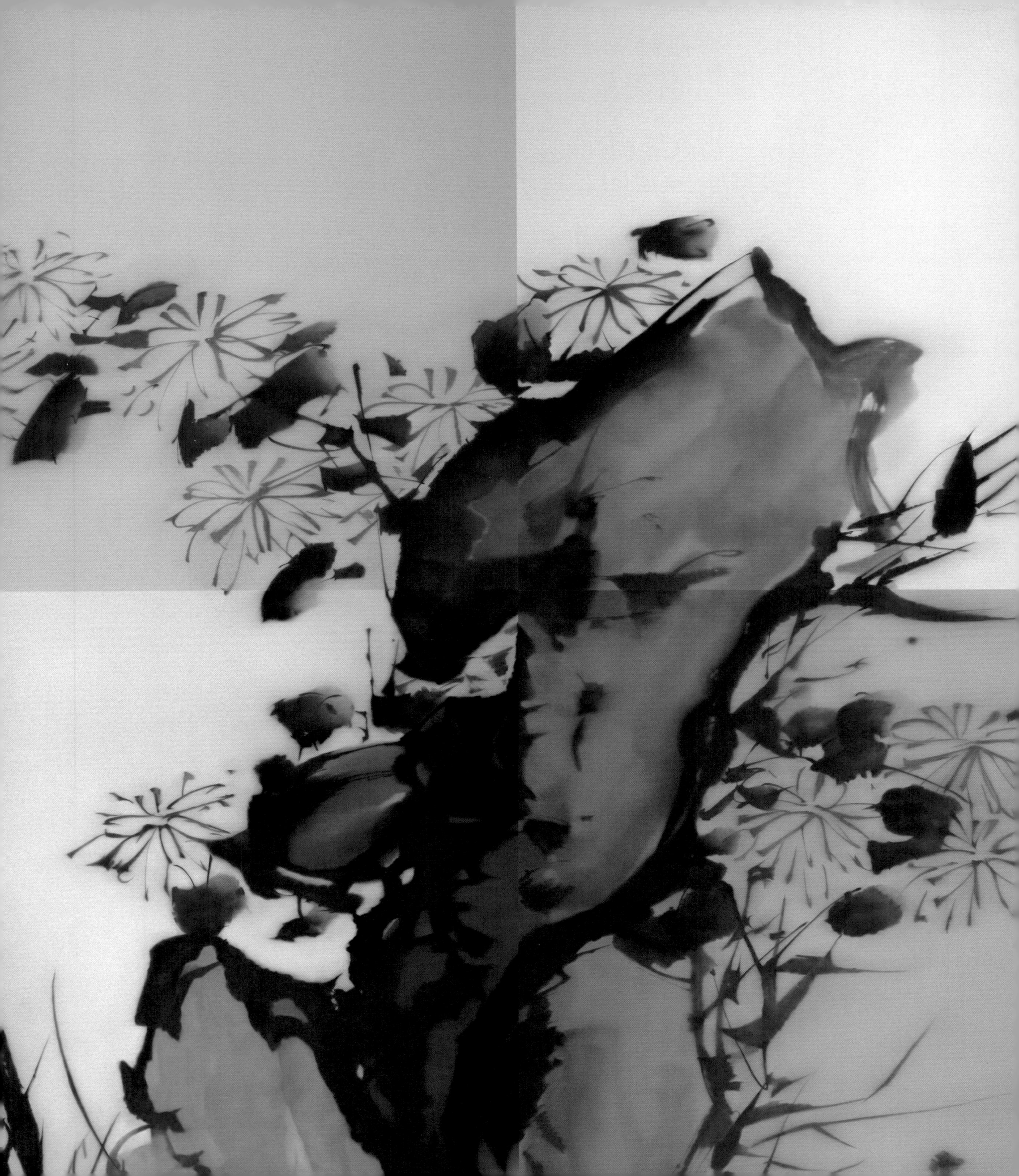

ested, with no particular purpose, even their unwillingness to answer the telephone gives a viewer the impression of an unbearable boredom; they also lack class and elegance in a public setting – all of this is the kind of thing that vulgar and unthinking artists like to represent. Under many circumstances, He Sen's compositions could easily attract voyeurism. At the same time, we notice that even as decorative props have been taken out of the photographs, the artist has kept or added toys which are usually white, on the ground, on sofas or being held by his subjects. When He Sen, answering a critic's probing, explained his reason for using the toys, he said, "Everyone's growth is accompanied by a sense of loss. Like the eyeless girls I paint, as well as the toys on the sofa in a closed space – all convey the emotions of childhood." ("My work is to understand others and myself through art" – interview with He Sen), of course this is a rather personal feeling and understanding. What needs to be emphasized now is that everyone has their own understanding of growth and time, such a fear is relevant to one's aging and the situation of one's path, no matter what the artist's life is like in particular.

In 1999, He Sen moved from Chongqing to Chengdu, he had always longed for the excitement of the Chengdu art world. Most of He Sen's important paintings were done after this year, he realized that his art was moving towards a greater clarity, he needed a new environment and more opportunities. After 2001, women with blinded eyes began to have clear eyes. Based on previous experiments He Sen began to leave subtle hints of sadness on his subjects' faces and bodies – with the abrupt brushstrokes used to accomplish this effect he seems to want to say that even the most bright and shining image or form can be hurt or be a sham. There is no fundamental difference with the artist's previous expressionist attitude, he has only changed his conduit of expression. In the years following, he has fully expressed the life and youth that he understood, all of which were related to time, related to the constant renewed understanding and probing of one's existence. Even though critics have covered up these questions with post-modern vocabularies, the works of the artist still reveal these things.

Women and the world in which we live seem rather similar in appearance, to put it in simple words, girls nowadays are prettier than before, and they seem to get even more beautiful. And the actual society we live in is also more beautiful, architecture and streets are also more beautiful. But our hearts and spirits are far less fulfilled than in the past, and the current beauty and progress is entirely illusion, in fact it is only an empty shell, an appearance covering a void; idealism is gradually diminishing in actual life, and this society is becoming very realistic and cool. (*My work is to get to know others and knowing myself through art – interview with He Sen*)

This is the kind of melancholy that can often be seen among southwestern artists; we can see the same contemporary tragedy in works by Zhang Xiaogang, Mao Xuhui, Zhao Nengzhi, Xin Haizhou, Zhang Xiaotao, Xie Nanxing and others. The time is "beautiful", but this "beauty" is precisely the symbol of degeneration and problems.
Just as a few years earlier He Sen had hopefully moved from Chongqing to Chengdu, in 2003 he moved to Beijing. And in the capital the artist attained the success he had long been hoping for. In the last few years, he has spent a lot of time on this degenerate "beauty", until 2005 when he restarted his reflections on art. Having flipped through many books of images of the past, he has returned to history. He attempts to use the medium of oil painting to express ancient scholar's paintings of birds and

flowers. Does he really want to explore the flavor and tone of the ancient painters? This is obviously not the case. He Sen has even abstracted Ma Yuan's twelve images on water, and dissected areas of his composition, using completely different manners of expression to complete the same piece of work. He Sen uses paintings of the ancient scholars as a given, editing them, not to achieve some kind of visual illusion, but rather to make an observation: when historical images are set in front of us, what should we be thinking? In fact, we saw a conceptual expansion through this difference of representation in composition. As an artist, He Sen is quite familiar with the uniqueness of images in Chinese art history, as many artists use densely ideological images to explicate issues of the contemporary, He Sen has set his inception point even further, he has thrown out allusions to political issues all together, instead he abandons the habit of ideological reflection and political allusion by creating a direct rapport with the ancients. This is the new direction for art in this century, we have already seen the beginning of many sensitive artists' return to history – in Zhou Chunya's peach blossoms and Zeng Fanzhi's landscapes – they have discovered an eternal quality in the works of the ancients, and they have sensed that this path of exploration could perhaps become a distinct contrast with western art and culture. In today's era of accessible global information, looking for genuine originality and uniqueness has once again become an artistic goal; this requires that concepts be combined with sensitivity and that the contemporary be married to history. From the beginning of new art in the eighties to today – thirty years later, besides one's own freedom of awakening, every other concept can be denied. For He Sen, New Art has just begun, but his instincts are healthy, he has already distinguished problems in this conceptual trend - wanton, dexterous to truckling to cynicism.

Obviously, among He Sen's works of different periods, we can sense the artist's early loneliness and his present melancholy. A person spends his early life pursuing something, but when he achieves what he has pursued, he feels new losses: naïve, beautiful and eternal. Ma Yuan's son Ma Lin has a painting titled *Holding a Candle Roaming at Night*, the ambiance of this image is both elegant and classy. At night, candlelight illuminating a garden in full blossom as if it's day, a person sitting in its midst; it is difficult to determine whether this person is enjoying reclusion or feeling a melancholy longing. We know that early 1279 was the last moment of the Song dynasty, before the Mongols invaded Hangzhou the literati all escaped to become recluses, and the quiet in each of their gardens came to an end – these little paintings by Ma Lin and other artists without recorded names of the Southern Song are records of the complexity of their mindset. Similar emotional states might also appear in today's works, in a period of drastic transition, perhaps symbolic melancholy could better remind us of the existing issues. He Sen and other artists have already realized the importance of sympathizing with history, and this is also the crucial characteristic of new art.

Lu Peng

SIMBOLIZZARE TRISTEZZA E PROBLEMATICHE.
LA PITTURA DI HE SEN

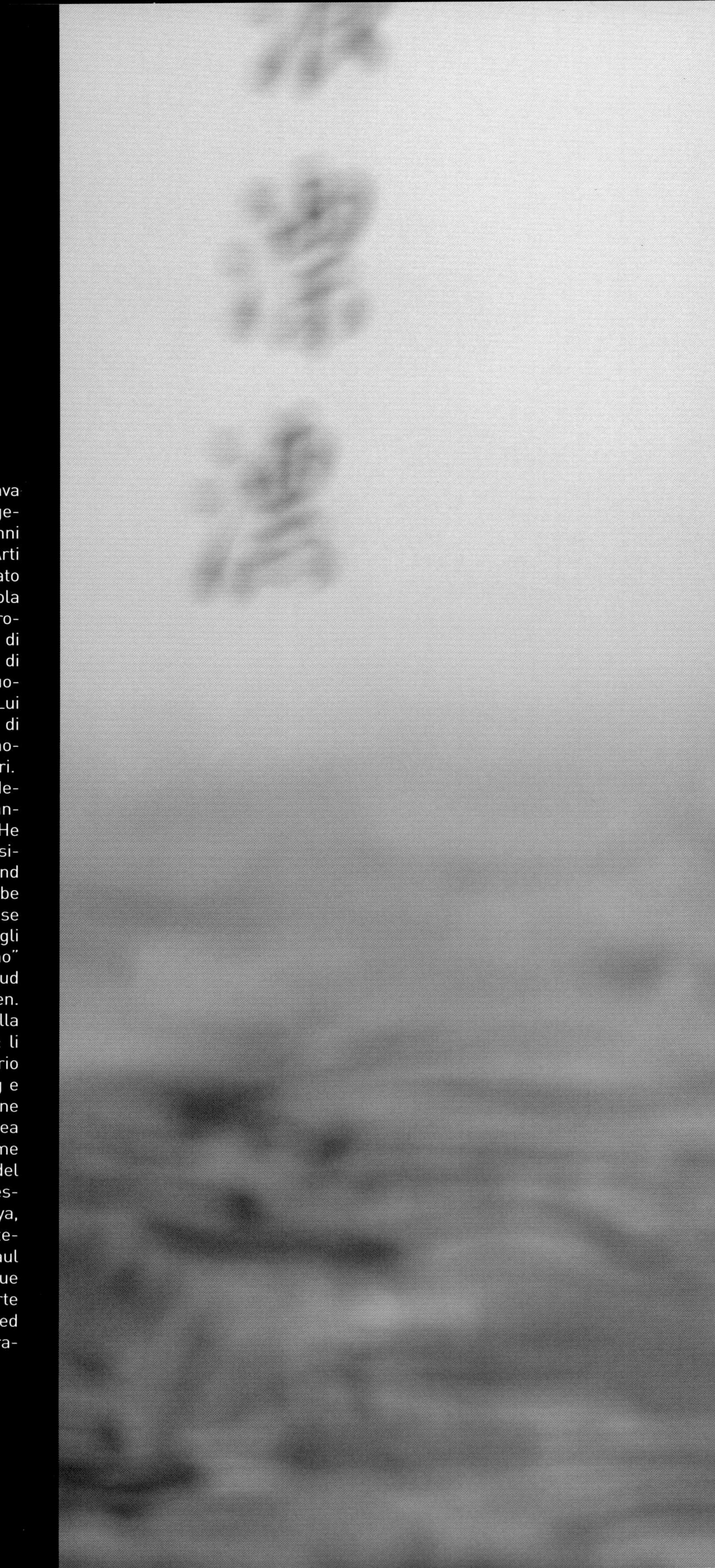

Nel febbraio 1989 la mostra "Arte Contemporanea Cinese" inaugurava alla National Art Gallery; durante l'inaugurazione, già caotica e energetica, i due colpi di pistola di Xiao Lu segnavano la fine dell'arte degli anni `80. Nel mese di giugno, He Sen si diplomava all'Accademia di Belle Arti del Sichuan.Come per la maggior parte dei laureati prima di lui, lo Stato predispose per lui una posizione di insegnante d'arte presso la Scuola Superiore n. 40 di Chongqing. Quello era un momento cruciale nel processo di formazione della memoria del giovane e nella sua capacità di comprensione. Il ventunenne diplomato aveva già una buona capacità di comprendere l'arte contemporanea che gli era stata illustrata a scuola, esattamente come accadeva a Chengdu, Kunming e in altre città. Lui stesso ricorda che fin prima di essere stato ammesso all'Accademia di belle arti del Sichuan, la visitava già spesso, intenzionato ad acquisire nozioni interessanti e guardare le opere degli artisti che gli erano familiari. Come lui stesso afferma: "La ragione per cui mi sono iscritto all'Accademia di Belle arti del Sichuan è che le classi dei laureati nel `77 e `78 hanno prodotto molti artisti influenti in Cina - Luo Zhongli, Cheng Conglin, He Duoling, Zhou Chunya, Zhang Xiaogang - che io tengo in altissima considerazione". Per un giovane artista come He Sen questo tipo di background fu determinante. E' difficile per noi avere un'idea di come He Sen sarebbe diventato se non avesse vissuto e lavorato a Congqing e Chengdu o se la "Scar art" del `79 e l`attivita` artistica del sud ovest nella metà degli anni `80 (il gruppo "Red, Yellow, Blue" di Chengdu, Il "Neofigurativismo" a Kunming così come altre differenti mostre e azioni dei gruppi del sud ovest) non ci fossero state. Zhang Xiaogang fu il professore di He Sen. In quanto uno dei membri rappresentativi del Movimento del `85 nella Cina del sud ovest, l'influenza di Zhang sui suoi studenti fu diretta: li incoraggiava a lavorare liberamente e a partecipare a mostre. Proprio per quell'atmosfera che era il risultato del clima unico di Chongqing e dell'ambiente speciale generato dall'Accademia di Belle arti, dalla fine degli anni `70 fino alla metà e la fine degli anni `80, l'arte contemporanea prodotta nel sud est mostrò grande complessità. Per esempio, il riesame storico ebbe inizio proprio con gli studenti dell'Accademia di belle arti del Sichuan– Gao Xiaohua, Cheng Conglin, Luo Zhongli, mentre una riflessione diretta sulla realtà dell'arte venne dalle sensibilità di Zhou Chunya, Zhang Xiaogang, and Ye Yongqing; la comprensione della solitudine interiore dell'essere umano iniziò con Mao Xuhui che aveva letto Sartre, Saul Bellow, Jose. E se non si trattava di compagni di classe erano comunque amici e proprio grazie alla condivisione del concetto di libertà dell'arte divennero compagni inseparabili. Questi artisti sono una fonte attuale ed indispensabile per tutti coloro che desiderano capire l'arte contemporanea.

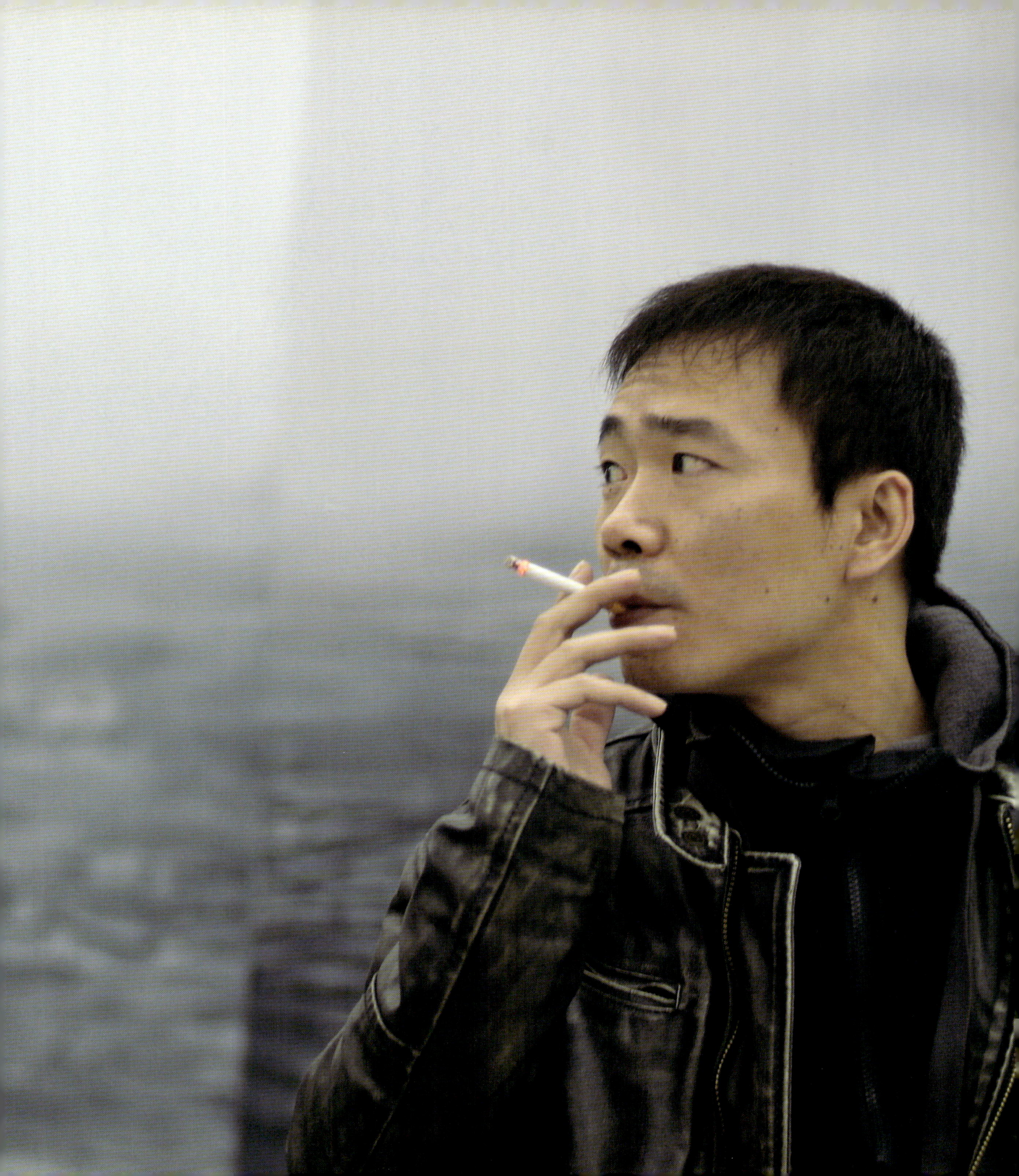

Alla volta del 1988, l'aria di riforma che aveva ormai pervaso le strade e si era infiltrata fin nei vicoli nel corso di quasi dieci anni, faceva di quell'anno un momento pieno di instabilità e di potenziale come mai era avvenuto prima. Le contraddizioni tra la rapida crescita economica e il lento cambiamento del sistema di riforme erano diventate più evidenti. Lo sviluppo dei meccanismi di mercato nell'economia nel corso degli anni precedenti avevano ulteriormente destabilizzato l'ordine sociale stabilito. Iniziarono ad emergere tutti quei tipi di fenomeni inquietanti che accompagnano le riforme: decine di migliaia di persone dalle zone rurali cominciarono ad abbandonare la produzione agricola e a confluire nelle grandi metropoli per perseguire i loro sogni; ci furono fallimenti di alcune fabbriche, il lavoro cominciò a diventare insufficiente e iniziarono a circolare voci sulla possibilità di una massiccia ed imminente ondata di disoccupazione, tutto ciò creava paura. Inoltre una gestione incompetente del sistema ferroviario portò ad una serie apparentemente incessante di incidenti, nei campus universitari un senso di surrealtà, indifferenza, superficialità, scoraggiamento e confusione riempiva l'aria, tutto ciò era accompagnato dall'inflazione, un fervore per "il rovesciamento dei funzionari", e il nepotismo tra i funzionari stessi. Tutto questo portò ad un insostenibile peso mentale e una forte pressione psicologica. Così gli artisti iniziarono a concentrarsi sull'individuo, a focalizzarsi su temi relativi a piccoli accadimenti. Finché, quando nel maggio del 1989, lo scontro tra società e politica arrivò ad un punto di rottura, la reazione si fece ancora più complessa.

I dipinti fatti da He Sen per la sua laurea mostrano una tendenza verso la pesantezza visiva. Mantiene la profondità e lo straniamento dello spazio nel suo "Shattered World". Certamente è stato influenzato dalle idee del Surrealismo, ma per quanto riguarda la sua formazione, lo straniamento sicuramente condivide analogie con la corrente "Scar" dei primi tempi - per esempio, il senso per l'oscurità sembra essere stato assorbito da *"Guards' Morning of Execution"* di Cheng Conglin, e il sentimento di paura sembra provenire da dipinti esemplari come *"Bed Sick "* di Zhang Xiaogang. Tali influenze sono state certamente sottili ed inconsce, ma anche molto naturali. Il Movimento del 1985 stabilì tutte le basi del modernismo; ogni individuo giovane poteva attingere a tali risorse. I lavori di laurea di He Sen sono stati eseguiti tra aprile e maggio del 1989, un periodo di confusione e ansia. Tuttavia, fu proprio tutta la tensione e la concentrazione che bisognava dare alle problematiche dello Stato e degli individui singoli a permettere all'artista di vincolare l'ansia facendola convogliare all'interno di un ambiente di abbandono e di stanchezza. Lo spazio che ci mostra l'artista è uno spazio ipotetico, un ambiente che probabilmente si avvicinava all'ambiente che lui viveva veramente e al quale era abituato. Tuttavia, il fatto che questo spazio compare solo sulla carta, dimostra che l'artista non vuole considerarlo come uno spazio reale, ma piuttosto considerarlo come un'ipotesi possibile. In questo periodo (fino al 1991), anche un altro compagno di classe, Shen Xiaotong, si focalizzò sugli effetti della "carta", e anche Guo Wei aveva presentato simili ambienti surreali. Vi era certo una contraddizione psicologica, una problematica riguardante il proprio ambiente di vita. Dopo aver lasciato la scuola ed essere entrato a tutti gli effetti nella società, He Sen ha portato a termine molte opere che rivelano simili sentimenti: in opere come *Still life and People* (1990), ha incorporato nelle sue composizioni oggetti che egli stesso usava nella sua vita quotidiana: borse, vestiti, tazze, posacenere e mozziconi di sigarette di varie lunghezze. Questi oggetti simboleggiavano il caos della sua vita personale dopo aver lasciato la scuola ed aver varcato il confine con la società. In realtà, la presenza di questi oggetti diventa anche per l'artista il modo per concentrarsi sulla sua vita personale e un sistema per rompere con il perseguimento dei principi fondamentali del Movimento

del 1985. Fino alla fine del 1991, He Sen ha utilizzato i suoi amici e compagni di classe come oggetto di rappresentazione, ma, a differenza della tradizione della corrente "scar", queste persone non ruotano intorno a un problema o a un obiettivo, anche se le composizioni sono le stesse, non vi è alcuna relazione tra le loro espressioni facciali e le azioni (*Two on a Chair, Joyful Years*, 1991).Così i dettagli psicologici tipici dell'Essenzialismo erano trascurati, anche se l'applicazione dell'artista di pennellate complesse era una traccia di nostalgia profonda per il suo professore - una nostalgia che non poteva essere rapidamente risolta. Sia che sia stato il suo sentimento a portare avanti la sua nuova coscienza, o che sia stato l'effetto di una nuova generazione artistica, in entrambi i casi la sensibilità di He Sen per la realtà di questo periodo deve aver avuto molte somiglianze con quella degli artisti di Pechino. Nel 1996, He Sen ha dichiarato all'editore della rivista "Gallery":
"La serie di opere tra il 1991 e 1992 sono sostanzialmente una raccolta di esperienze personali, un accumulo di cultura, e una sintesi di molti anni di bisogni indefiniti. Ho attribuito a persone familiari, amici e oggetti personali significati sacri. Il linguaggio di rappresentazione in cui ho reso il mio linguaggio naturale è diventato il mio portavoce. In quelle immagini, la distanza "stretta" nell'espansione illimitata del sentimento personale è in linea perfettamente con i metodi della "nuova generazione" di artisti a Pechino in seguito classificati come "pop art" dopo la mostra Post-89. Tuttavia, a mio parere, l'impressione eroica e il linguaggio di rappresentazione sono in contraddizione con l'atteggiamento del "realismo cinico". Ma, a parte la comunicazione di emozioni personali, queste opere mancano di più ampi significati sociali. Così, nel 1993, gli unici adeguamenti che ho fatto sono stati nella mia ricerca."

La poetica introspettiva di He Sen rivela analogie con la nuova generazione di artisti, lui stesso aggiunge anche, "oltre all'espressione di emozioni personali, queste opere sono prive di più ampi significati sociali". Tuttavia, la sua enfasi sulla "impressione eroica" dimostra una conservazione dei suoi sentimenti particolari, che credeva fossero valsi per ottenere l'approvazione dei professori nella regione sud-occidentale. Nel 1992, He Sen dipinge *Two Artists* sulla base di una fotografia di Zhang Xiaogang e Chen Weimin. He Sen dipinge freneticamente e usa toni di grigio per rappresentare i suoi due professori. Nell'angolo in alto del quadro, He Sen scrive, "Ponendo una stele e stabilendo un primato per i venerabili Chen e Zhang". Ciò dimostra il suo rispetto per i professori che dissentivano con un atteggiamento di "non serietà". Infatti in *Life Triptych* (1992), anche se i soggetti hanno le labbra inarcate, i loro sorrisi sono costretti, in *Centered Landscapes* (1992) i sorrisi delle donne non sono sufficienti ad alleviare il cuore pesante e l'ansia degli uomini. L'artista ama la musica, dice anche che la musica è "più arricchente ed energica dei dipinti". Tuttavia, anche nelle sue composizioni legate alla musica, la "musica " che vi sentiamo è un elemento molto pesante; questa è l'anima della tradizione degli artisti del sud-ovest. Grezze e ripetitive pennellate, composizioni imponenti, così come toni del grigio marcano una distanza evidente con la "nuova generazione". Questa situazione è legata alla percezione che l'artista ha della sua stessa esperienza, il lessico espressionista appare spesso nella pittura di artisti che si sentono repressi o si trovano in difficoltà reali. Infatti, nelle opere dei suoi amici più stretti di questo periodo - Zhang Nengzhi, Yin Ruilin, e Du Xia – l'ansia, la violenza anonima e un senso di oppressione costituiscono un substrato che sta alla base delle opere, anche se ognuno lo esprime secondo il proprio metodo. Tale fenomeno spiega anche ciò che ha portato l'artista a rappresentare il fortemente simbolico "copper bird": l'uccello incatenato esprime l'impotenza dell'artista. La ragione per la scelta dell'artista di questo uccello particolare è in realtà poco chiara, tuttavia, dal momento che egli usa pennellate e colori pesanti, e che copre con uno spesso strato di pigmento l'immagine, sarebbe meglio considerare l'uccello dipinto come una ipotesi possibile, non è un'allusione al triste presagio della mistica occidentale, tanto meno un richiamo al buon auspicio orientale, piuttosto, si tratta semplicemente di una registrazione dello stato della sua vita, una sorta di diario che, riguardato molti anni dopo, avrebbe portato via la tristezza ed il dolore. Dopo questo lavoro, He Sen riscopre la speranza e immagina di rompere le catene e volare via, consapevolmente o meno, crea un rapporto con la società. Come lui stesso afferma:

"Successivamente l'esperienza di essere un ospite in una stazione TV in Chongqing mi ha permesso di sperimentare di persona il senso del potere dei media, aggiungendo a questo i miei ideali esagerati che appartenevano a un periodo precedente, in linea con la mia ribellione contro gli "ismi", nel 1994, ho dipinto la serie *Stage* . Questa serie era destinata a svelare la realtà sociale della gente contemporanea, consapevole o inconsapevole del proprio "agire", nonché la reciproca influenza dei media. In un primo momento, enfatizzavo la reazione immediata dell'artista al suo ambiente. Tuttavia, proprio come una scelta individuale diventa limitante, quando si penetra una certa struttura, il modello eccessivamente diretto e determinato, aggiunto al mio carattere piuttosto introverso, formavano una grave contraddizione."(Gallery Magazine, saggi combinati di 5, 6, 1996)

Qui l'artista entra in contatto con il realismo cinico popolare e l'arte pop di questo periodo, così come l'arte kitsch che si diramava da queste due correnti. La descrizione di He Sen è verosimile, la sua introspezione lo fa essere avvezzo e incline al gusto espressionista, ma l'ambiente intorno a sé lo richiama immediatamente al fatto che la società sta subendo un cambiamento evidente. La serie *Stage* rappresenta la rottura di He Sen con l'eccessiva enfatizzazione del sé, e l'ingresso in una fase in cui prestare maggiore attenzione ai cambiamenti sociali e il tentativo di esprimere meglio i propri sentimenti. Ha riconosciuto i problemi derivanti da un "esagerato idealismo" e da "l'ideologia", ha notato gli infiniti "singhiozzi" di anime apparse alla fine degli anni Ottanta, non ritiene più che l'acclamazione a gran voce dell'idealismo sia opportuna o significativa. Sulla base dei ricordi, della realtà e del suo ambiente particolare, ha costruito un nuovo palcoscenico, con un microfono, una televisione, uno studio degli striscioni. Tuttavia, non importa quanto l'artista tenti di presentare un ambiente rilassato e dissipare tracce di espressionismo e di composizioni complesse, comunque porta i telespettatori a fare una connessione con la storia recente , con la contemporaneità dell'arte "scars" e del romanticismo. Quando le composizioni delle nuove generazioni pulite e ordinate divennero popolari, He Sen, che viveva nella città di Chongqing e lavorava nel grigio smog e negli angoli unti di Huangjiaoping, non aveva davvero modo di essere coinvolto in questo fenomeno. Questo ambiente unico impedì e preservò He Sen e gli altri amici dall'utilizzare le campiture piatte e gli effetti di gusto commerciale, in linea con la manipolazione utilizzata dagli artisti provenienti dal nord.
Nel dicembre 1994, He Sen ha collaborato con i suoi amici e compagni di classe Yin Ruilin, Chen Wenbo, Du Xia, e Zhao Nengzhi alla mostra *Slice*. Ciò avvenne nel corso di un momento particolarmente difficile per la vita e l'opera di He Sen e dei suoi amici. Il catalogo della mostra che realizzarono era molto semplice, non solo la stampa delle fotografie era in bianco e nero, ma oltretutto non era affatto chiara. Eppure in questo catalogo hanno espresso una visione nitida e tagliente: nella sezione intitolata "slice selection" hanno dichiarato le loro opinioni sull'arte. Secondo Yin Ruilin, "i colori della nostra pittura stanno diventando luminosi... non è un'espressione diretta di emo-

zioni e sentimenti personali, ma una posizione al di fuori delle opere e un resoconto relativamente oggettivo di un patrimonio comune e condiviso"; Zhao Nengzhi si esprimeva così," la maggior parte delle nostre opere sono documentative, siamo contrari e riluttanti a mostrare chiaramente una posizione critica palese o altri atteggiamenti "; Chen Wenbo poneva l'accento su l'influenza della Pop art, anche se sottilmente disprezzava l'influenza diretta del Pop art sul proprio lavoro come in "Mao Amin's Songs". Messo di fronte al problema dell'influenza della cultura pop, He Sen concluse che la questione per lui presupponeva una certa complessità interiore, "Tutti sanno che ciò che è più contemporaneo è più diretto, ad esempio i film più visti fanno uso di modi di espressione diretti e scioccanti. Tuttavia, le persone più diventano contemporanee, più complessa è la loro psicologia, questo contrasto certamente diventerà più grande, e la loro complessità interiore sarà impossibile da districare. Tradotta in forma artistica, siamo in grado di esprimere tale complessità, ma ciò naturalmente andrà a discapito dell'immediatezza. Questa è la contraddizione ".
Pertanto, lo stato psicologico di incertezza che divenne dominante nella metà degli anni 1990 non portò a immagini e simboli memorabili. Come i pittori del Nord parlavano direttamente della loro noia ed impotenza, He Sen utilizzava immagini popolari per comunicare alla gente che né il palcoscenico né tanto meno la vita vera sono reali; la finzione dovrebbe essere messa in evidenza, tuttavia, He Sen sembra aver espresso il suo attaccamento alla realtà.

Il bello della messa in scena: la gente può vedere la verità attraverso la finzione.
Il pericolo della messa in scena: la gente può scorgere la finzione che è nella realtà.
La serietà della messa in scena: la gente può scorgere la forza invincibile della logica stringente.
La sicurezza della messa in scena: tutto ciò che viene messo in scena è tutto irreale.

Il modo di pensare di He Sen viene dalla tradizione del suo professore, questa tradizione ha avuto inizio nell'analisi storica dell'arte del movimento "scar", e poi è stata influenzata dai principi della filosofia esistenzialista occidentale. Fino alla prima metà degli anni Novanta, gli artisti che lavoravano e vivevano nel sud-ovest hanno mantenuto la ricerca legata ai temi alla realtà.

In effetti, dopo il 1989, la logica esistenzialista aveva perso la sua ragione d'esistere, la gente non fu più d'accordo sul fatto che a quel punto ci fossero delle reali questioni di collettività. Un tipo di vita sociale prodotta da eventi politici unici mise chiaramente in guardia la gente: non c'è alcun reale significato nella ricerca della verità. Non solo eventi emozionanti possono venire fuori in modo naturale, ma le persone possono creare una messa in scena in qualsiasi momento e in ogni luogo, e recitare uno spettacolo. Non è una questione di essere disposti o no, se ogni persona non assume un ruolo e non partecipa, tutto diventa inutile. Pertanto i nodi e dolori del proprio cuore diventano insignificanti. Negli anni Ottanta, il dolore e la solitudine divennero risorse per gli artisti, divennero l'evidenza della necessità di resistenza e preservazione della propria vita - questo era il tema comune espresso da Mao Xuhui e Zhang Xiaogang nei dieci anni precedenti al 1992. Ma, in questo momento, un'ottica di questo tipo era messa in discussione, il rapporto tra l'individuo e la società fu ancora una volta preso sul serio. Nel 1994, Zhang Xiaogang aveva già dipinto la matura serie "Familiy". L'opera *"Parents"* di Mao Xuhui si era già evoluta in una forbice che andava dall'insoddisfazione alla comodità; Ye Yongqing aveva iniziato i graffiti con i quali sposava un'attitudine letteraria; Zhou Chunya, ispirato dai predecessori, si innamorò degli studi del *"Rock"*... questo è stato un cambiamento generale, anche se, rispetto al fenomeno nel nord, è stato un cambiamento che non aveva fatto deragliare dal suo binario principale. Tuttavia, He Sen accettò l'influenza della Pop-Art: bandiere rosse, attestati di merito, fazzoletti rossi, e tutte queste immagini non furono solo prese in prestito, funsero allo stesso tempo anche da documentazione di ricordi e realtà. Come l'artista combinava simboli della politica, della storia e della società, così combinava liberamente differenti correnti, in realtà infatti fu coinvolto nella ricerca su questioni storiche e di vita insieme alla "new generation" al "cinical realism" e alla "Pop-Art". Epurata dal modernismo, la composizione di He Sen era fatta di espressione, surrealtà, collage, pubblicità così come di fotografia. Naturalmente, come la maggior parte degli artisti del sud-ovest, ha mantenuto un atteggiamento vigile nei confronti dell'ingresso del modernismo.

Il rapporto tra emozioni e razionalità è difficile da spiegare. Allo stesso tempo, l'influenza di un'aerea sull'artista non si limita a questioni di stile, lo stile è generato dall'"interiorità" e dalla "prudenza". Fino a che punto ciò è opportuno, in termini di tendenza? Per He Sen questo è un problema. Chiarezza e semplicità rendono queste immagini distinguibili e facili da ricordare, anche se sono comuni dipinti "kitsch", sono diventati popolari. Una situazione del genere fece diventare He Sen ansioso, quindi fino al 1996 He Sen ha vagato tra il suo espressionismo e il suo mondo complesso ed esitante. Si concentra sulla parte interna, ma si accorge che l'anima non è tutto, egli è interessato alla realtà, ma si rende anche conto che l'arte non è la realtà, egli aspira ad essere riconosciuto, ma è consapevole del fatto che questo non è un vero e proprio problema artistico; come si risolve tutto ciò?

Nel 1996, Huang Zhuan ha chiesto, "a partire dalla metà degli anni 1990 si è registrata una tendenza verso il concettuale nell'arte cinese, qual è la tua opinione a proposito di questa tendenza? Le tue opere hanno questo tipo di carattere o di esito?"
He Sen ha risposto: "Questa tendenza concettuale ha fornito un nuovo punto di ingresso per gli artisti figurativi nella loro ricerca di un nuovo campo dopo la Pop-Art e il Cinical Realism. Esso ha anche beneficiato dell'impatto stimolante e vivace della performance e delle installazioni. Se i dipinti non servono più come portatori di senso, non possono essere affiancati a installazioni, performance e video arte come autentici mezzi d'espressione d'arte contemporanea. Un tale cambiamento riflette una disconnessione con il vecchio modo di reagire. Comunque questa è solo una premessa, che è già diventata un nuovo inizio, ed è solo su questa base che l'artista può cominciare a ri-esplorare e riconsiderare le questioni di interesse, consentendo al metodo artistico e alla rotta culturale di essere nuovamente rielaborate, in questo caso può nascere nuova forza per l'arte. Abbiamo ancora immaginazione? Questa è la premessa per la fine della morte dell'arte. Io continuo ad avere un sacco di lavoro da fare su questo punto. La riorganizzazione della struttura compositiva e del linguaggio di base, mi fa sperare che la pittura non sarà più una semplice reazione al mondo esterno. Nel mio linguaggio di base, è necessario liberare il linguaggio più espressionista dal pericolo di essere un semplice mezzo per sfogare emozioni, e quindi riportarlo in una struttura razionale, liberandosi del caos visivo, non aggiungendo significato attraverso il processo della pittura e della pennellata stesse, altrimenti l'essenza del concetto sarà del tutto trascurata. Qui, la presenza, la tipicità e la trama non hanno alcuna funzione, il problema è come ridurre al minimo le relazioni di eredità, e rendere ciò pittorico.

Utilizzare metodi espressionisti per moltiplicare un oggetto, raggiungere un livello di raffinatezza in cui ci saranno contraddizioni con il significato di questo corpo linguistico, contraddizioni con un unico significato spirituale; rendere ambiguo ciò che è significante. Alla fine, ciò che risalta è l'effetto, le immagini. Non è più semplicemente la feccia della liberazione emotiva, ma piuttosto il significato è sottoposto all'osservazione storica.

Nella sua risposta a questa domanda, He Sen è ovviamente molto chiaro sul futuro del suo lavoro, ha davvero cominciato a indagare obiettivamente sui pericoli dei metodi abituali di espressione d'arte contemporanea. Entra così in una nuova fase artistica.

Forse non c'è un grande significato nell'unicità psicologica di un individuo, ma una volta che questa unicità è trasformata in una lingua, vi è la possibilità di produrre significato. Già in *Space Inside* del 1990, He Sen aveva iniziato a porre alcune macchie ambigue in un angolo in alto dello sfondo. Non vi è alcun significato particolare in queste macchie, sono solo un effetto del trattamento dell'artista. Volerle osservare in termini di esplorazione psicologica, forse potrebbe essere considerato come una manifestazione di "completa ignoranza". Nella serie *Still life* del 1991's e nel suo lavoro sulle figure, le macchie indistinte producono un senso di espressionismo malinconico. La cosa interessante è che anche altri artisti dello stesso periodo - Shen Xiaotong, Haizhou Xin, Guo Wei ed altri - presentato questi grumi galleggianti in forme diverse. Sotto quale tipo di circostanze questi sentimenti ambigui sarebbero diventati una sorta di linguaggio, invece di essere semplicemente una auto-iniziativa di presentarsi? Non sappiamo le circostanze particolari, ma un giorno nel 1996, He Sen ha trasposto queste masse indistinte in figure, in una certa misura ha mantenuto la loro "forma", però queste masse hanno cominciato a diventare evidenti e rigide, le forme sono state fossilizzate, hanno cominciato ad assumere l'aspetto di pietre. Quando l'artista si innamorò di questo effetto, anche le teste potevano essere viste come delle specie di pietre. Le opere completate nel 1996 sono uniformemente allusive: esse rivelano contraddizioni interne, un'espressione della pesantezza e della risposta necessaria che esige la realtà. Queste opere fossilizzate e la fissa vita quotidiana del soggetto, potrebbero indurci a creare una connessione con la storia di Pompei, ma le pietre sotto le pennellate di He Sen ci ricordano molto più facilmente le pietre cinesi. Non importa quanti sforzi l'artista abbia compiuto in materia di stile o a livello linguistico, il suo tono stilistico tende ancora verso l'espressionismo: complessità, incomprensibilità, serietà d'analisi. Tale stile ha chiaramente aumentato la distanza tra He Sen e gli altri artisti. Eppure l'effetto ottenuto solo con tecniche particolari non ha permesso all'artista di trasmettere chiaramente il suo intento: si tratta di una dipendenza dal modernismo, o è un tentativo di rompere seriamente con il groviglio di legami psicologici? In gran parte questo era un segno di distinzione, uno spartiacque indicato dai critici tra modernismo e post-modernismo, che cancellava l'attitudine individuale metafisica.

Sulla base di un'estetica "fossile", l'artista comincia a rilassarsi, la complessità del suo pensiero dà modo ad un sondaggio di congetture e di interesse. Tra i lavori fatti nel 1997, gli oggetti rigidi (comprese le teste delle persone) improvvisamente iniziano ad emettere luce, in netto contrasto con le rocce senza vita del passato. Chi o che cosa è stato il motivo che consente a oggetti "fossilizzati" di emettere luce?
Ciò su cui He Sen si concentrava veramente non erano quelle immagini orrende tipo "adesivi", immagini che sembravano essere intagliate con un coltello non erano necessariamente quello che lui voleva. Che tipo di mi-

racolo poteva essere creato con le tecniche e l'illuminazione accumulate nel corso degli anni - la questione poteva essere chiarita solo mediante la continua sperimentazione. Se questo tipo di manipolazione ripetitiva ancora non riusciva a farlo rompere con i dettagli del passato, allora forse solo scartando completamente il passato si sarebbe potuti arrivare a una nuova direzione. Cominciò a diminuire la complessità e gli strati delle sue immagini, non è chiaro quale tipo di luce diede l'input all'artista, se tramite luci soffuse in grado di diminuire la complessità dell'immagine e portare avanti altre possibilità, l'artista avrebbe trovato un efficace percorso per disancorarsi dai dettagli dell'espressionismo. He Sen iniziò a rievocare la propria storia artistica, ritornò addirittura allo sperimentalismo del 1990; a lavori ultimati nel 1998, in *Girl biting hands, Wandering, Scream, Self-portrait – Hiding face*, vediamo un riassunto delle sue opere precedenti: un ritorno alla "carta", alla pulizia del realismo così come alle pennellate espressive. Tuttavia l'artista cominciò a studiare con calma le sue composizioni, coraggiosamente abbandonò contenuti complessi e poco chiari, e ha ridotto la sua pennellata espressiva al minimo. La luce è diventata un elemento fondamentale che influenza la sua composizione - in particolare quella luce improvvisa che fa sparire gli occhi delle persone. Questa era l'epoca in cui la fotografia digitale ha sostituito la pellicola, il libero e arbitrario uso della macchina fotografica è divenuto possibile. Non è importante quando He Sen ha cominciato a prestare attenzione agli effetti di luce sulle immagini e nelle fotografie, soprattutto in ambiti di intervento specifico, ma questo senza dubbio ha dato all'artista input importanti. Non siamo sicuri neanche di quando He Sen abbia iniziato a prestare attenzione al lavoro di Richter, fu comunque lui stesso a dichiarare che fu molto impressionato dall'arte dell'artista tedesco. Ovviamente, l'esperienza dell'artista occidentale è servita ad He Sen anche come fonte di incoraggiamento e di ispirazione per sperimentare. Nel complesso, tra tutte le possibilità, He Sen ha scelto gli effetti della fotografia, così come Richter ha detto una volta, "la fotografia, una volta tentava di ottenere gli effetti della pittura, oggi, le opere su tela stanno cominciando a ispirarsi alla fotografia." Tale parere è anche supportato da osservazioni di Duchamp: le immagini dipinte in forma di fotografie possono anche produrre nuove composizioni concettuali. *The girl lying on a sofa* è stato il primo tentativo di questo genere con effetti fotografici - completato nel 1998, è stata un'azione senza una pianificazione, è stato un lampo spontaneo. Fino al 1999, questa sorta di coincidenza fu di grande aiuto per He Sen che completò un gran numero di opere di questo tipo. Abbandonò completamente i metodi espressivi, e sembrava pensare che l'aggiunta di fattori casuali direttamente sulla tela sarebbe stata sufficiente - questo era il nuovo punto di svolta per He Sen.

Certo, a differenza di altri artisti che utilizzano le fotografie nella loro pittura, He Sen rimane più cauto, nota gli effetti di luce, tuttavia, mettendo in evidenza tali effetti, e soprattutto evidenziando la semplificazione delle forme data dal flash, crea un'atmosfera unica. Quindi, se verifichiamo le fotografie a cui He Sen fa riferimento, si comprende che l'artista si basa su un'inerzia visiva, portato dalla semplificazione della forma e dall'atto intenzionale di eliminare lo sguardo dei soggetti umani. He Sen ha detto una volta, "La serie precedente *Accumulation* ha preso inspirazione da sculture in pietra, e le sculture in pietra non hanno gli occhi, così, quando sono passato alle ragazze, anche loro non avevano gli occhi". Quindi, ciò non è necessariamente dovuto al fatto che "con il flash, gli occhi diventano indefiniti", l'artista vuole solo ricreare la percezione che le persone hanno del flash cancellando intenzionalmente gli occhi. Questa manipolazione è molto importante, perché attraverso di essa He Sen ha l'opportunità di sottolineare il timore che è sempre stato presente nella sua spirituali-

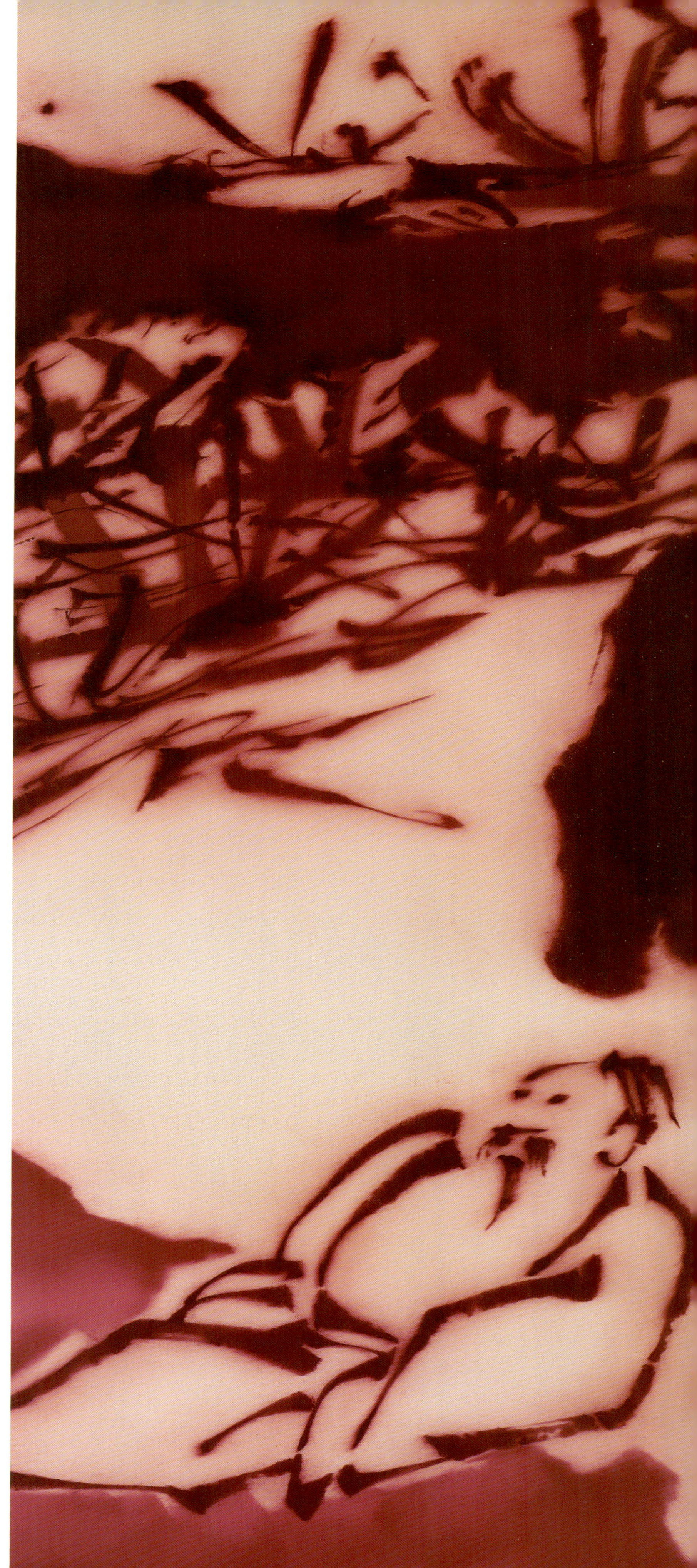

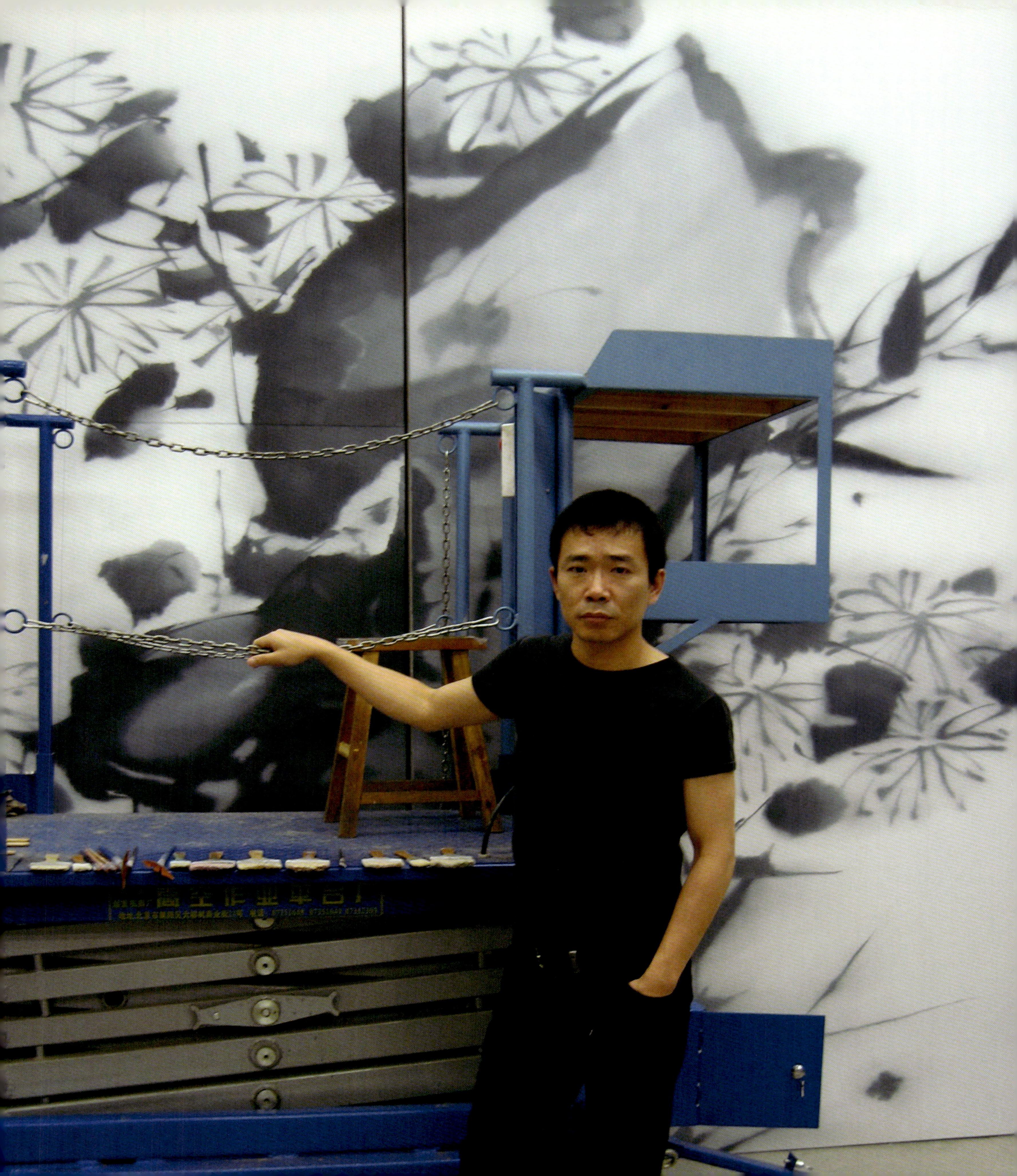

tà - questo tipo di stato mentale era stato dichiarato direttamente nella fase dell'espressionismo. In seguito, l'artista aggiunge un'altra considerazione sulle immagini, "le ragazze nei miei dipinti non hanno gli occhi, perché credo che ci sia una distanza irraggiungibile tra le persone, che li rende incapaci di riconoscere chiaramente la realtà. Sono confusi, freddi, guardano la realtà senza reale attenzione. "(*Female Portraits, Social Projection?* Ke Ning, June, 2006)

He Sen ha finalmente trovato un filone di sperimentazione in cui si sente a suo agio, il concetto di pittura fotografica gli consente di applicare la sua abilità e la tecnica realistica senza ostacoli, l'oggetto e il suo contenuto gli permettono di allontanarsi da quella caricatura eterna che è la rappresentazione del "bello". Con tale sostegno concettuale ha iniziato una produzione infinita di ragazze: le pose sono apatiche e indifferenti, senza alcuno stimolo particolare, anche la loro indisponibilità a rispondere al telefono dà l'impressione di noia insopportabile, mancano di classe e di eleganza in scene pubbliche - tutto questo è il genere di cosa che artisti volgari e non impegnati amano rappresentare. In molte circostanze le composizioni di He Sen possono facilmente suscitare voyeurismo. Allo stesso tempo, ci si accorge che se anche i supporti vengono presi dalle fotografie, l'artista ha aggiunto giocattoli di solito bianchi posti per terra, su divani o tenuti in mano dai soggetti. Quando He Sen, rispondendo a un critico, ha spiegato la ragione dell'uso dei giocattoli, ha detto, "la crescita di tutti è accompagnata da un senso di perdita. Come le ragazze senza occhi che dipingo, così i giocattoli sul divano in uno spazio chiuso - tutti trasmettono un senso di infanzia. ("My work is to understand others and myself through art", interview with He Sen), naturalmente questo è un sentimento piuttosto personale. Ciò che deve essere sottolineato è che ognuno di noi ha la propria personale cognizione della crescita e del tempo, è questo sentimento di timore ad essere rilevante rispetto all'invecchiamento di ognuno e al percorso di ognuno, non ha importanza l'esperienza particolare dell'artista.

Nel 1999, He Sen si spostò da Chongqing a Chengdu, cosa che aveva sempre desiderato per l'entusiasmo del mondo dell'arte di Chengdu. La maggior parte dei dipinti più importanti di He Sen sono stati fatti dopo questo anno, quando si accorse che la sua arte si stava muovendo verso una maggiore chiarezza e che aveva bisogno di un nuovo ambiente e maggiori opportunità. Dopo il 2001, le donne con gli occhi annullati cominciarono ad avere gli occhi chiari. Sulla base di esperimenti precedenti He Sen ha cominciato a lasciare sottili note di tristezza sui volti e sui corpi dei suoi soggetti - con le pennellate brusche utilizzati per realizzare questo effetto egli sembra voler dire che anche l'immagine o la forma più luminosa e radiosa può essere rovinata o essere offesa. Non vi è alcuna differenza fondamentale con l'atteggiamento del pittore espressionista precedente, ha solo cambiato il suo canale di espressione. Negli anni seguenti, egli ha espresso pienamente quello che ha capito della vita e della giovinezza, legato al tempo, legato alla comprensione e speculazione costantemente rinnovata della sua esistenza. Anche se i critici hanno risposto a queste domande con un vocabolario post-moderno, le opere dell'artista rivelano ancora tutto ciò.

Le donne e il mondo in cui viviamo sembra abbastanza simile in apparenza, per dirla in parole semplici, al giorno d'oggi le ragazze sono più belle di prima, e sembra che diventino sempre più belle. E anche la società in cui viviamo è più bella, l'architettura e le strade sono più belle. Ma i nostri cuori e gli spiriti sono molto meno soddisfatti rispetto al passato, e la bellezza in corso e il progresso è del tutto illusorio, in realtà è solo un guscio vuoto, un aspetto che copre un vuoto; l'idealismo sta gradualmente diminuendo nella vita reale, e questa società sta diventando molto realistica e fredda. *(My work is to get to know others and knowing myself through art – interview with He Sen)*

Questo è il tipo di malinconia che spesso può essere ritrovata tra gli artisti del sud-ovest, possiamo vedere la stessa tragedia contemporanea nelle opere di Zhang Xiaogang, Mao Xuhui, Zhao Nengzhi, Haizhou Xin, Zhang Xiaotao, Xie Nanxing e altri. Il tempo è "bello", ma questa "bellezza" è appunto il simbolo di degenerazione e di problemi.

Così come qualche anno prima He Sen si era spostato da Chongqing a Chengdu, nel 2003 si trasferì a Pechino. E nella capitale l'artista raggiunse il successo che aveva a lungo sperato. In questi ultimi anni ha speso molto tempo su questa "bellezza" degenerata, fino al 2005 quando ha riavviato le sue riflessioni sull'arte. Dopo aver sfogliato molti libri di immagini del passato, è tornato alla storia. Egli utilizza il mezzo della pittura ad olio per esprimere dipinti antichi di uccelli e fiori. Ha davvero voglia di esplorare il sapore e il tono dei pittori antichi? No, ovviamente. He Sen ha anche realizzato l'astrazione delle 12 immagini sull'acqua di Ma Yuan, e sezionato le aree della sua composizione, usando mezzi completamente diversi di espressione, per completare lo stesso lavoro. He Sen utilizza dipinti di antichi maestri come un dato di fatto, l'elaborazione dei loro dipinti non tende a raggiungere alcun tipo di illusione, ma piuttosto costituisce un'osservazione: quando le immagini storiche sono stagliate di fronte a noi, quale dovrebbe essere il nostro pensiero? In effetti, abbiamo visto un'espansione concettuale attraverso questa differenza di rappresentazione nella composizione. Come artista, He Sen ha familiarità con l'unicità delle immagini nella storia dell'arte cinese, come molti artisti utilizzano le immagini con un alto valore ideologico per dispiegare questioni legate alla contemporaneità, He Sen ha messo posto il suo punto di avvio ancora oltre, ha eliminato tutte le allusioni alla politica, ha abbandonato la pratica della riflessione ideologica e allusione politica, creando un rapporto diretto con gli antichi. Questa è la nuova direzione per l'arte in questo secolo, abbiamo già visto molti artisti sensibili alla riproposizione storica – i fiori di pesco di Zhou Chunya e i paesaggi di Zeng Fanzhi - hanno scoperto una qualità eterna nelle opere degli antichi, e hanno intuito che questo percorso di esplorazione potrebbe forse portare a un netto contrasto con l'arte e la cultura occidentali. In un'epoca di accessibilità delle informazioni a livello mondiale, la ricerca di originalità e unicità è diventata nuovamente un obiettivo artistico, questo richiede che il concetto sia combinato con la sensibilità e che la contemporaneità si sposi con la storia. Dall'inizio della nuova arte negli anni Ottanta fino ad oggi - a trenta anni di distanza, oltre alla libertà del risveglio di se stesi, ogni altro concetto può essere negato. Per He Sen, la New Art è appena iniziata, ma il suo istinto è in buona salute, ha già distinto i problemi di questa tendenza concettuale: lascivia, propensione al servilismo e al cinismo.

Ovviamente, tra le opere di He Sen di epoche diverse, possiamo percepire la precoce solitudine dell'artista e la sua malinconia. Una persona che trascorre la sua giovinezza perseguendo qualcosa, ma che quando ottiene ciò che ha perseguito, sente una nuova perdita: ingenuo, bello ed eterno. Ma Yuan, figlio di Ma Lin ha un dipinto intitolato *Holding a Candle Roaming at Night*, l'atmosfera di questa immagine è elegante e di classe. Di notte, la luce di una candela illumina un giardino in fiore come se fosse giorno, una persona è seduta nel mezzo del giardino, ma è difficile stabilire se questa persona stia godendo della solitudine o se abbia una sensazione di melanconia. Sappiamo che l'inizio del 1279 è stato l'ultimo periodo della dinastia Song, prima che i mongoli invadessero Hangzhou tutti i letterati scapparono per diventare eremiti, e sparì la quiete nei loro giardini - questi dipinti di Ma Lin e di altri artisti anonimi dei Song meridionali sono le testimonianze della complessità della loro mentalità. Simili stati emotivi possono apparire anche nelle opere di oggi, in un periodo di transizione drastica, forse una malinconia simbolica potrebbe meglio richiamare i problemi esistenti. He Sen e altri artisti hanno già capito l'importanza di capire la storia, e questa è anche la caratteristica fondamentale della nuova arte.

BEYOND APPEARANCES: MELANCHOLY AND UNEASE

Dirk Steimann

The Chinese painter He Sen was born in the Yunnan province in 1968, that is at the beginning of the Cultural Revolution. Twenty years later he began his artistic training at the Sichuan Academy of Fine Arts, in 1989, the year the democratic movement in China was put down. He Sen's career has therefore been – whether consciously or unconsciously – permeated by transformations which have shaped Chinese society until the present, and ultimately coincided with the ongoing phase of rapid urban and economic growth. During these years He Sen has developed a visual language in his painting which, even though it does not take such an obvious stand as that of the representatives of China's Cynical Realism and Political Pop movements in the early Nineties, it is hardly less focused on life in a continuously changing China.

Hints of melancholy and sensuality emanate from the artist's most recent paintings. The poster-sized oil paintings have an allure of cool sleekness displaying a complete lack of emotion. This is additionally emphasized by the obvious artificiality of these pictorial creations. The motifs are inscribed with an erotic as much as a melancholic atmosphere and convey an underlying feeling of loss and loneliness. He Sen's gaze is male and voyeuristic, the style of depiction being forceful evidence of this. He Sen is, however, not interested in these particular women in themselves.

Since 1998 the painter has been (almost) exclusively interested in the portrayal of girls and women, pictures which are distinguished by their exact finishing as much as their detailed depiction. By 2000 this precision had achieved such perfection that any further development was hardly possible. He Sen's paintings show anonymous young women alone with no further description, always placed against an undifferentiated and monochrome background. A few props such as an armchair, table, sofa

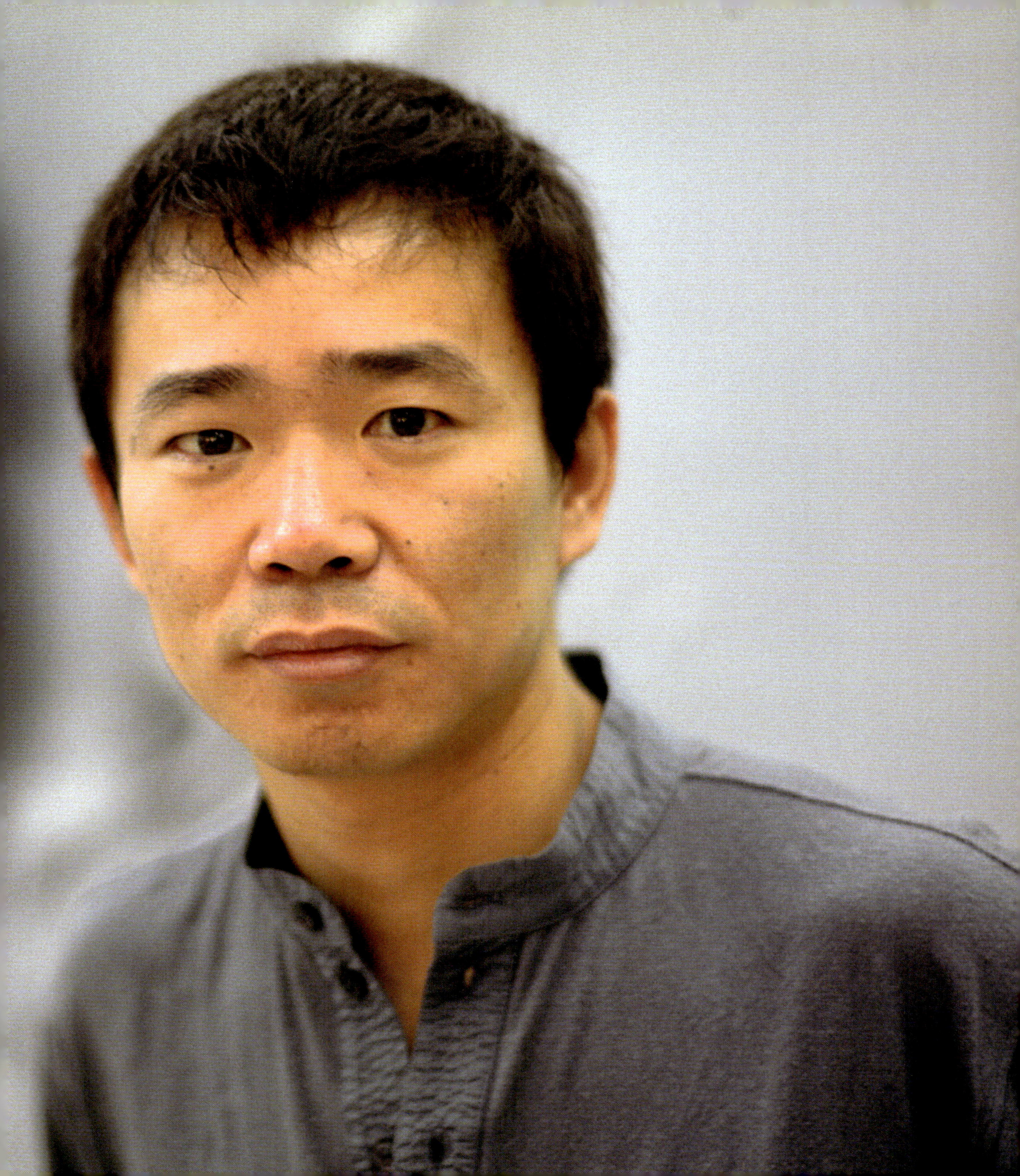

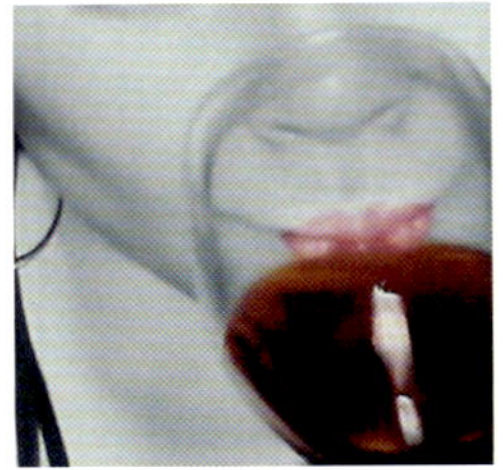

Inflammation
cigarette
oil on canvas
250x200 cm
2008

or bed as well as accessories such as a single bottle of whiskey, a glass, a packet of cigarettes, a mobile telephone or occasionally a cuddly toy suffice the painter to depict his models within a space which at most only hints at a room, embellished only by vague shadows or occasionally visible cigarette smoke.

He Sen depicts these young and attractive women as being unequivocally sensual. Additionally, expression, gaze and posture allow no doubt that what they are projecting is absolutely self-conscious. This is emphasised through the use of the colour red, which functions here not only as a warning or signalling colour but also has erotic connotations. Sometimes it is a red blouse or dress, at other times a cover, but always it is the strong bright red of the women's lips that contrasts with the otherwise muted and largely grey tones of the oil paintings.

The women are always depicted alone in rooms with no discernable boundaries. Their postures appear as a latently aggressive mixture of calm and tension; rarely caught in movement, they are always either crouching, sitting, squatting or sprawling whilst drinking or smoking. The viewer senses, however, that these moments of peace and relaxation will quickly pass. Even though the models mostly take up poses facing the viewer and their gaze appears to be directed towards the viewer, on the whole they seem to be interested more in themselves. It is this bored and sad, sometimes laconic and aloof, but always impersonal gaze that obviously contradicts the occasional appearance of a tired smile. This observation is reflected in the women's postures. In fact their poses which initially appear casual and composed, have stiffened to become inhibited and deeply insecure.

At first these young women seem to conform to the stereotype which has become a cliché as much in the East as the West, that of the post-feminist, meaning a self-confident as well as an attractive and successful, woman. Given a society which hardly offers any support and is subject to continuous change and alienation, their reaction is one of being remote and disillusioned. However, it is only at first glance that the women He Sen shows are tough and self-confident; in fact they have no illusions and are sceptical and insecure in an unsupportive and directionless present. Even though the cropping of the picture appears to make the women approachable, no further bond is really possible beyond a vague eye contact. He Sen's women are unapproachable and remote, they remain insulated. Although their gaze, which superficially is directed towards the viewer,

in fact passes through him and into the void. The seemingly provocative and self-confident attitude is merely camouflage and proves to be both directionless and insecure. In view of this, the grabbing of a cigarette and a glass of whiskey is rather more a helpless search for stability.

The narrative potential of these paintings probably works especially on the imagination of male viewers, which certainly is largely due to the subject matter and He Sen's interpretation of it, because the artist, who is aware that even contemporary painting remains a medium mostly shaped by an explicitly male point of view, returns in his paintings to traditional and popular roles of femininity, as reinforced by the mass media. Furthermore, these motifs are well-suited as screens of projection for the viewer's longing and desire, even though his yearning will remain unfulfilled.

He Sen's depictions of women are based upon a knowledge of old academic traditions of craftsmanship as well as an awareness of recent social discourses within the arts. At first glance his paintings suggest no particular conclusions concerning an imaginable narrative lying beyond that which is depicted, and so from a certain point onwards his pictures abandon the viewer to their own thoughts. Any approach to content that lies beyond that which is portrayed, can only be tentative and cautious. In his portrayals of women He Sen neither criticises nor denounces. Instead he has decided upon depictions of anonymous individuals in order to illustrate his observations of young people's lives in contemporary Chinese society. In a subtle way, by means of his portrayals of women he visualises the individual's changing self-image and self-esteem in a society subjected to enormous transformations. He thereby provides an up-to-date inventory of contemporary life and highlights the huge insecurities arising from an aggressive, almost limitless market economy and excessive consumer culture. These consequences of the new economic freedom and the dwindling support provided by society are accompanied by a growing awareness of the threat to and the insecurity of independent existence. It appears as if He Sen's women have come to terms with their loneliness and dislocation in a disillusioning present. Even more so his works are evidence of an unfulfilled desire for a happy life, a desire to achieve an existence which has to offer more than merely disillusionment and unease.

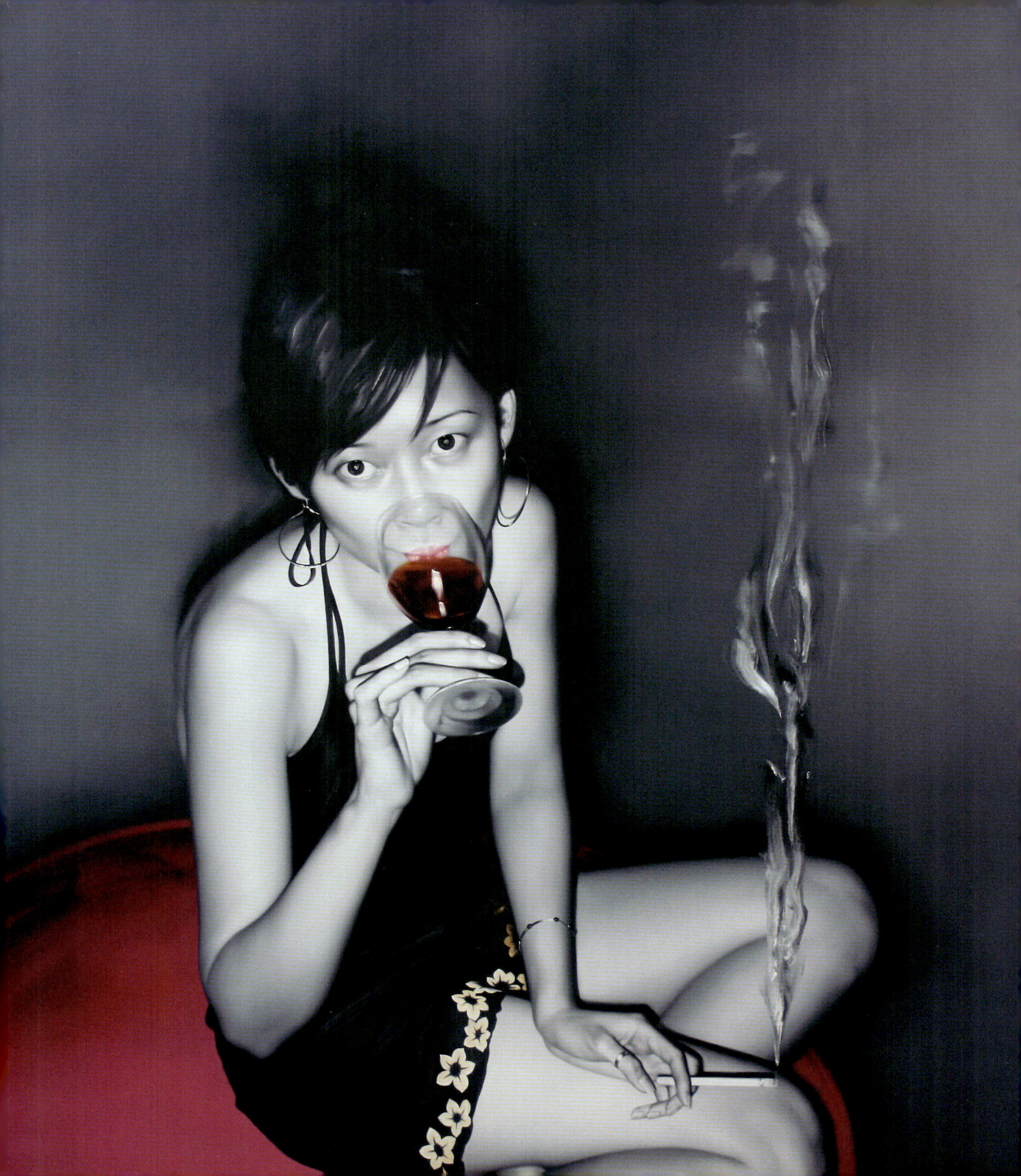

OLTRE LE APPARENZE: LA MALINCONIA E IL DISAGIO

Dirk Steimann

Il pittore cinese He Sen è nato nella provincia dello Yunnan, nel 1968, cioè all'inizio della Rivoluzione culturale. Venti anni più tardi, ha iniziato la sua formazione artistica presso l'Accademia di Belle Arti del Sichuan, nel 1989, l'anno della caduta del movimento democratico in Cina. La carriera di He Sen è stata quindi - consapevolmente o inconsapevolmente - permeata dalle trasformazioni che hanno plasmato la società cinese fino ai giorni nostri, e in ultima analisi, ha coinciso con l'attuale fase di rapida crescita urbana ed economica. Durante questi anni He Sen ha sviluppato un linguaggio visivo nella sua pittura che, anche se non prende una posizione così evidente come quella dei rappresentanti del Realismo Cinico e del movimento del Pop Politico dei primi anni Novanta, di certo non è meno concentrato sulla continua evoluzione della Cina.

Accenni di malinconia e sensualità emanano i dipinti più recenti dell'artista. I dipinti a olio delle dimensioni di poster hanno un fascino di fredda lucentezza che trasmette una totale mancanza di emozioni. Ciò è ulteriormente sottolineato dalla artificiosità evidente di queste creazioni pittoriche. I motivi sono disegnati tanto con erotismo quanto con un'atmosfera malinconica e trasmettono una sensazione di fondo di perdita e di solitudine. Lo sguardo di He Sen è maschile e voyeuristico, lo stile pittorico ne è una forte prova. He Sen, tuttavia, non è particolarmente interessato a queste donne.

Dal 1998 il pittore è stato (quasi) esclusivamente interessato alla rappresentazione di donne e ragazze, le immagini si distinguono per la loro esattezza nella finitura e per la loro rappresentazione dettagliata. Dal 2000 questa precisione ha raggiunto una perfezione tale che ogni ulteriore sviluppo è stato quasi impossibile. I dipinti di He Sen mostrano anonime giovani donne sole, senza ulteriore descrizione, sempre collocate su uno sfondo indifferenziato e monocromo. Pochi oggetti di scena, come una poltrona, un tavolo, un divano o un letto, come anche gli accessori quali una sola bottiglia di whisky, un bicchiere, un pacchetto di sigarette, un telefono cellulare o occasionalmente un peluche, sono sufficienti al pittore per dipingere le sue modelle all'interno di una spazio che consiste solo in una stanza, impreziosita solo da ombre vaghe o di tanto in tanto dal fumo di una sigaretta.

He Sen descrive queste donne giovani ed attraenti come esseri inequivocabilmente sensuali. Inoltre, l'espressione, lo sguardo e la postura non consentono alcun dubbio sul fatto che ciò che stanno proiettando è un'assoluta auto-consapevolezza. Questo è enfatizzato dall'uso del colore rosso, che funge qui non solo come un avvertimento o una segnalazione di colore, ma ha anche connotazioni erotiche. A volte si tratta di una camicetta rossa o di un capo di abbigliamento, altre volte una coperta, ma sempre è il forte rosso brillante delle labbra delle donne che contrasta con i toni altrimenti in sordina e in gran parte grigi dei dipinti ad olio.

Le donne sono sempre rappresentate da sole in camere senza dettagli riconoscibili. Le loro posizioni appaiono come un misto latentemente aggressivo di calma e di tensione; raramente prese in movimento, sono sempre o accovacciate, sedute, o intente a bere e fumare. Lo spettatore, tuttavia, sente che questi momenti di pace e relax passeranno rapidamente. Anche se le modelle per lo più assumono pose di fronte allo spettatore e lo sguardo sembra essere orientato verso lo spettatore, nel complesso sembrano essere più interessate a se stesse. E' questo sguardo annoiato e triste, a volte laconico e distante, ma sempre impersonale che contraddice, ovviamente, la comparsa occasionale di un sorriso stanco. Questa osservazione si riflette nelle posture delle donne. In realtà le loro pose, che inizialmente sembrano casuali e composte, sono irrigidite fino a diventare inibite e profondamente insicure.

In un primo momento queste giovani donne sembrano uniformarsi allo stereotipo che è diventato un luogo comune tanto in Oriente come in Occidente, quello della donna post-femminista, ossia una donna sicura di sé, attraente e di successo. Tenuto conto di una società che non offre praticamente alcun sostegno ed è soggetta a continui cambiamenti e alienazioni, la loro reazione è quella di essere distanti e disilluse. Tuttavia, è solo a prima vista che le donne che dipinge He Sen sono dure e sicure di sé, in realtà non hanno illusioni e sono scettiche e insicure in un presente ostile e privo di una direzione. Anche se il taglio dell'immagine sembra rendere accessibili le donne, nessun altro legame è davvero possibile, al di là di un incrociarsi vago di sguardi. Le donne di He Sen sono inavvicinabili e lontane, rimangono isolate. Anche il loro sguardo, che superficialmente è diretto verso lo spettatore, in realtà passa attraverso di lui e si perde nel vuoto. L'apparentemente provocazione di un atteggiamento sicuro di sé è solo una maschera e dimostra di essere forzata e insicura. In considerazione di ciò, l'afferrare una sigaretta e un bicchiere di whisky è piuttosto un gesto disperato di ricerca di stabilità.

Il potenziale narrativo di questi dipinti è probabilmente incentrato in

The girl in red
oil on canvas
120x150 cm
2009

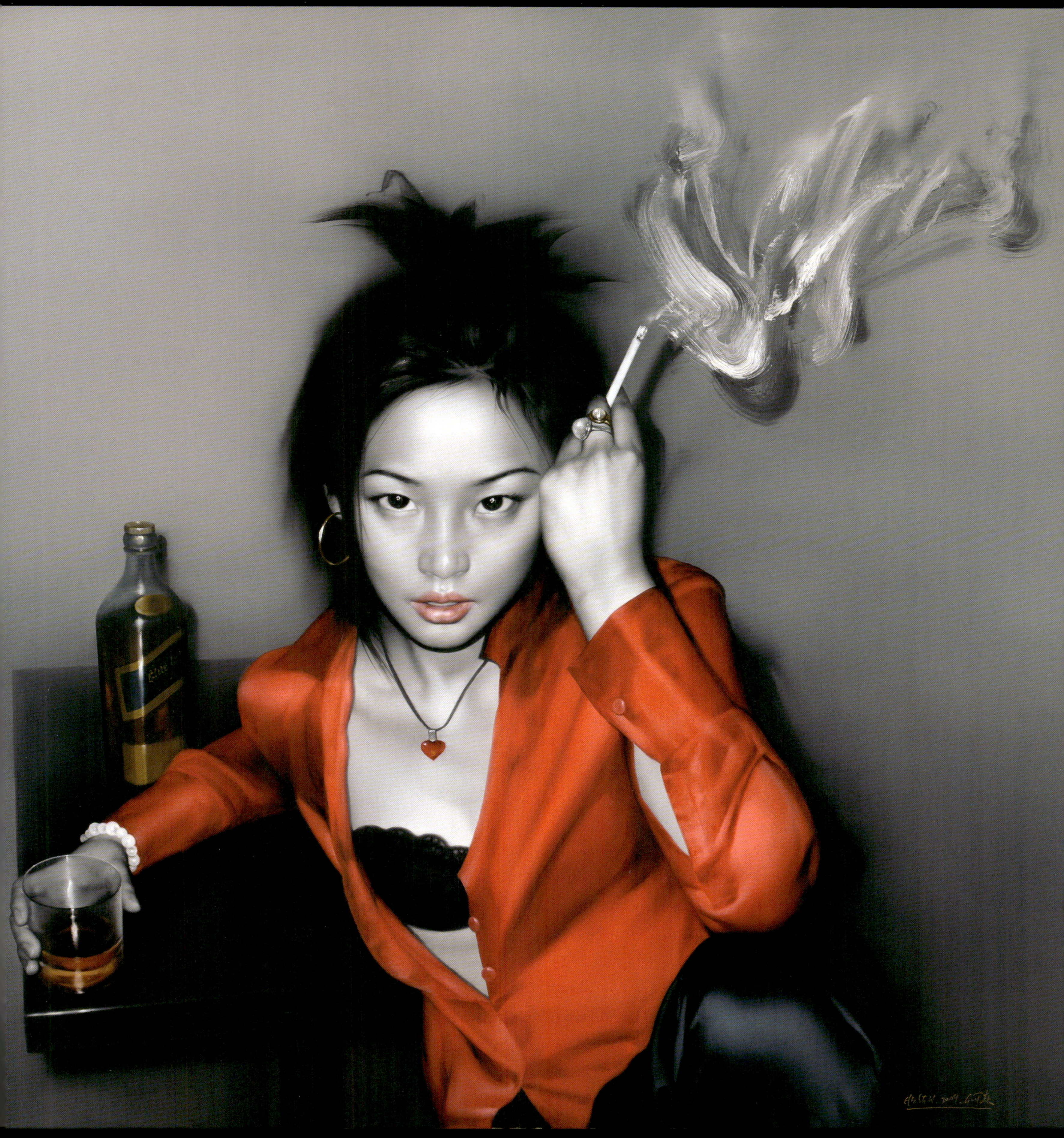

particolare sulla fantasia degli spettatori di sesso maschile, certamente dovuto in gran parte all'interpretazione di He Sen, perché l'artista, che è consapevole che la pittura contemporanea rimane un mezzo per lo più formato da un punto di vista esplicitamente maschile, torna nei suoi dipinti ai ruoli tradizionali e popolari della femminilità, come rafforzata dai mass media. Inoltre questi motivi sono ben adattati ad essere schermi di proiezione dei desideri dello spettatore, anche se i suoi desideri rimarranno insoddisfatti.

Le raffigurazioni di donne di He Sen sono basate sulla conoscenza dell'antica tradizione accademica d'arte, nonché sulla consapevolezza dei recenti discorsi sociali all'interno delle arti. Al primo sguardo i suoi dipinti suggeriscono che non vi sono conclusioni particolari per quanto riguarda una narrazione che si possa immaginare vada oltre a ciò che è rappresentato, e quindi da un certo punto in poi le sue immagini abbandonano lo spettatore ai propri pensieri. Qualsiasi approccio ai contenuti che si trova al di là di ciò che viene rappresentato, non può che essere provvisorio e cauto.

Nei suoi ritratti di donne, He Sen non contesta né denuncia. Piuttosto ha deciso di raffigurare individui anonimi, al fine di illustrare le sue osservazioni a proposito della vita dei giovani nella società cinese contemporanea. In modo sottile, attraverso i suoi ritratti di donne, visualizza il cambiamento che l'individuo compie su se stesso e sulla propria autostima in una società sottoposta a trasformazioni enormi. Egli, pertanto, offre un inventario aggiornato della vita contemporanea e mette in luce le insicurezze enormi derivanti da un'aggressiva quasi irrefrenabile economia di mercato e da un'eccessiva cultura consumistica. Queste le conseguenze della nuova libertà economica e di un appoggio sempre in calo fornito dalla società, accompagnati da una crescente consapevolezza della minaccia e dell'insicurezza di essere indipendenti. Sembra come se le donne di He Sen vengano a patti con la loro solitudine e la dislocazione in un presente deludente. Ancor di più le sue opere sono la testimonianza di un desiderio insoddisfatto di una vita felice, il desiderio di realizzare un'esistenza che ha da offrire più di una semplice delusione e del disagio.

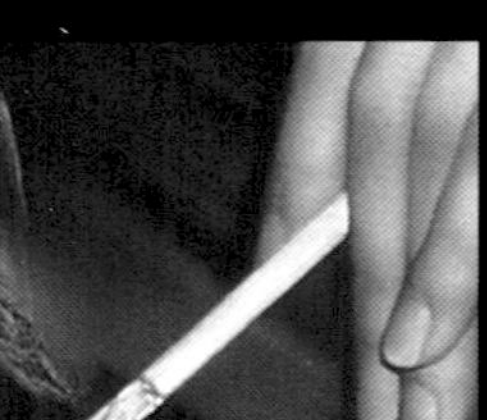

Soft sofa
oil on canvas
250x300 cm
2009

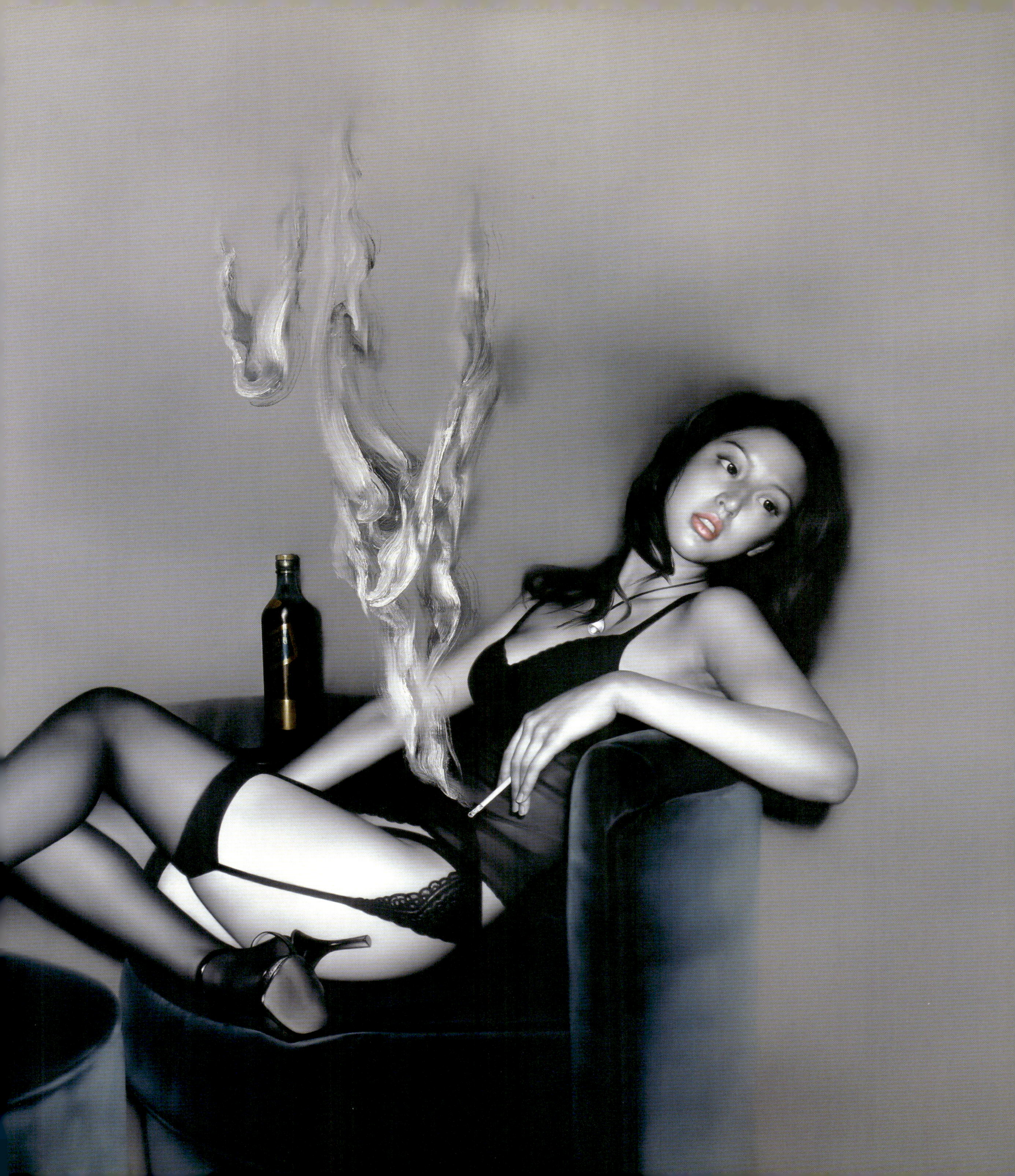

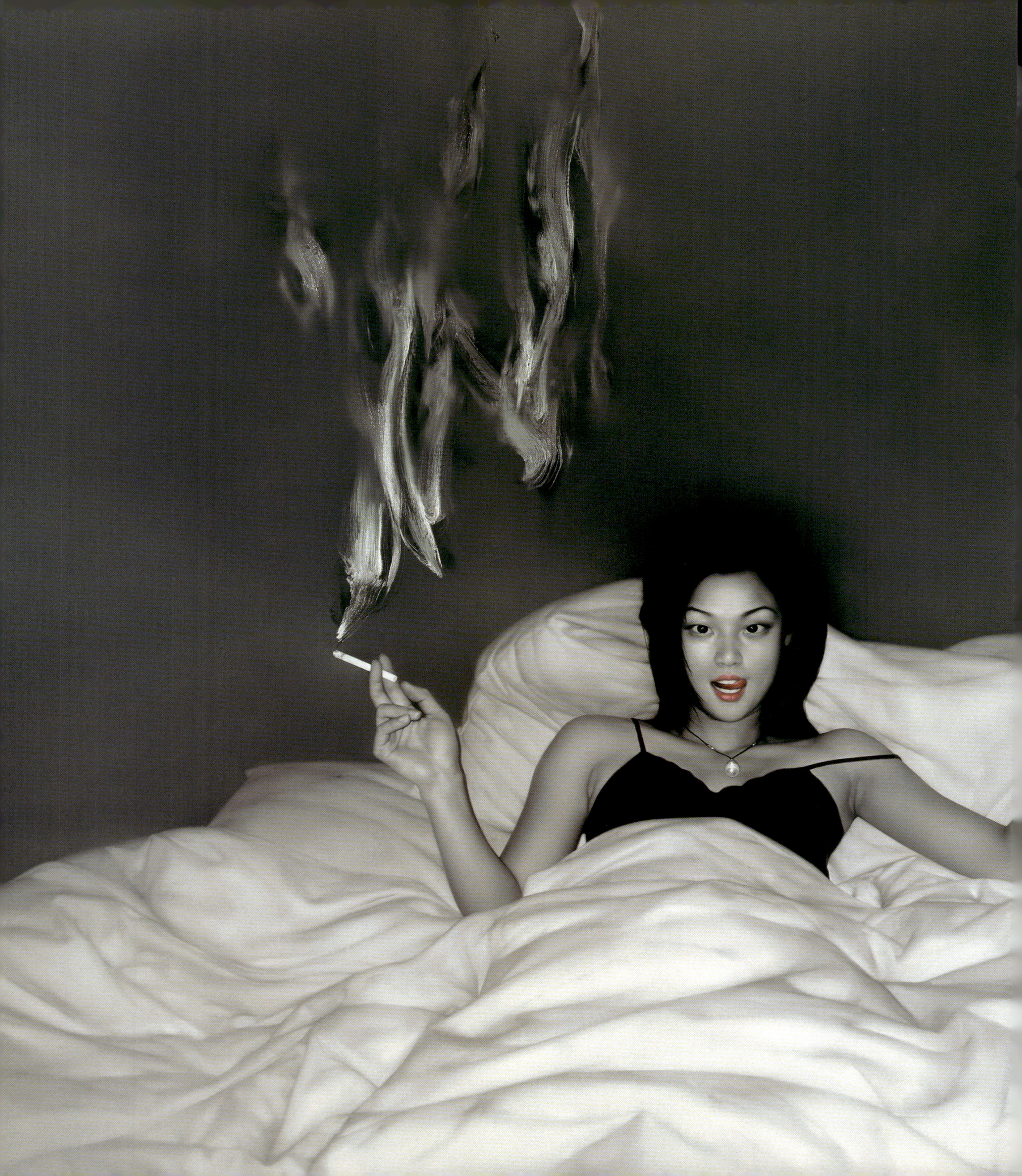

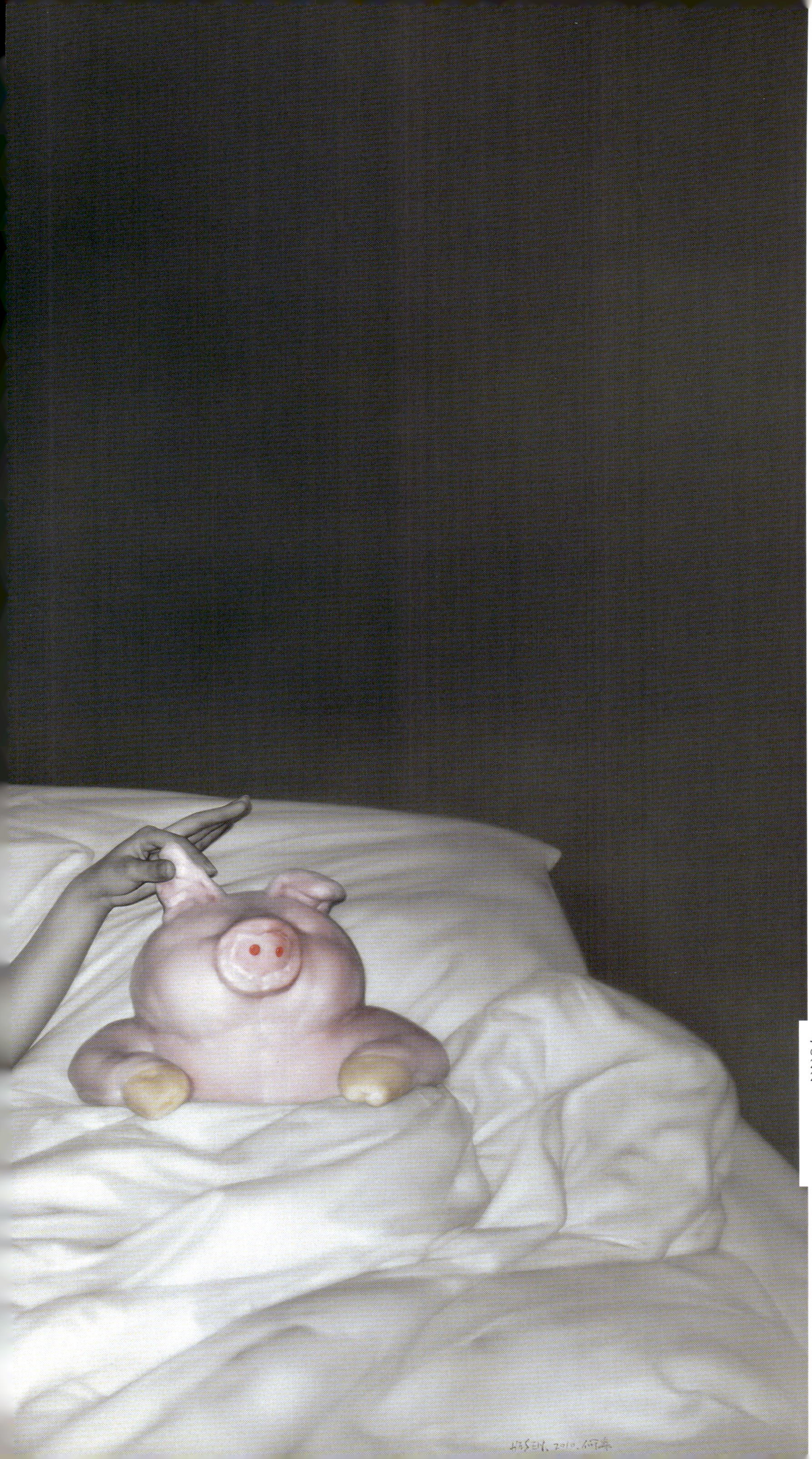

Just be happier
oil on canvas
200x250 cm
2010

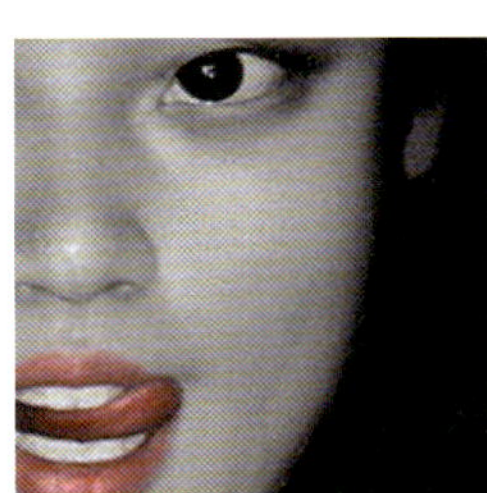

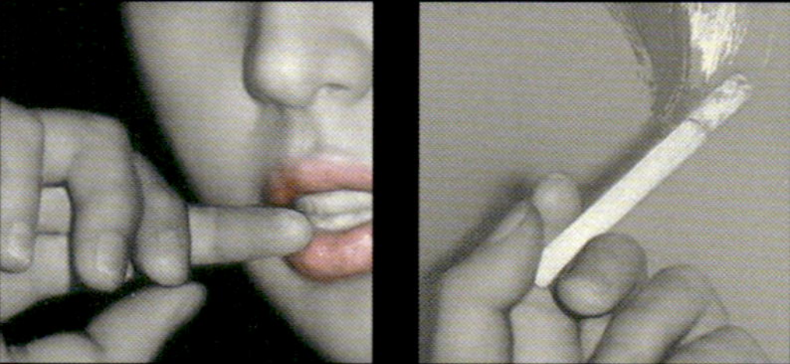

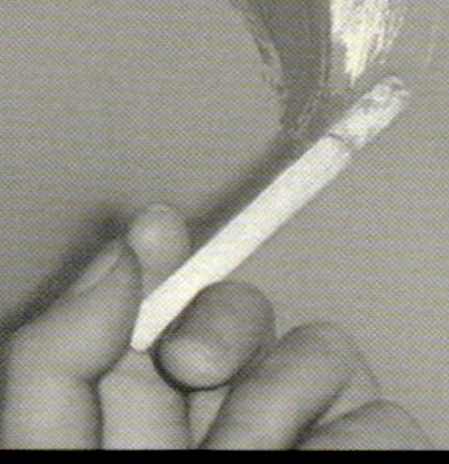

Sofa in Green
oil on canvas
200x150 cm
2010

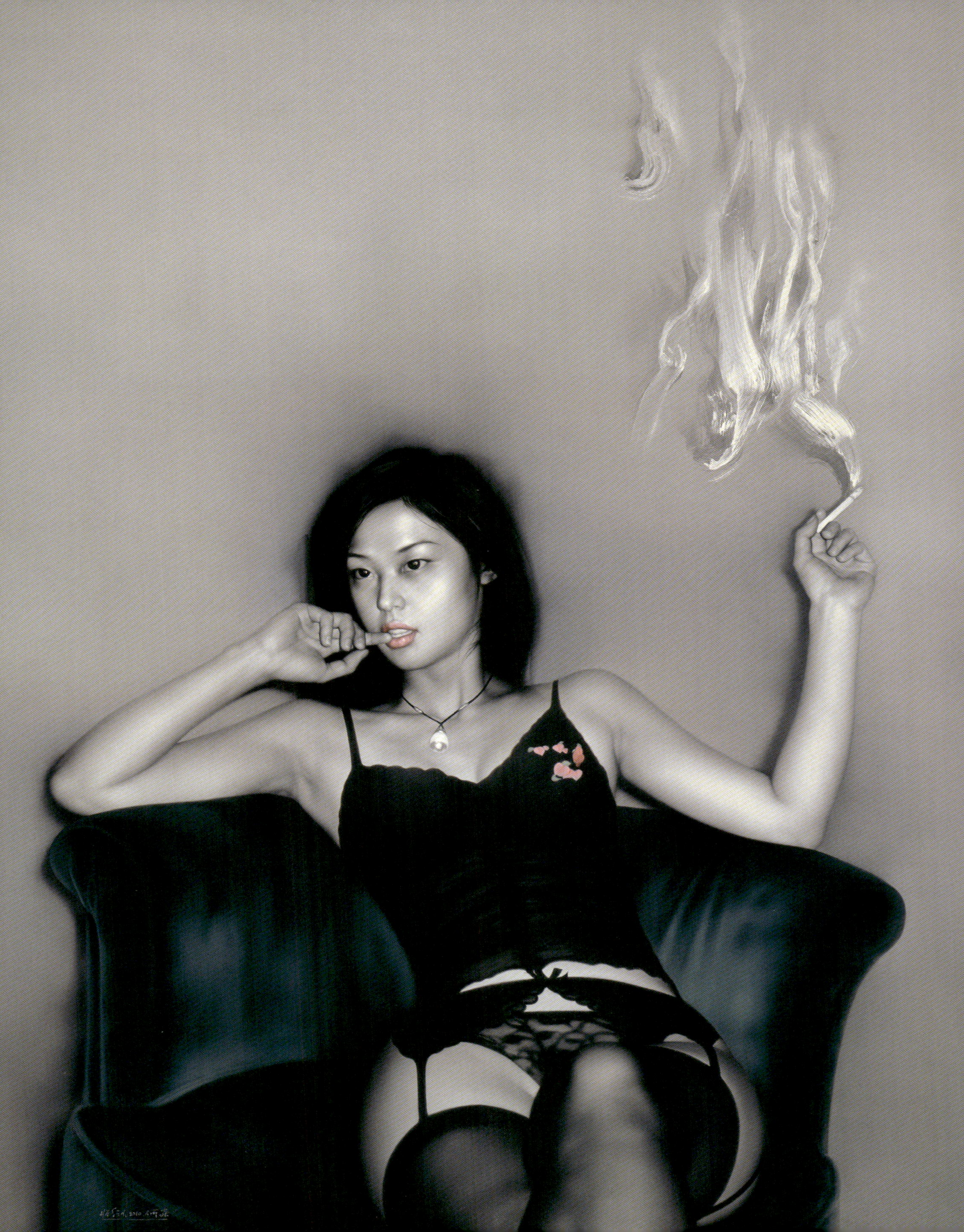

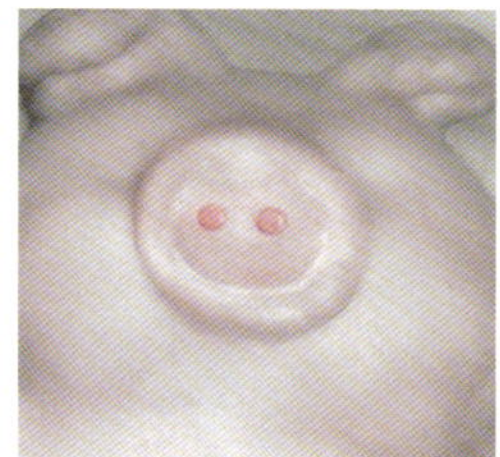
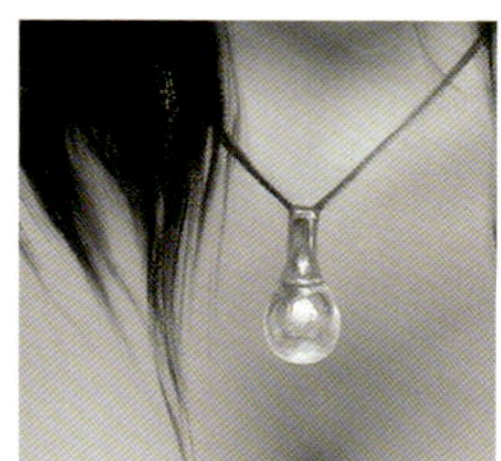

Lie with me
oil on canvas
150x200 cm
2009

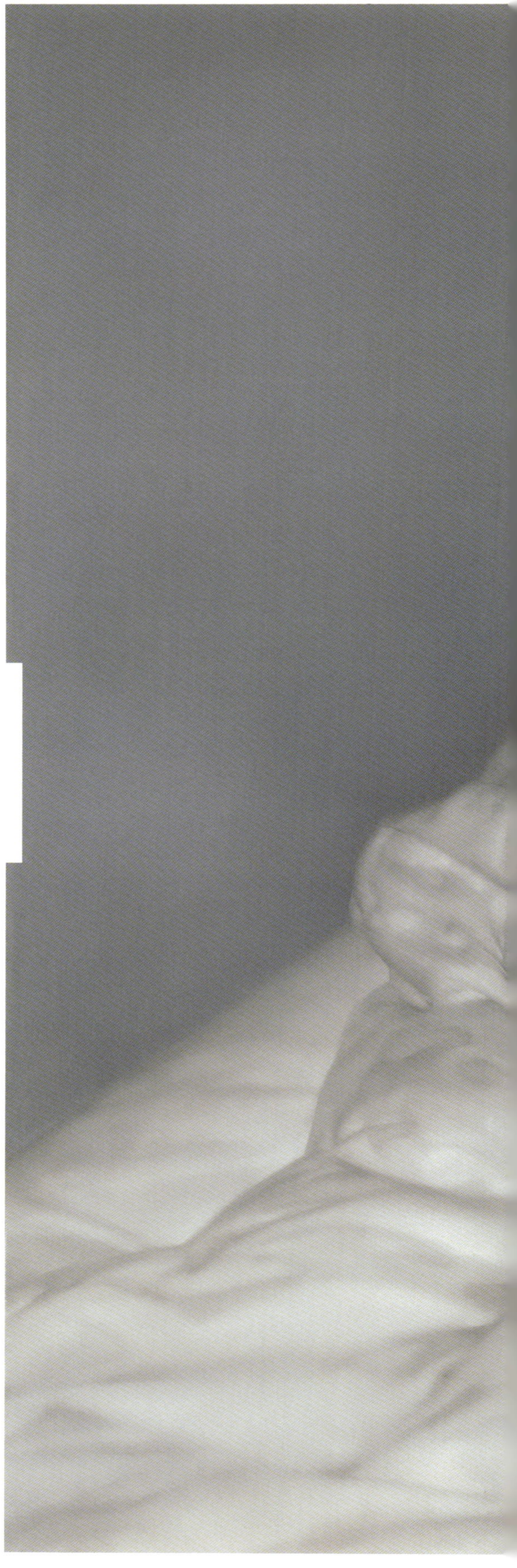

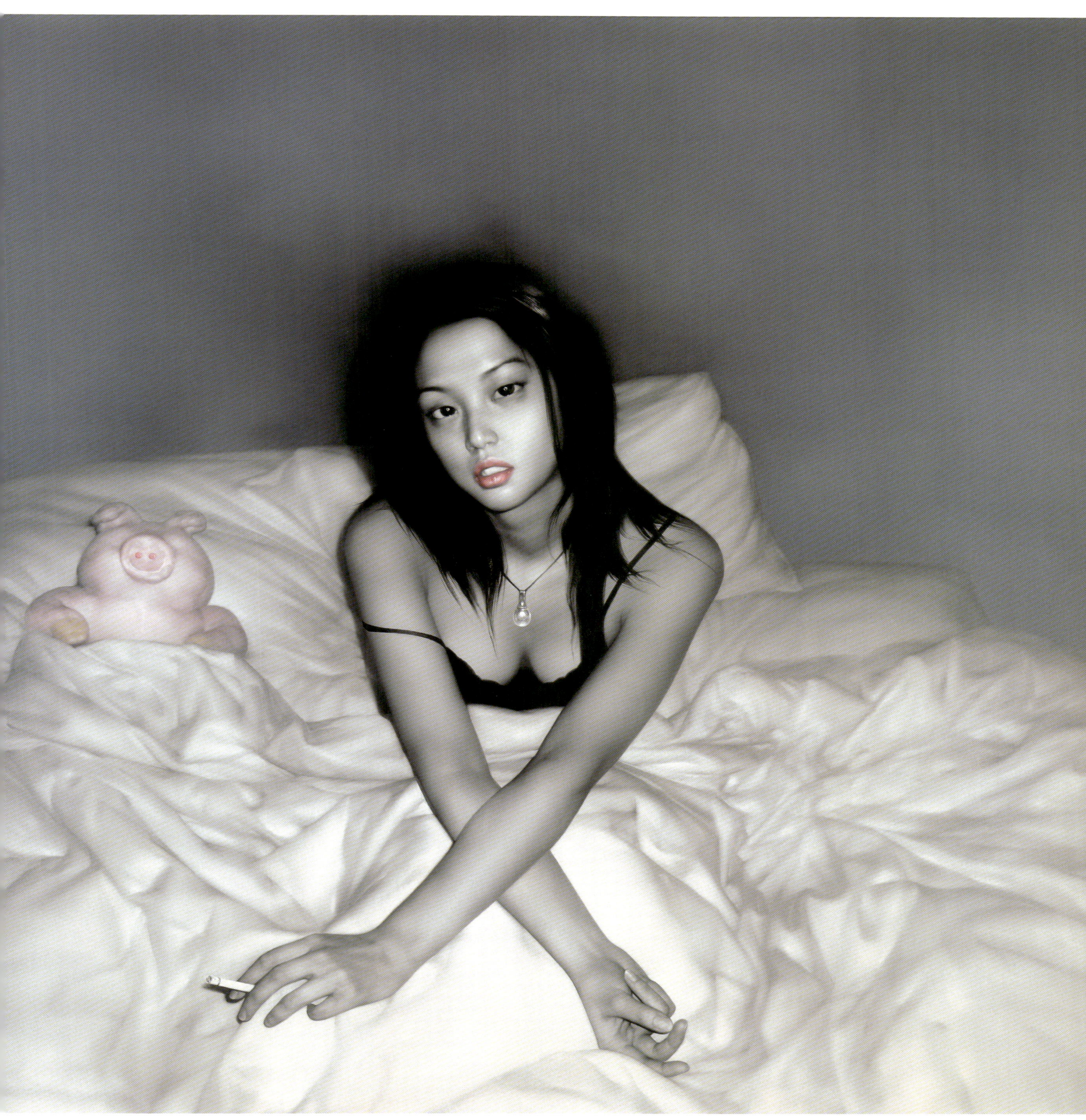

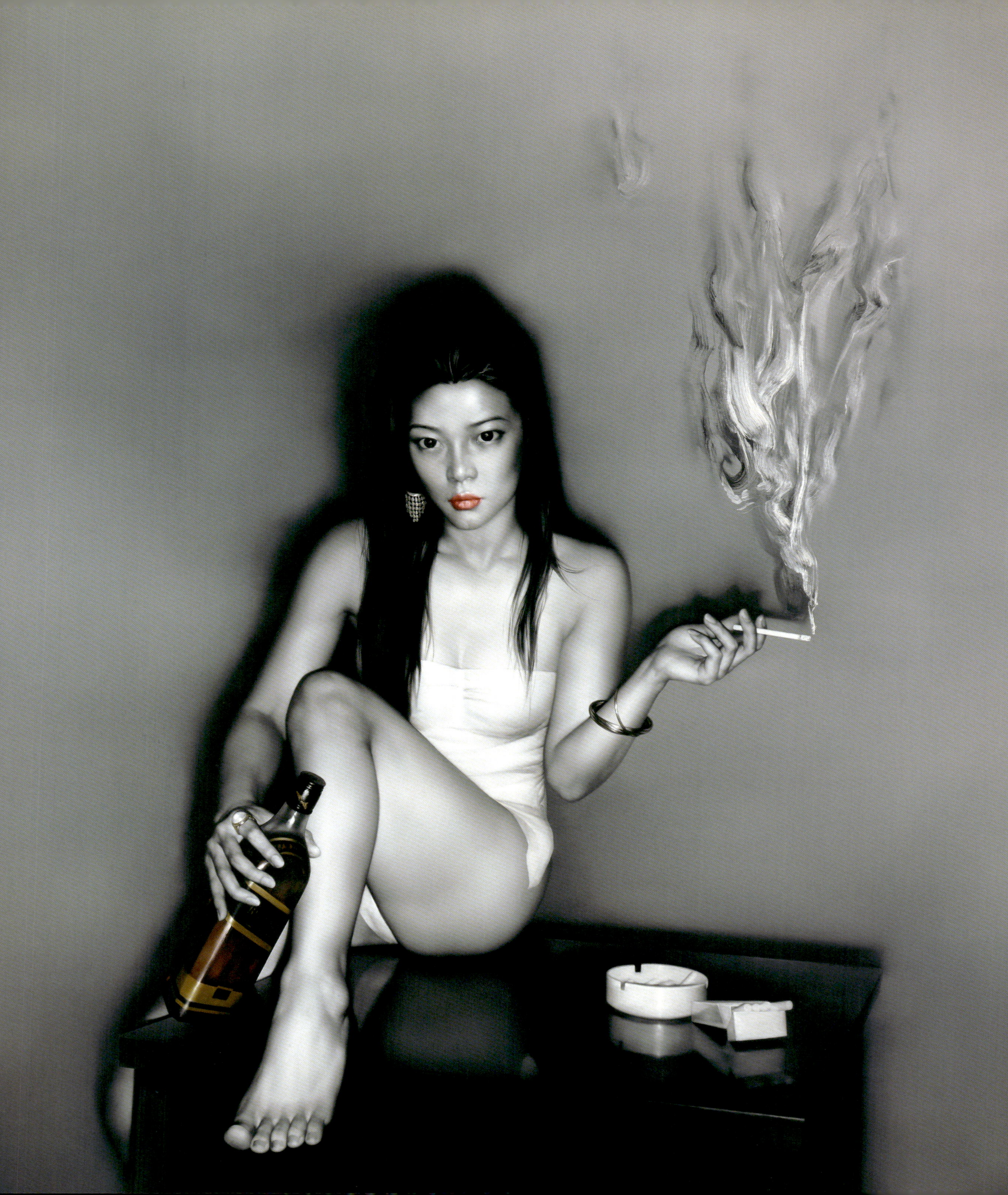

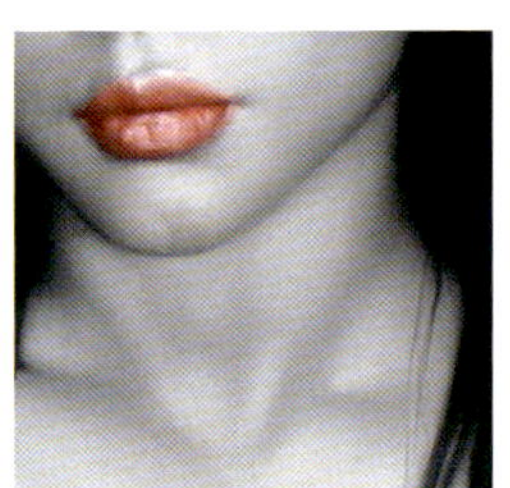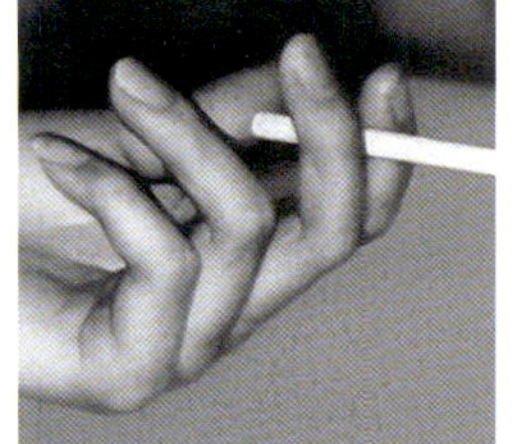

**Du Du sitting
on the table**
oil on canvas
250x200 cm
2009

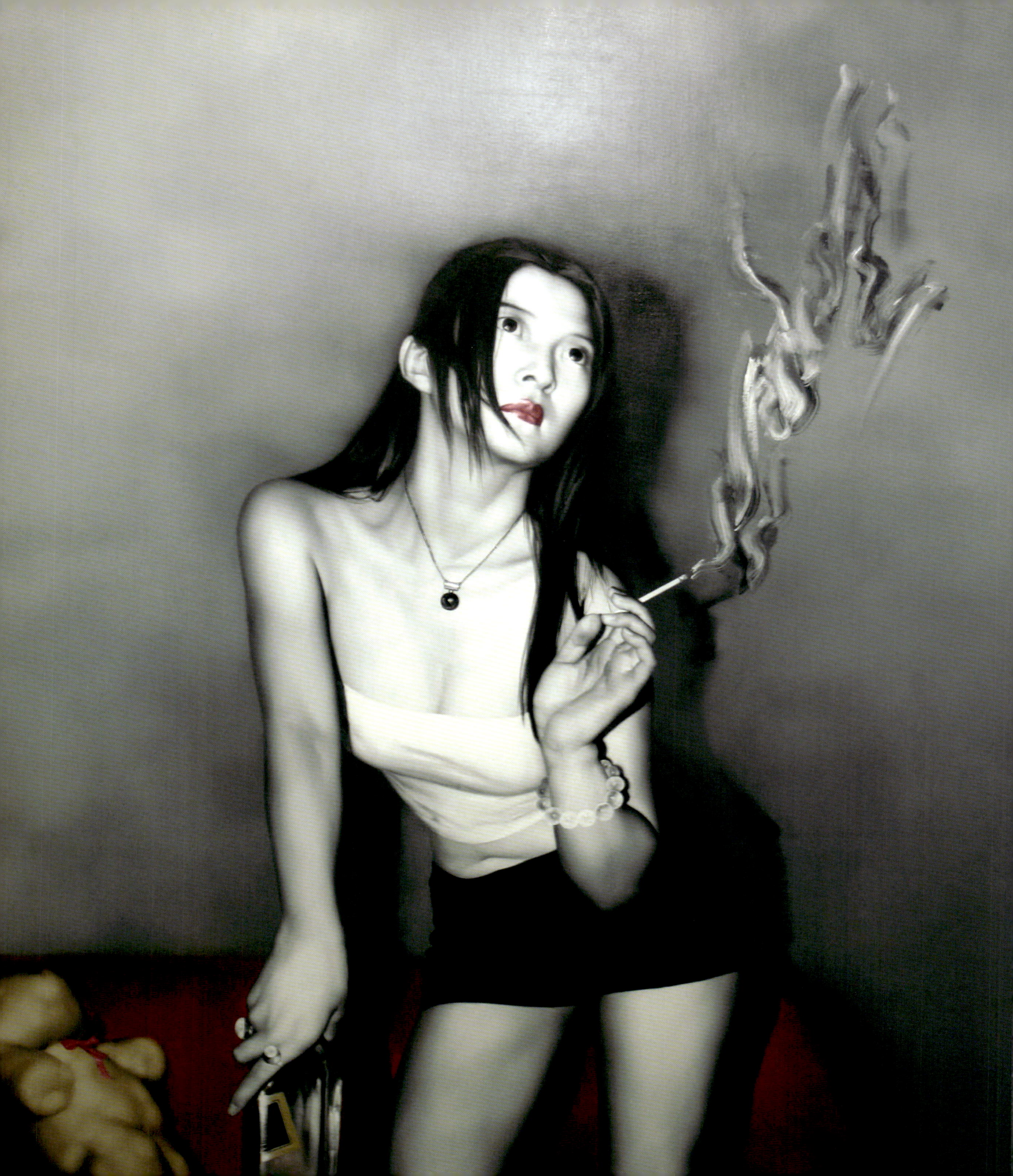

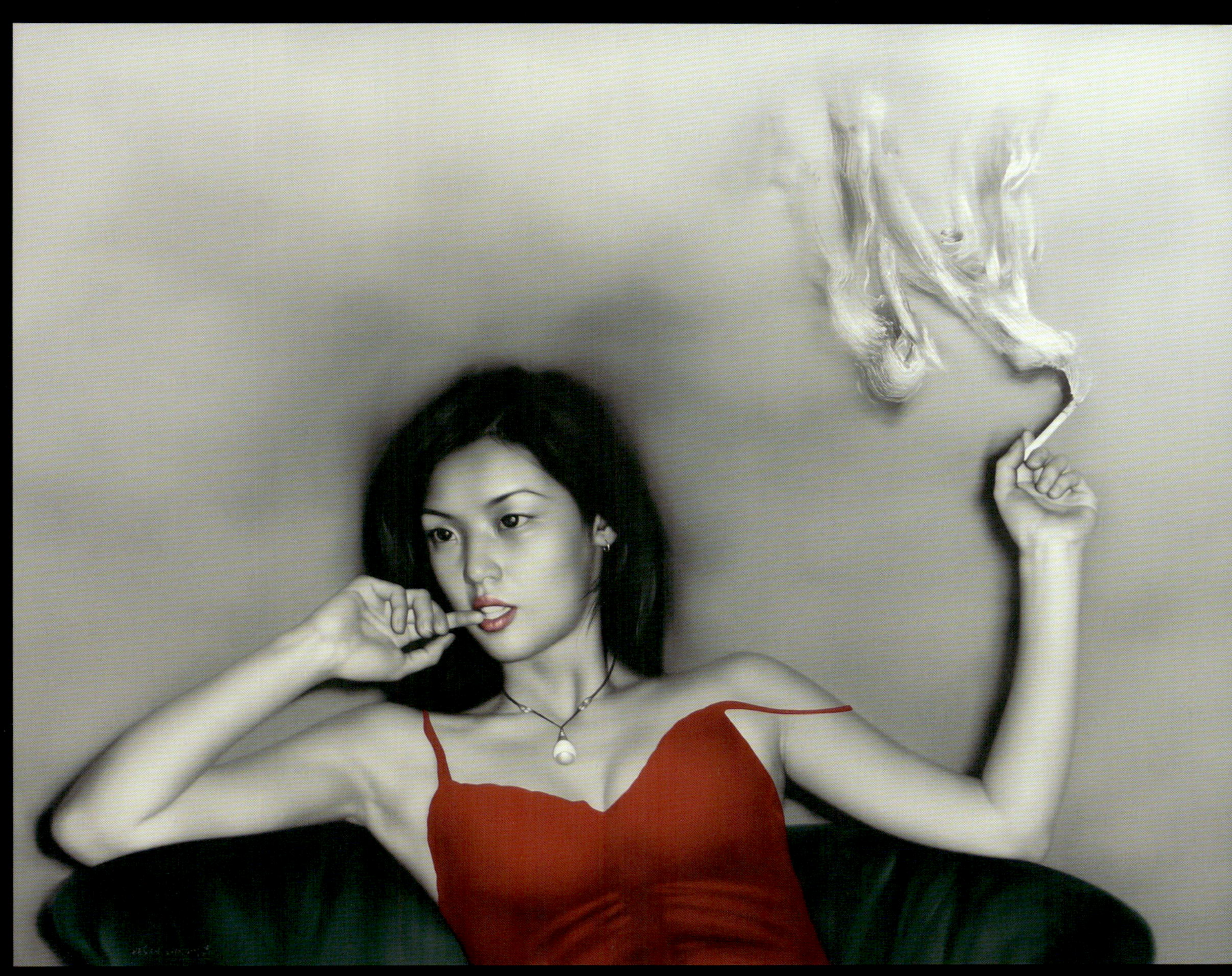

Du Du's worry
oil on canvas
250x200 cm
2008

Alone
oil on canvas
120x150 cm
2010

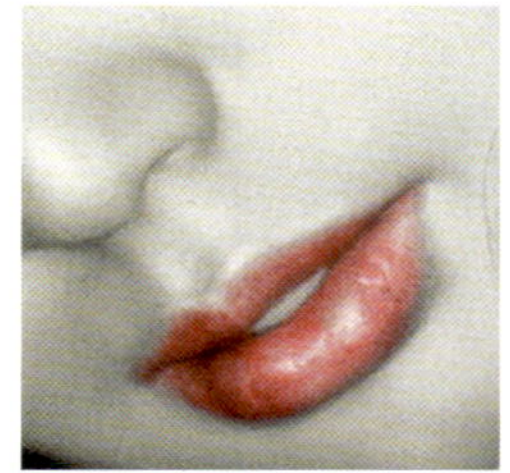
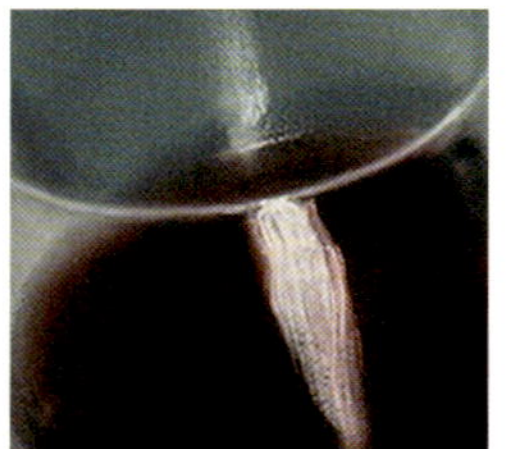
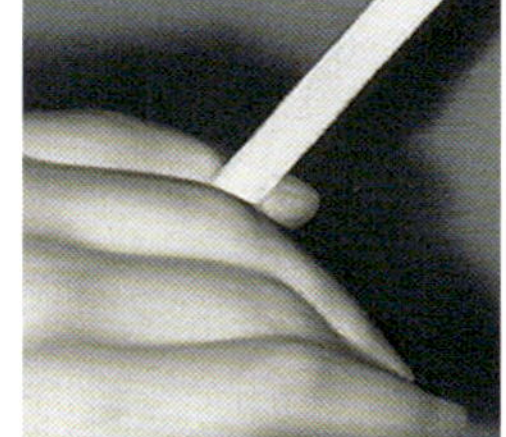

Glass of Wine
oil on canvas
150x120 cm
2009

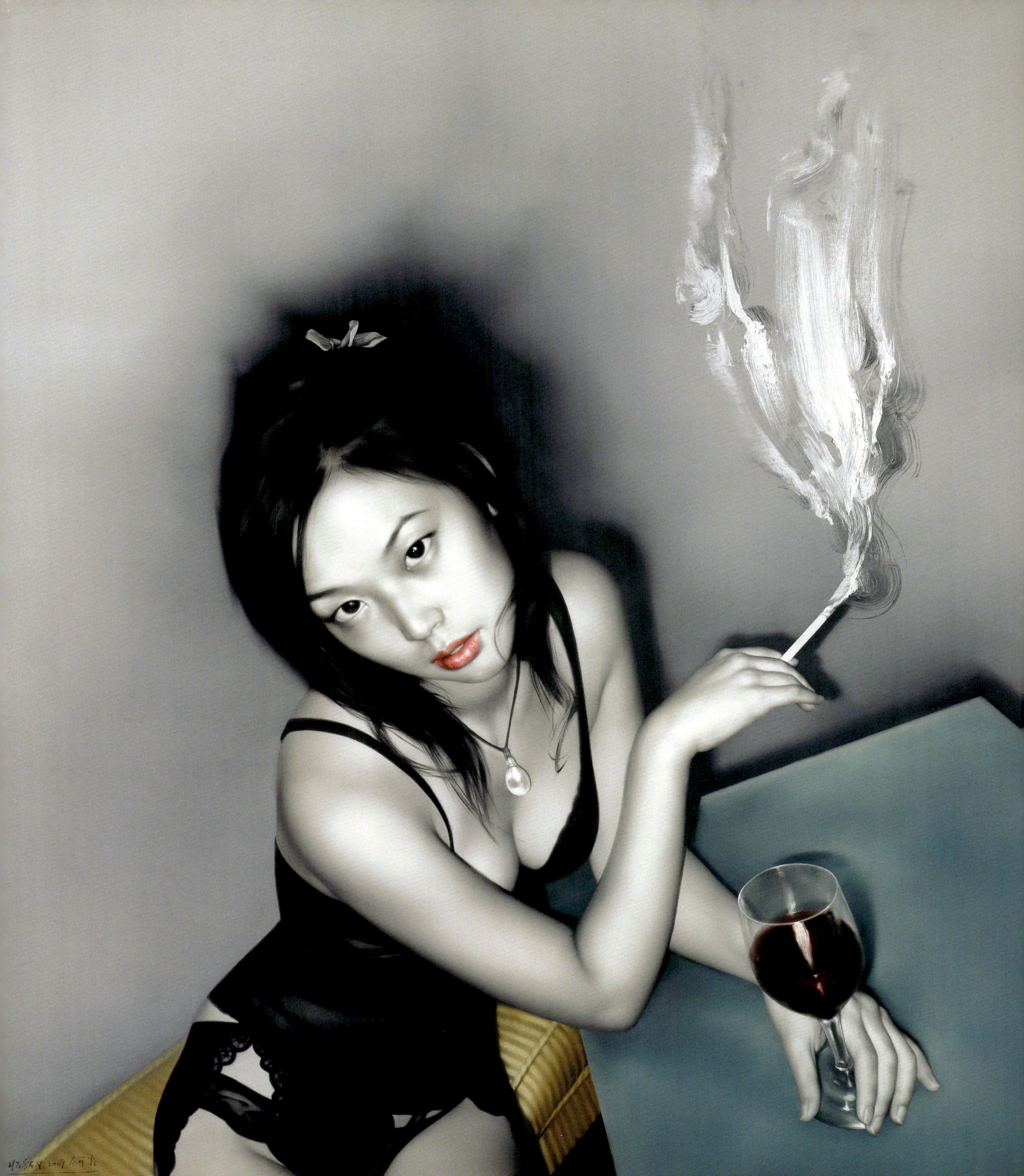

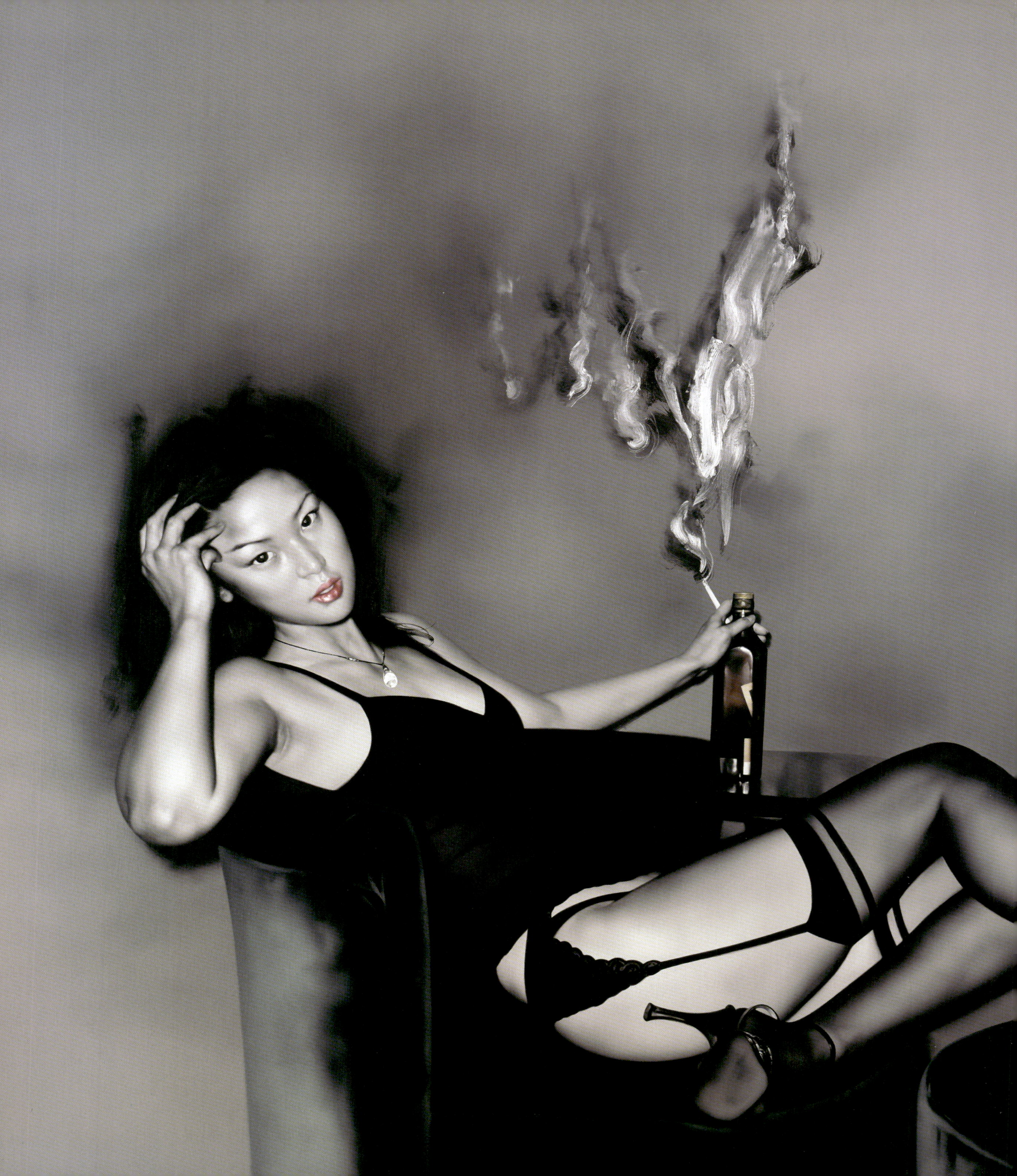

Enjoy
oil on canvas
250x300 cm
2009

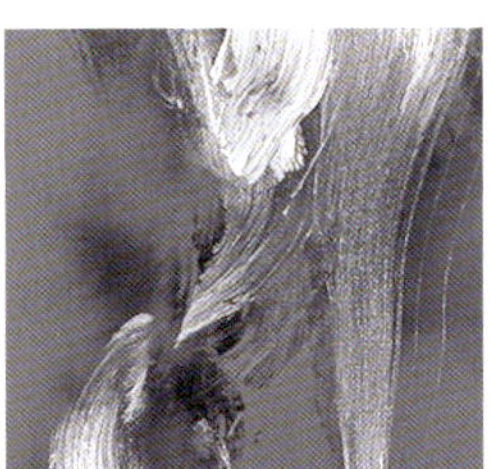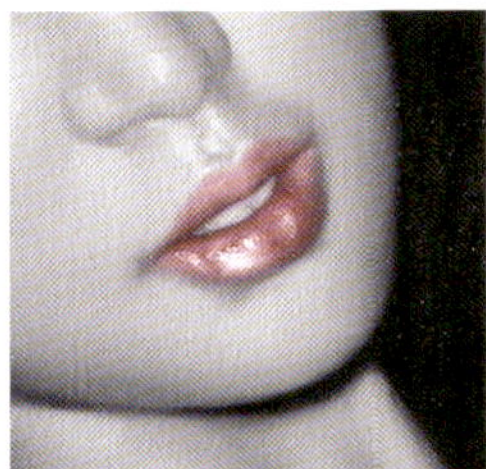

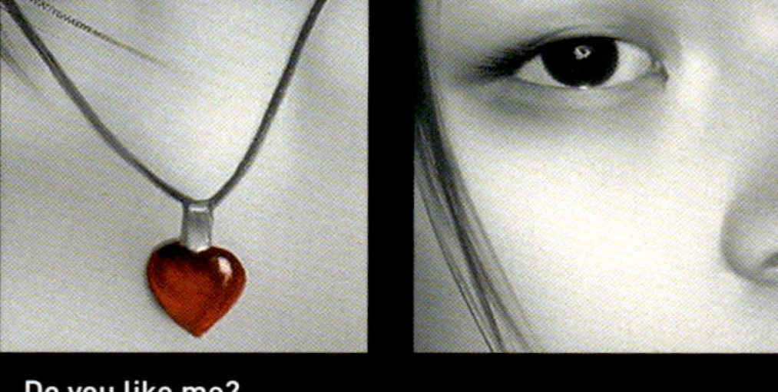

Do you like me?
oil on canvas
150x120 cm
2010

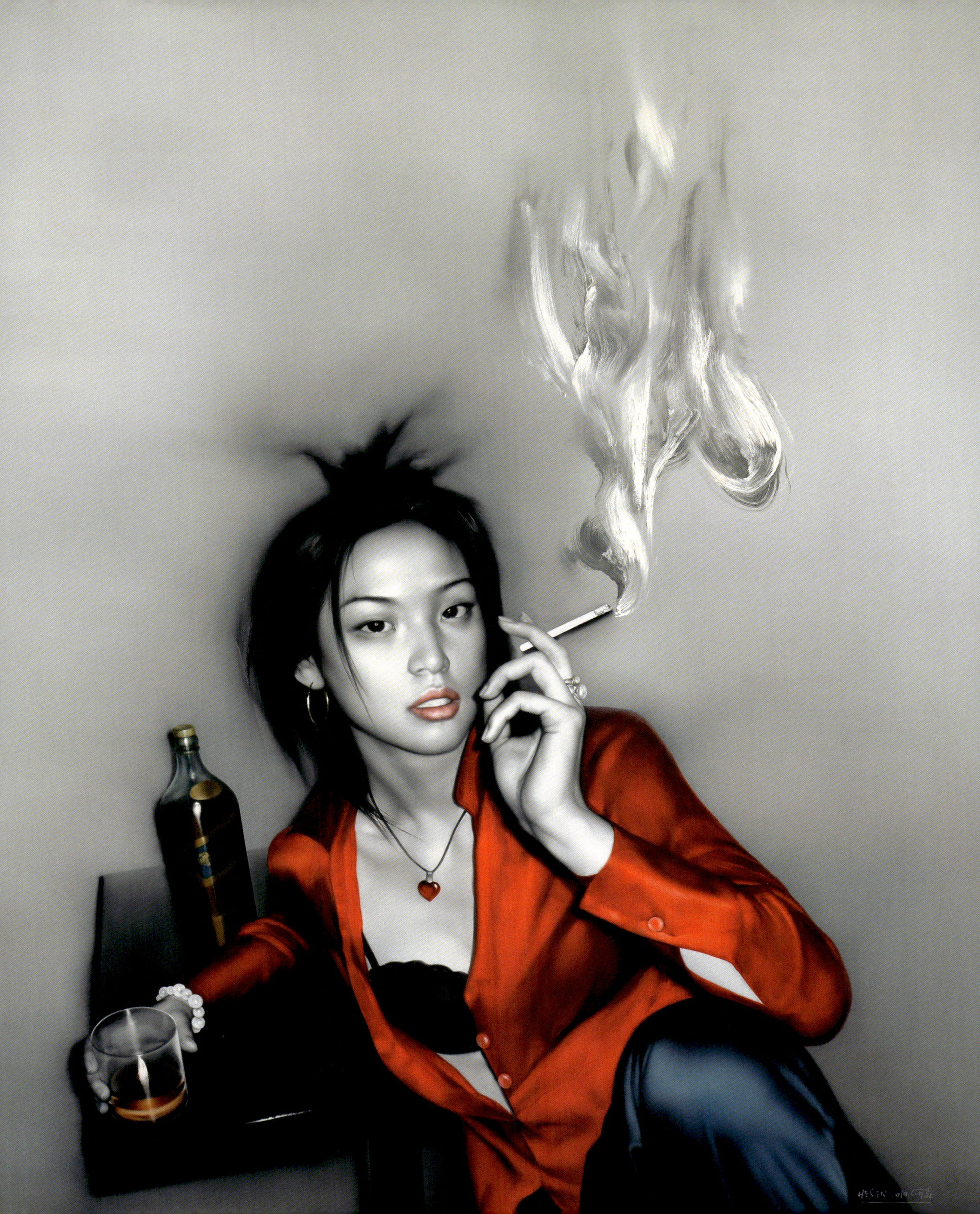

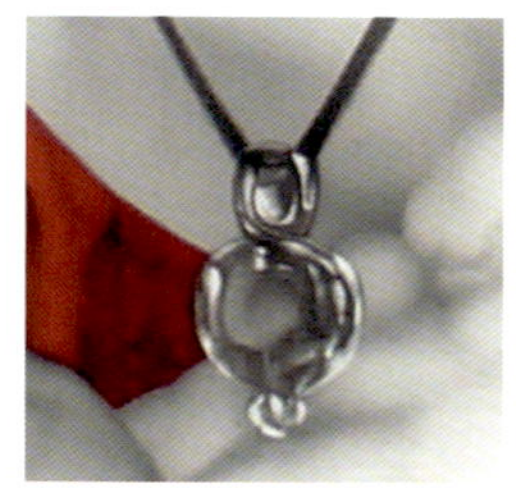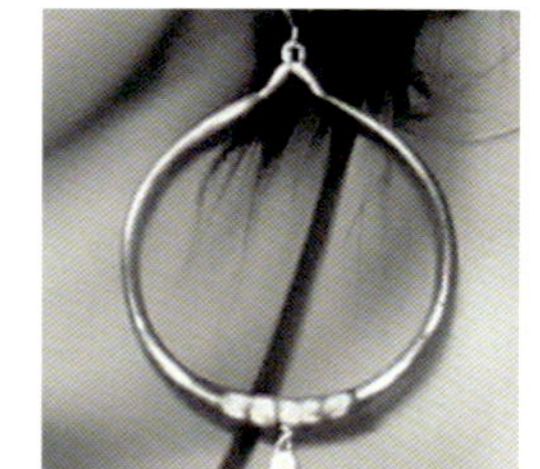

Is it interesting?
oil on canvas
150x120 cm
2009

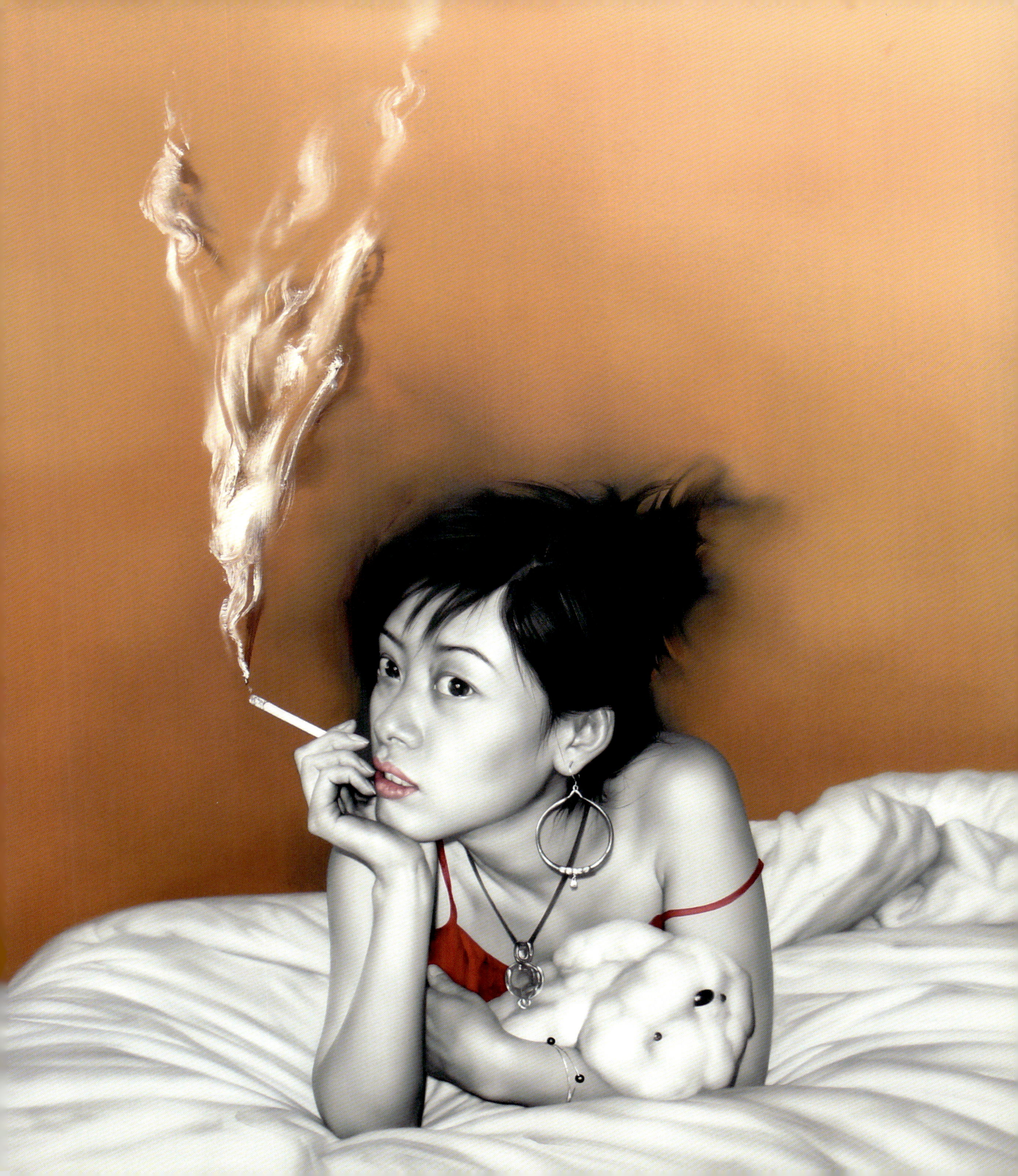

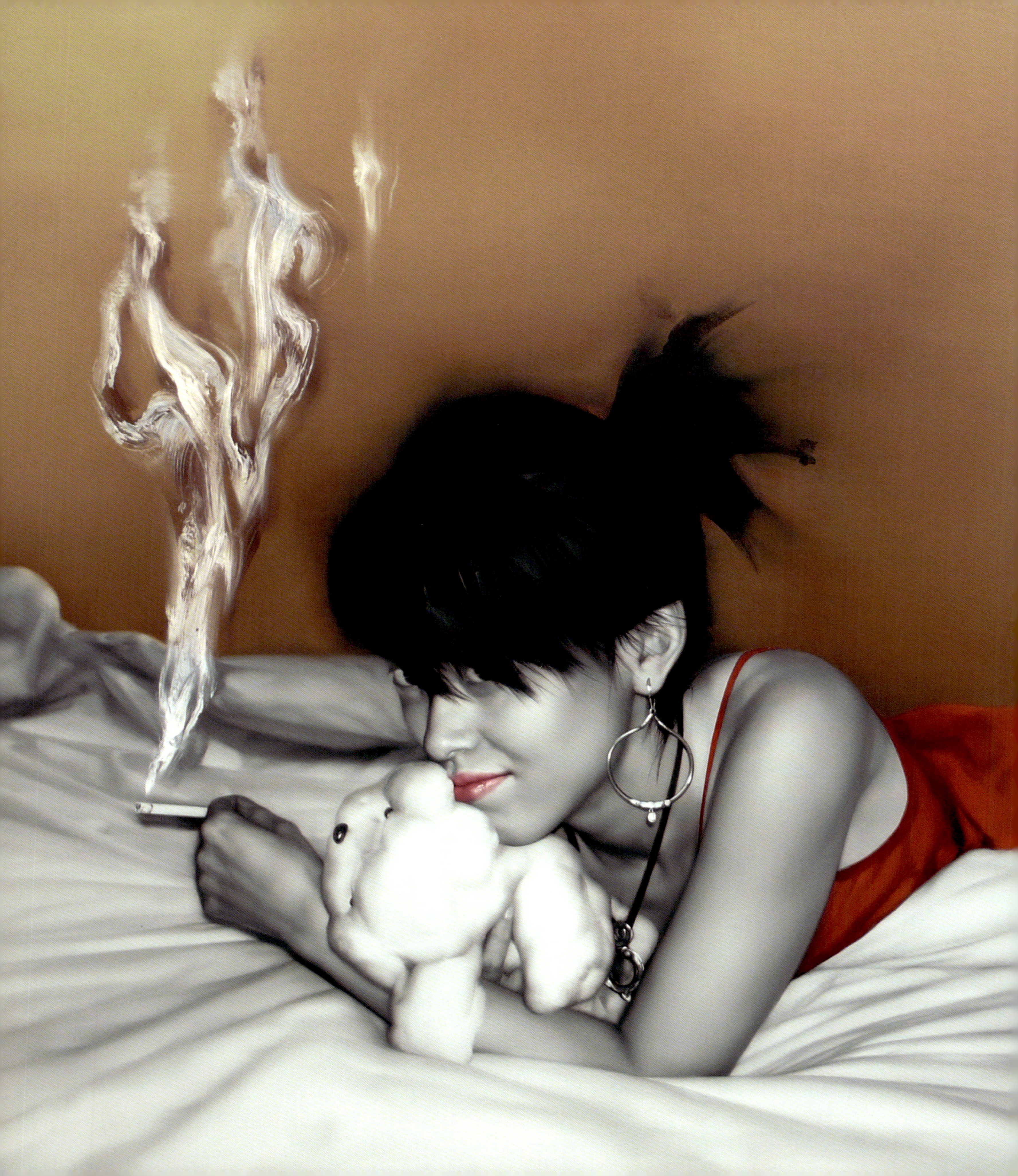

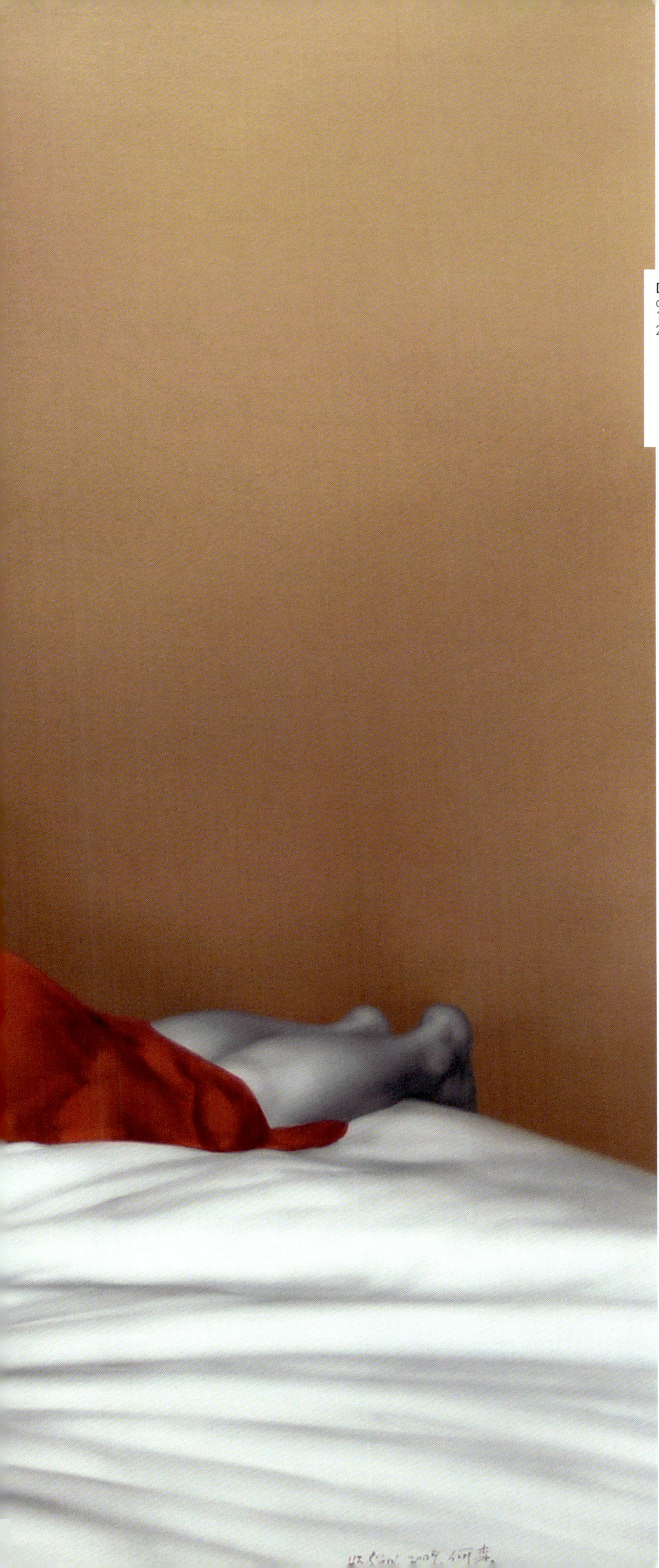

Don't look at me
oil on canvas
120x150 cm
2009

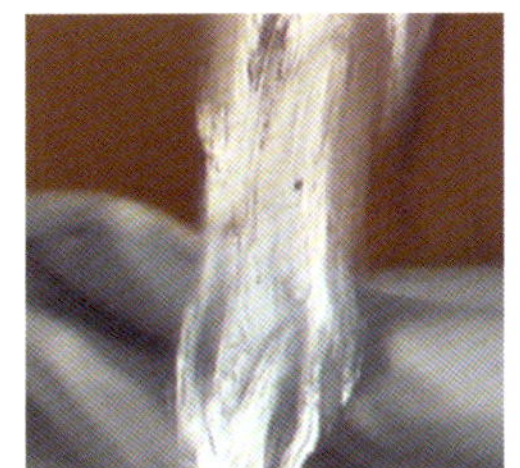 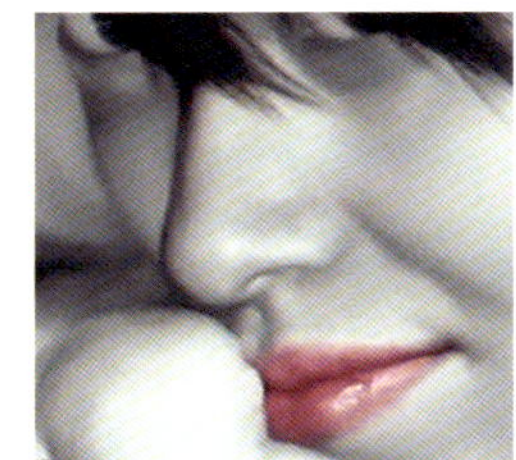

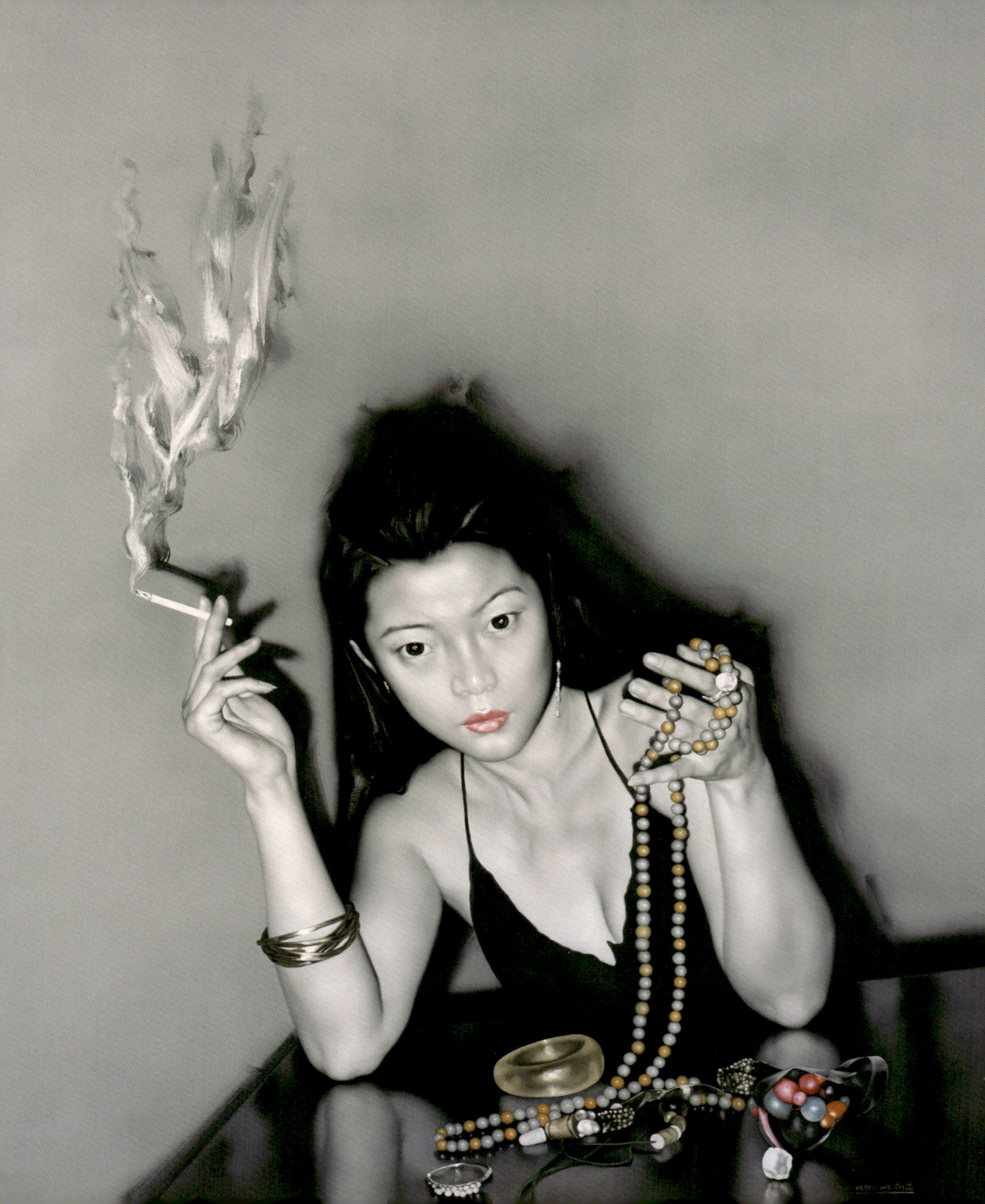

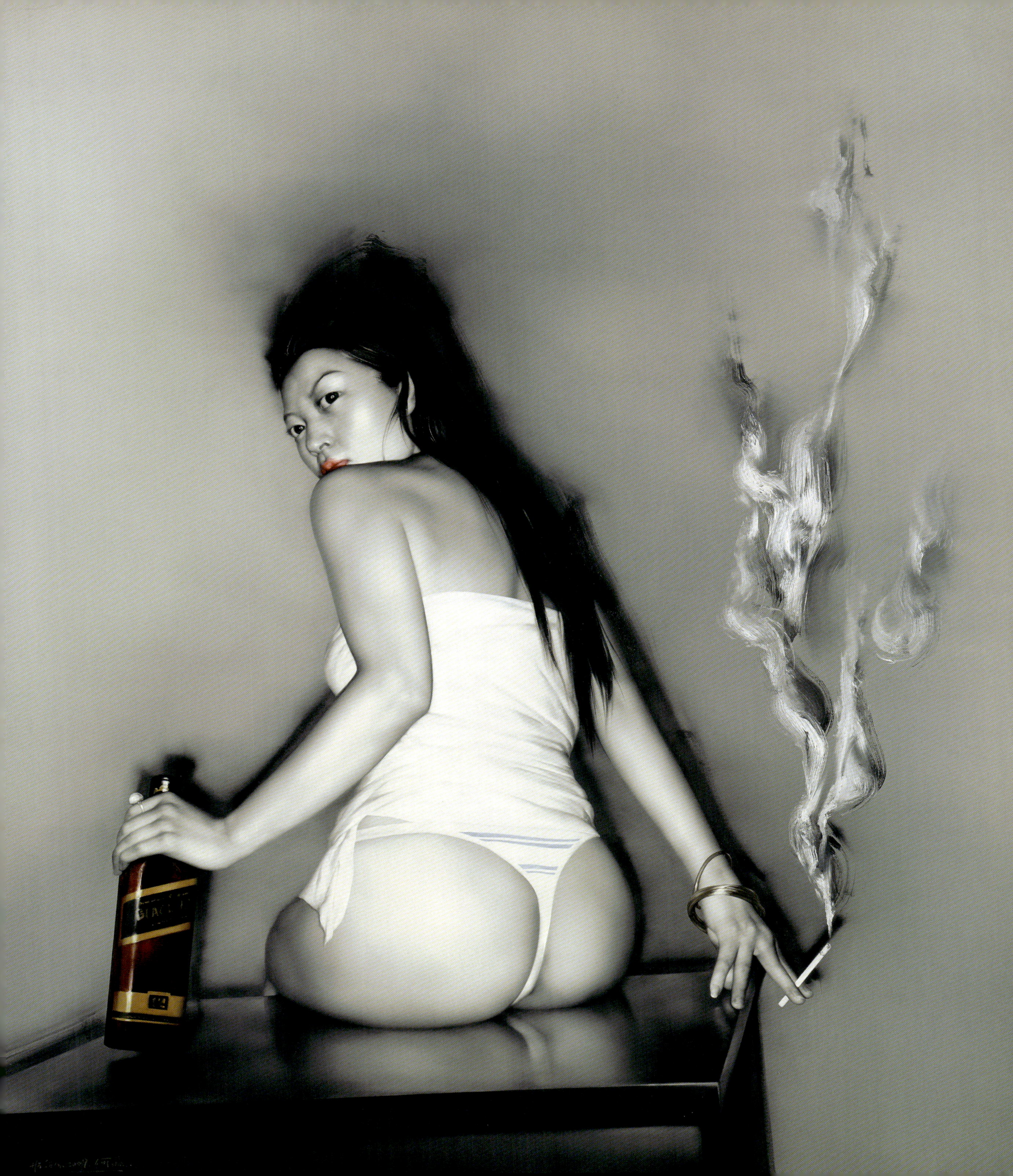

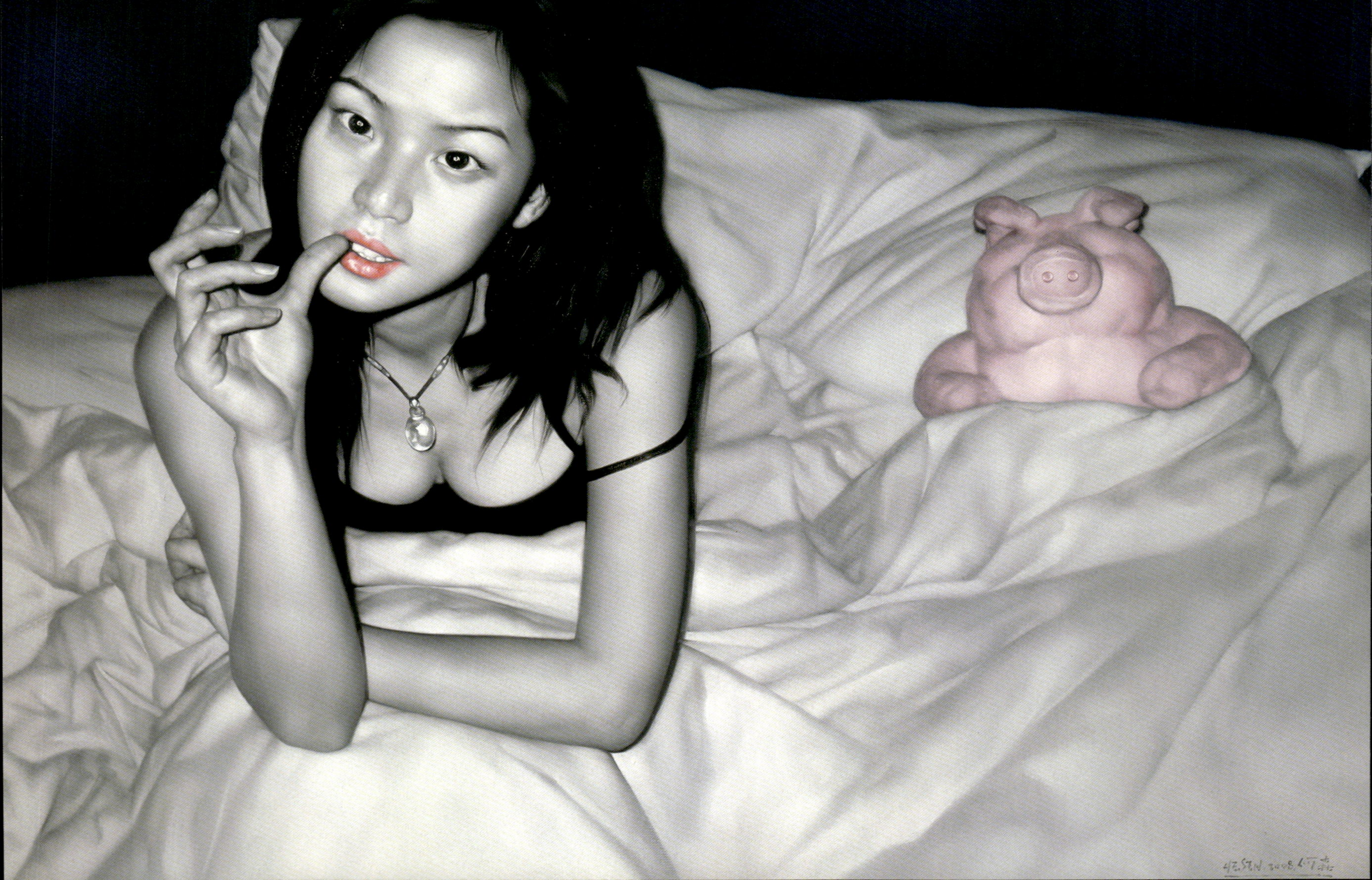

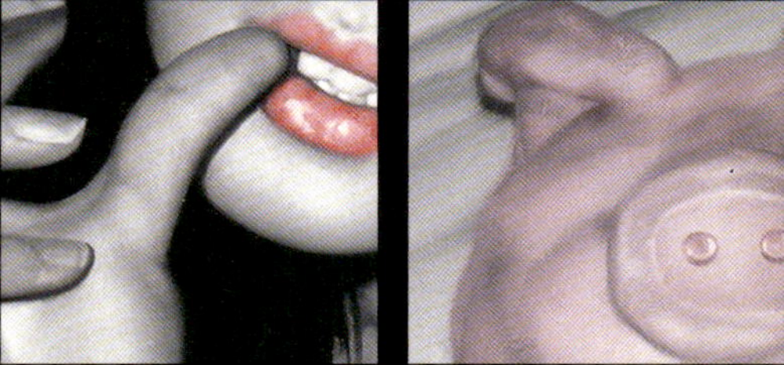

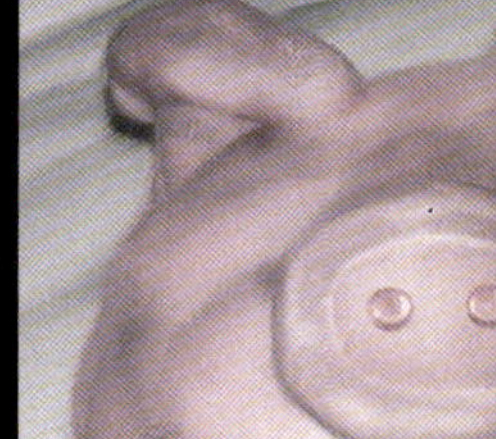

Sleeping with the toy
oil on canvas
170x150 cm
2008

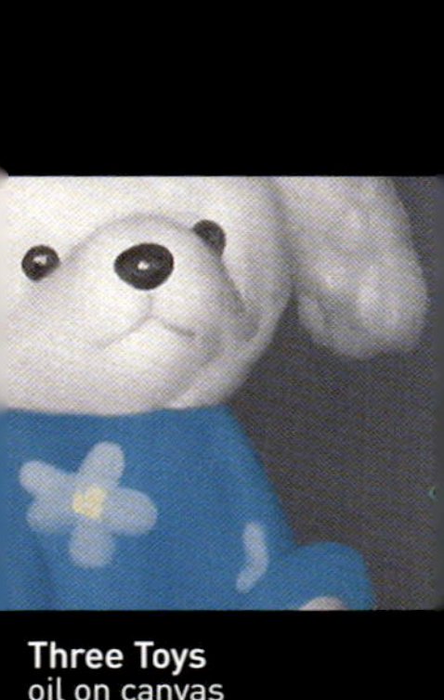

Three Toys
oil on canvas
250x200 cm
2007

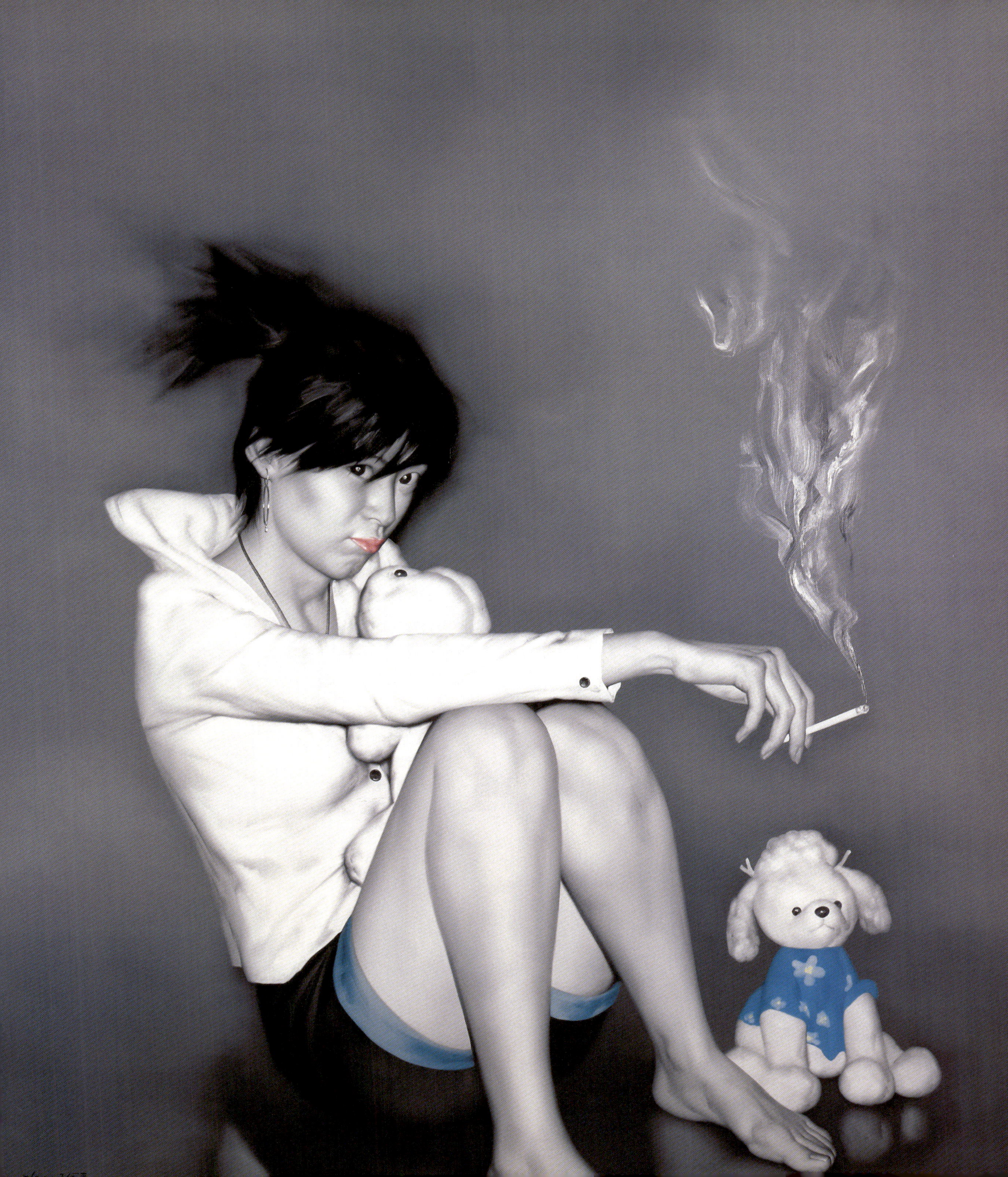

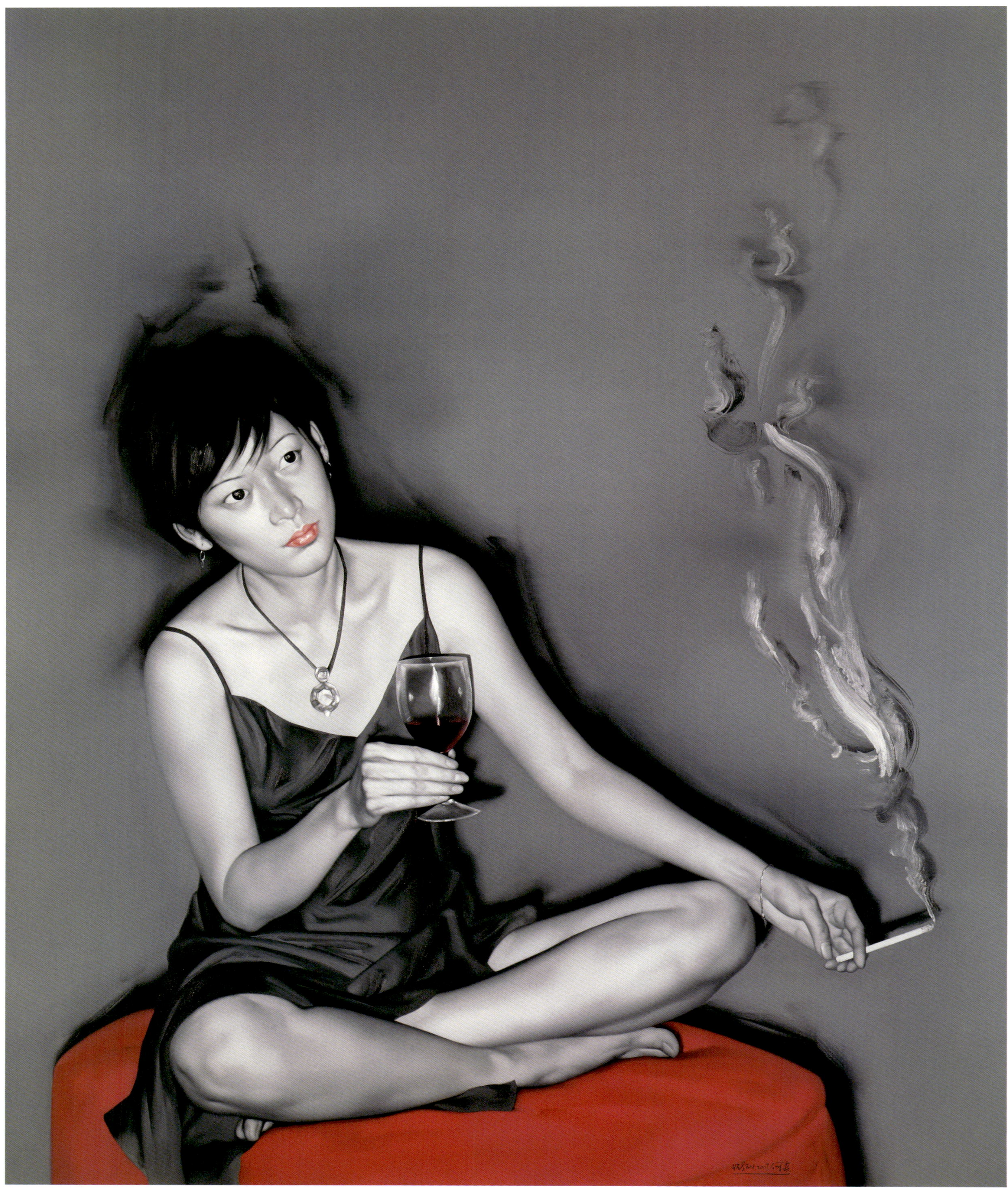

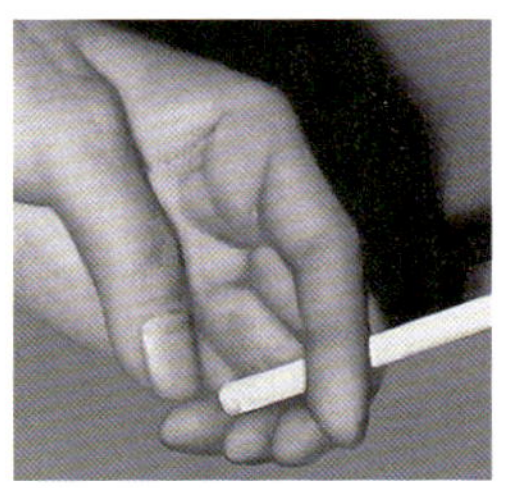

Smoking woman
with wine
oil on canvas
250x200 cm
2007

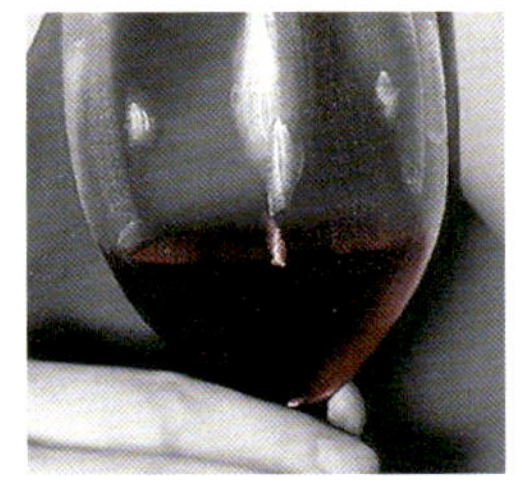

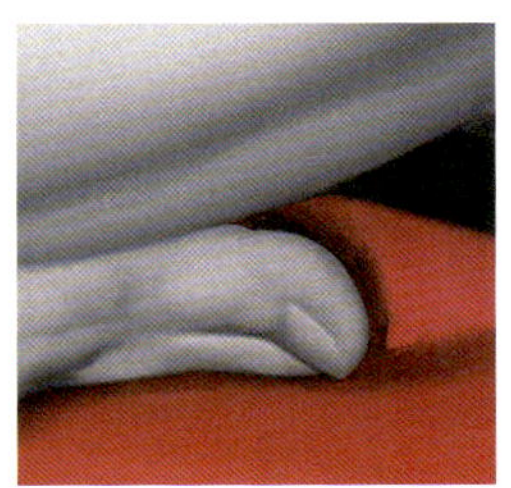

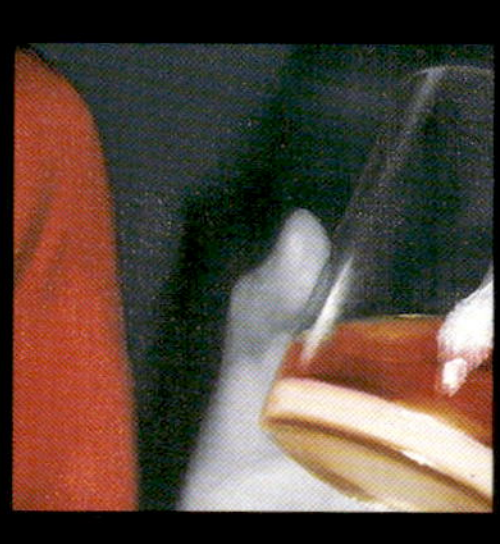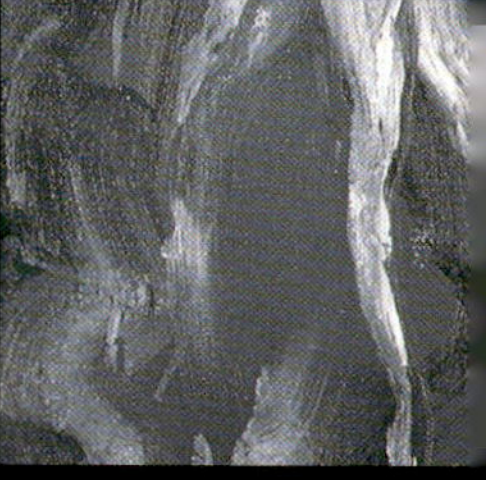

Come on. Let's drink
oil on canvas
250x200 cm
2008

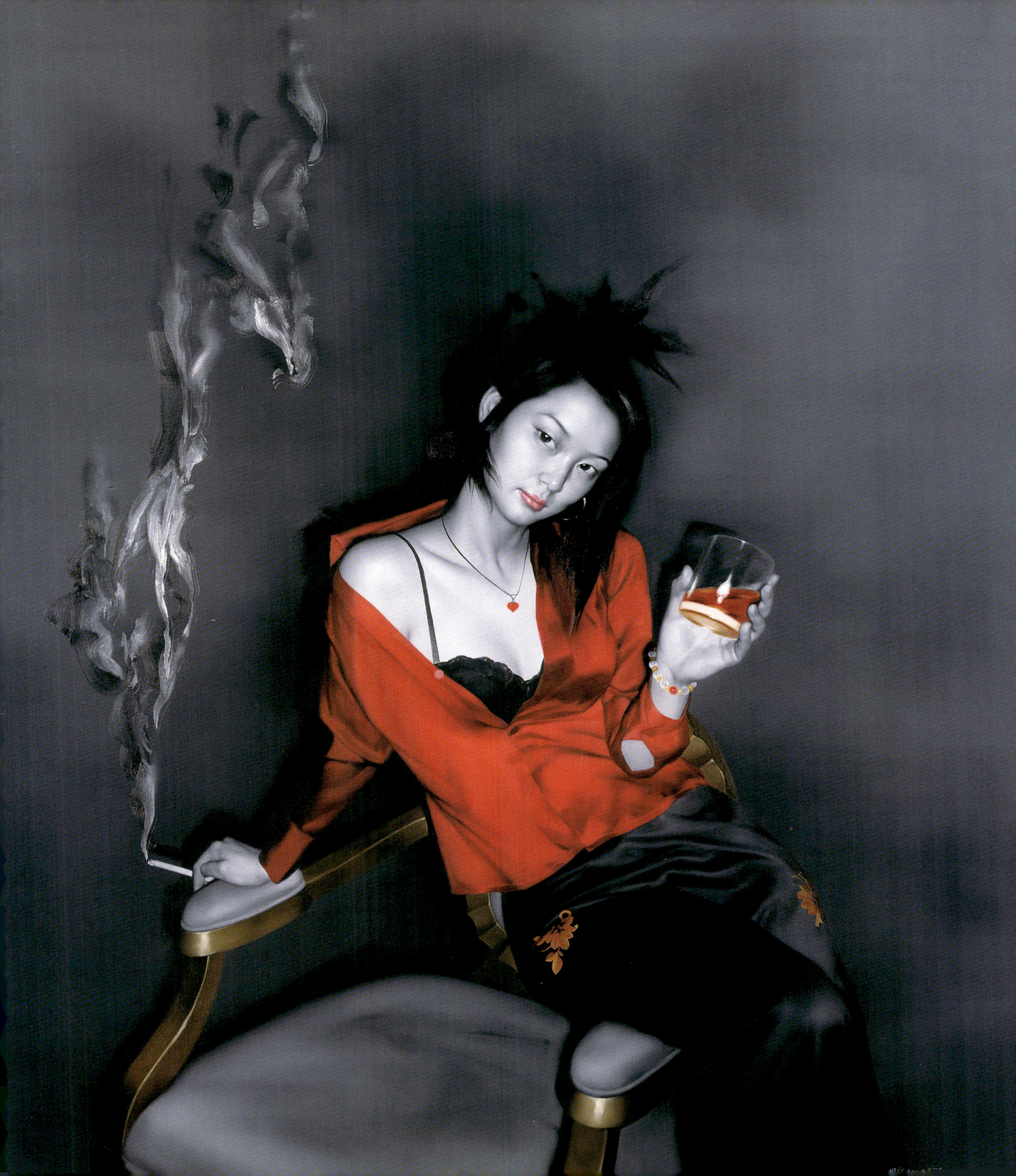

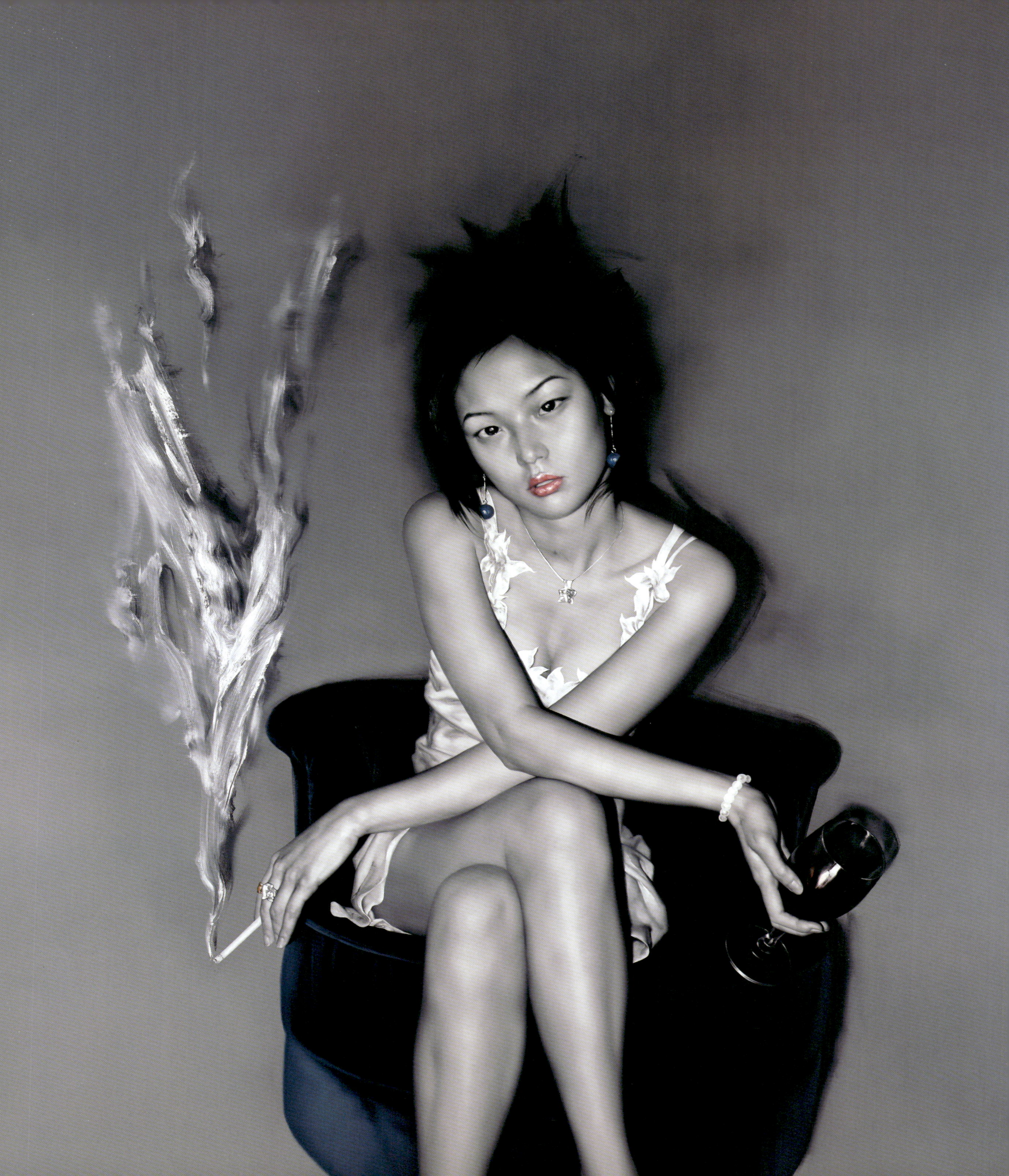

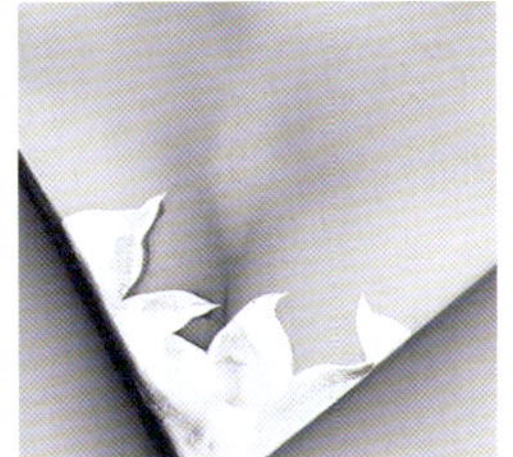

Are you tired?
Take breaks
oil on canvas
300x250 cm
2008

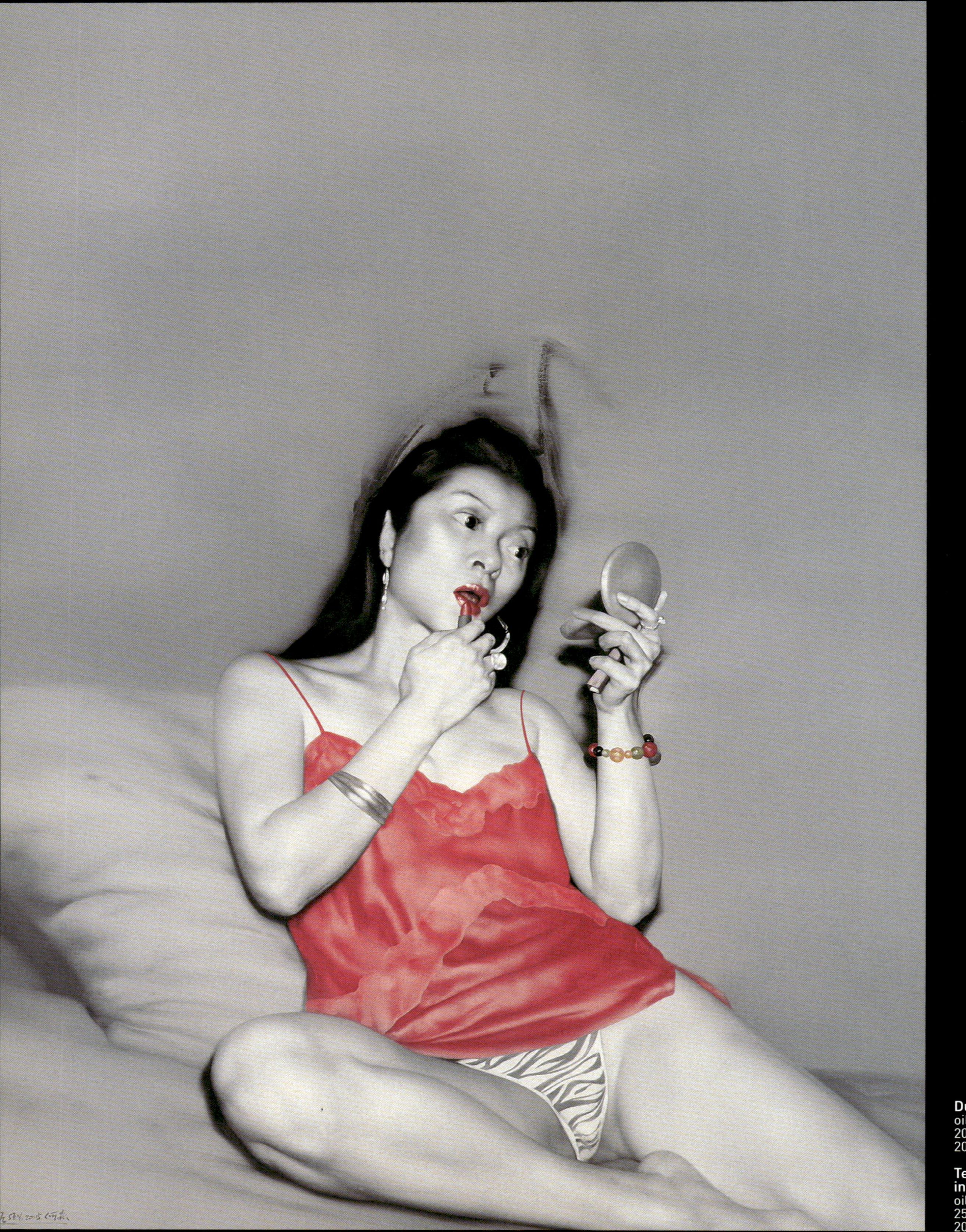

Du Du with make-up
oil on canvas
200x150 cm
2005

**Temptation is
innocent**
oil on canvas
250x200 cm
2009

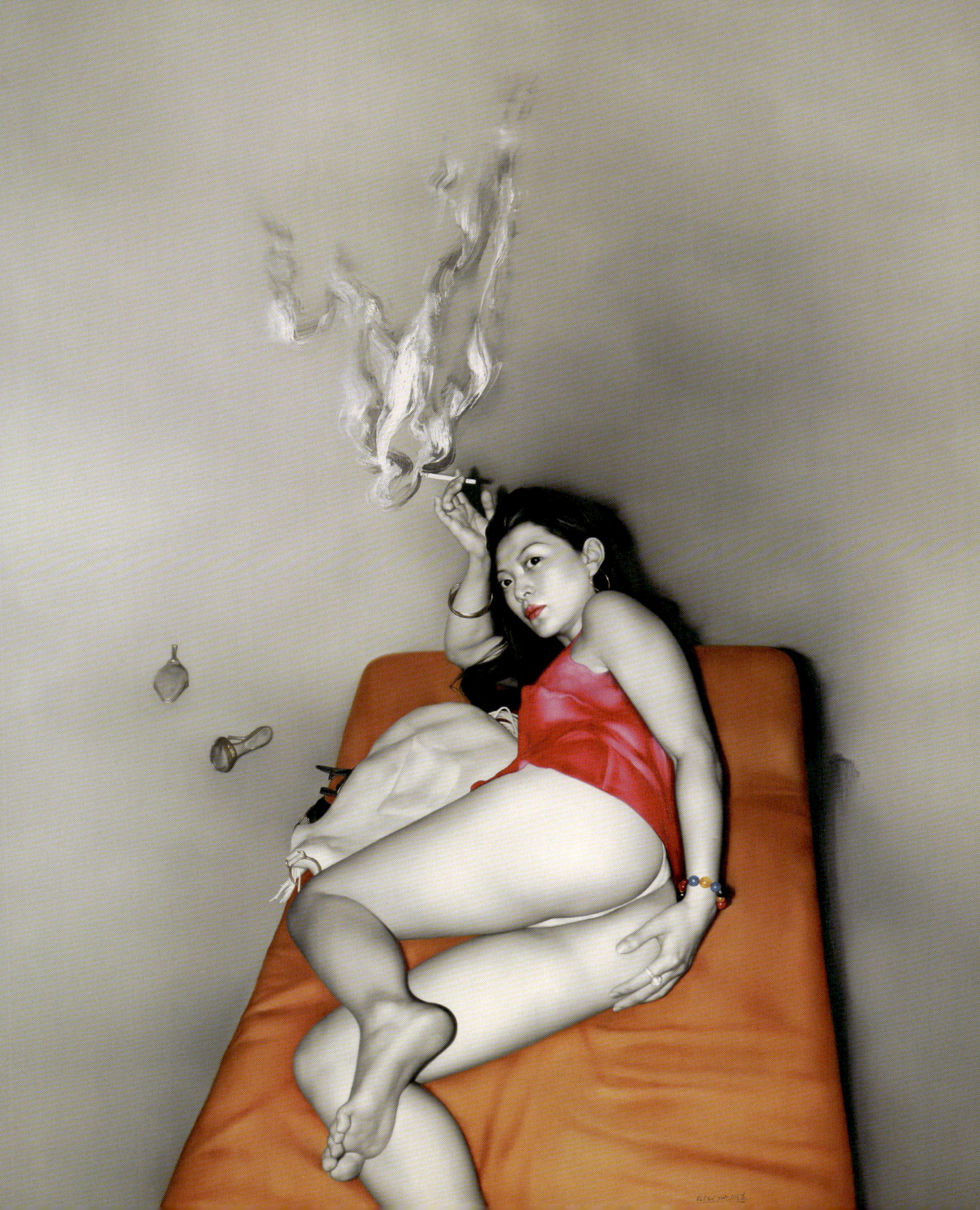

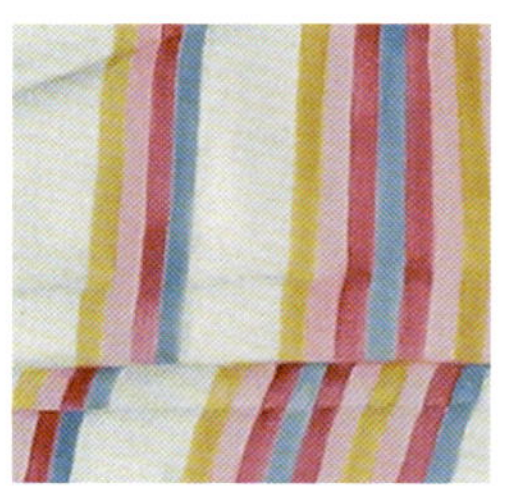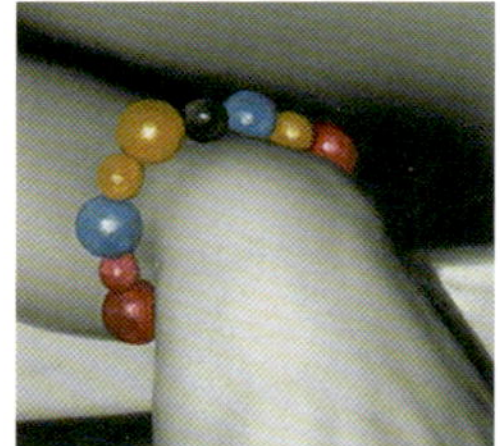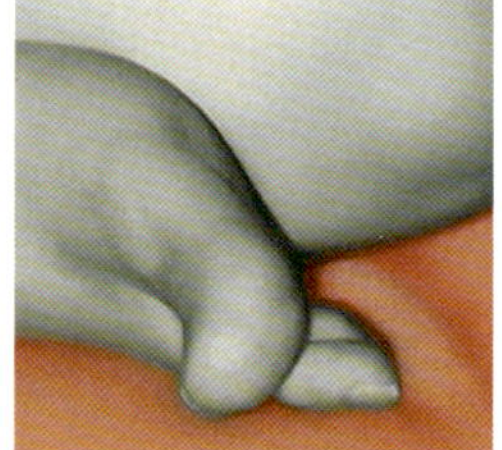

Inelegant Du Du
oil on canvas
250x200 cm
2009

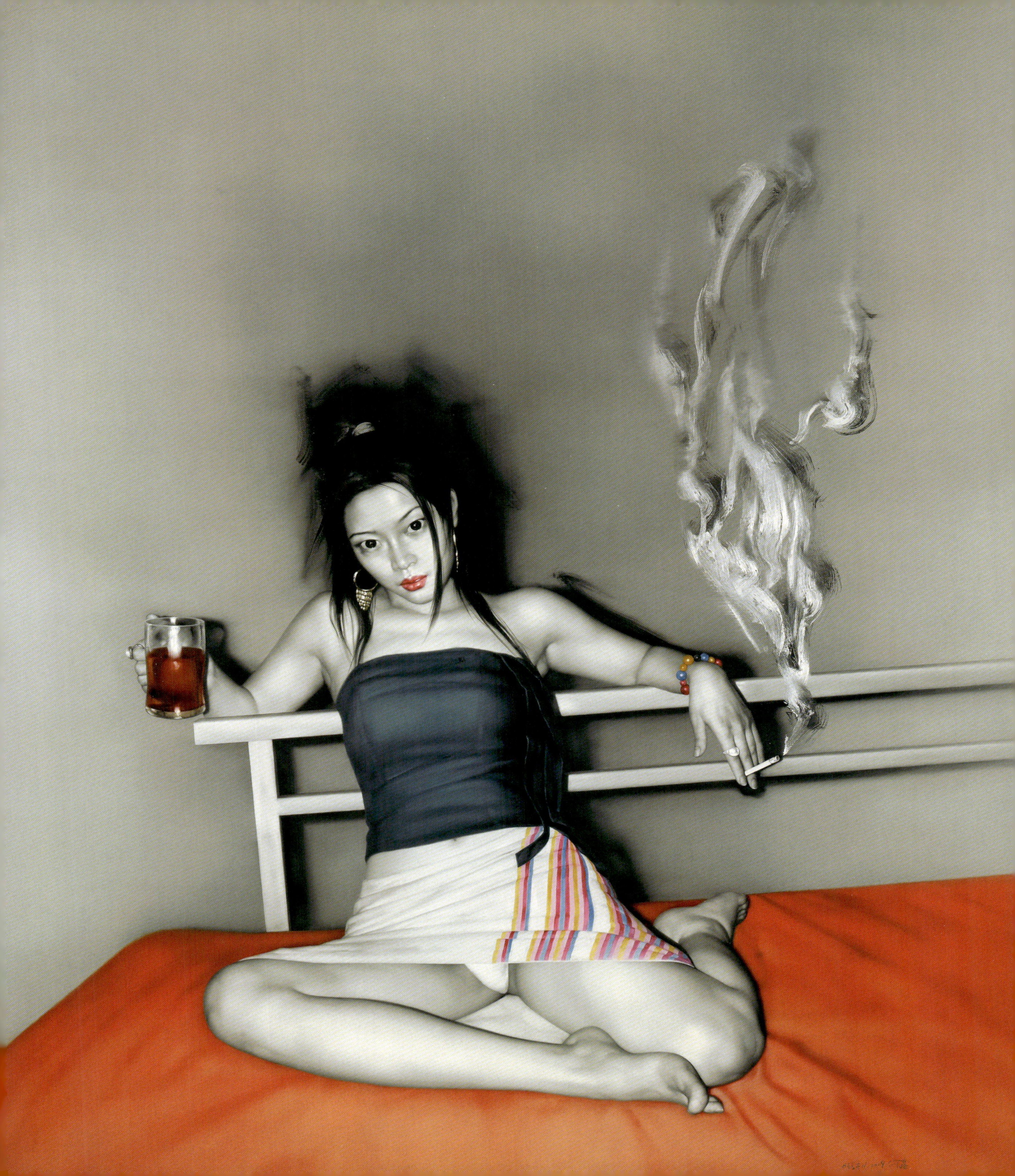

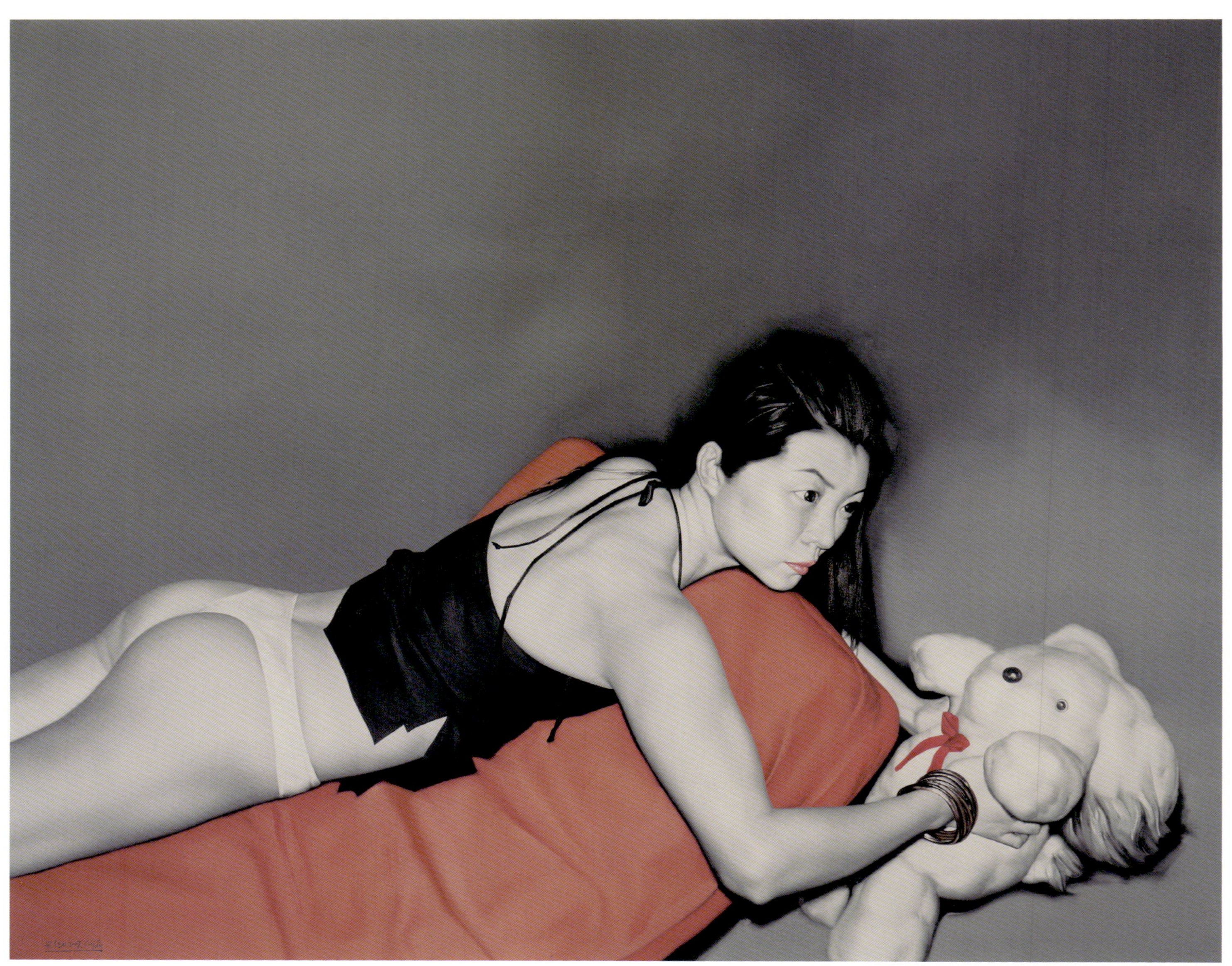

Du Du's Toy
oil on canvas
200x250 cm
2007

Girl with Toy
oil on canvas
250x200 cm
2007

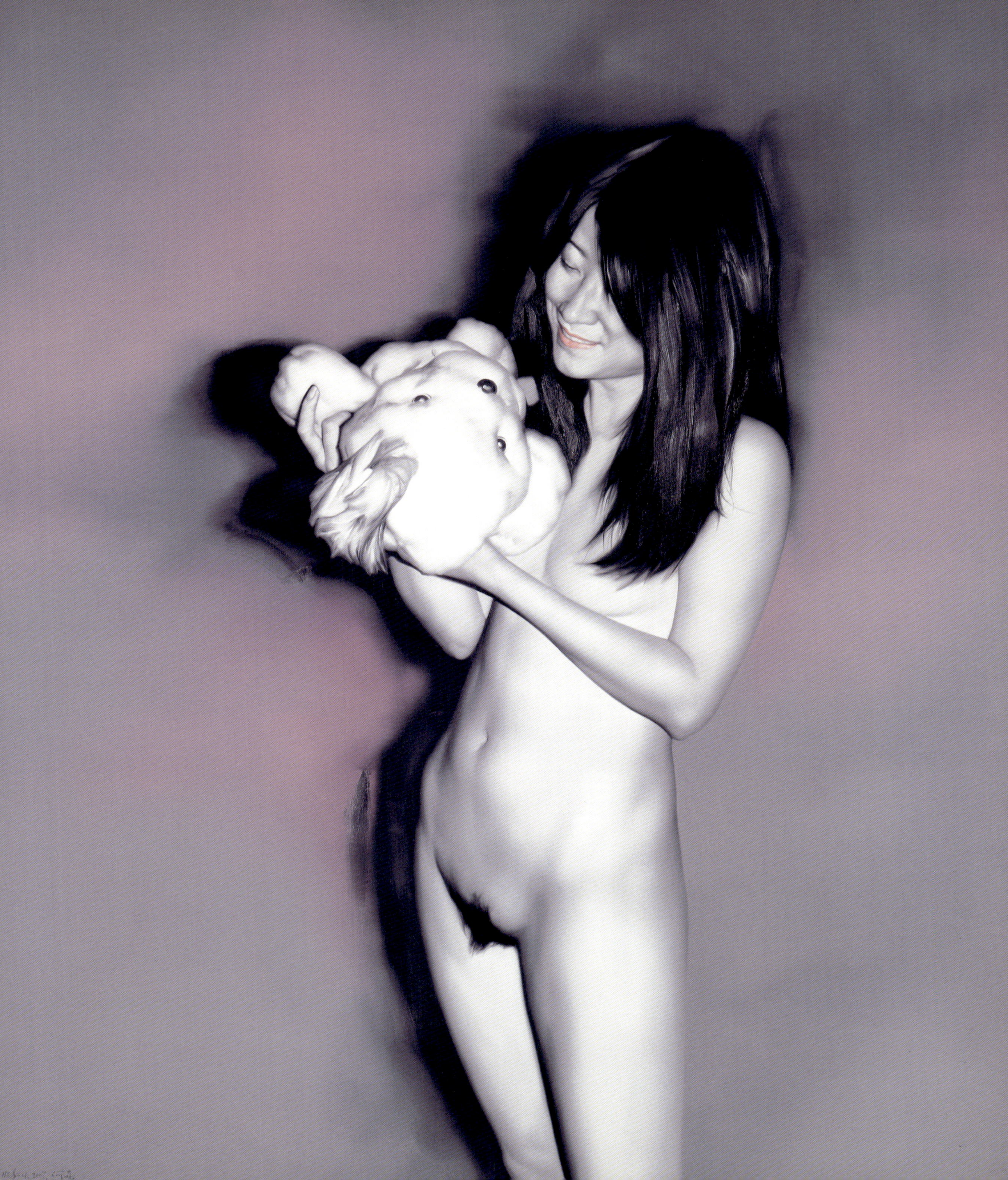

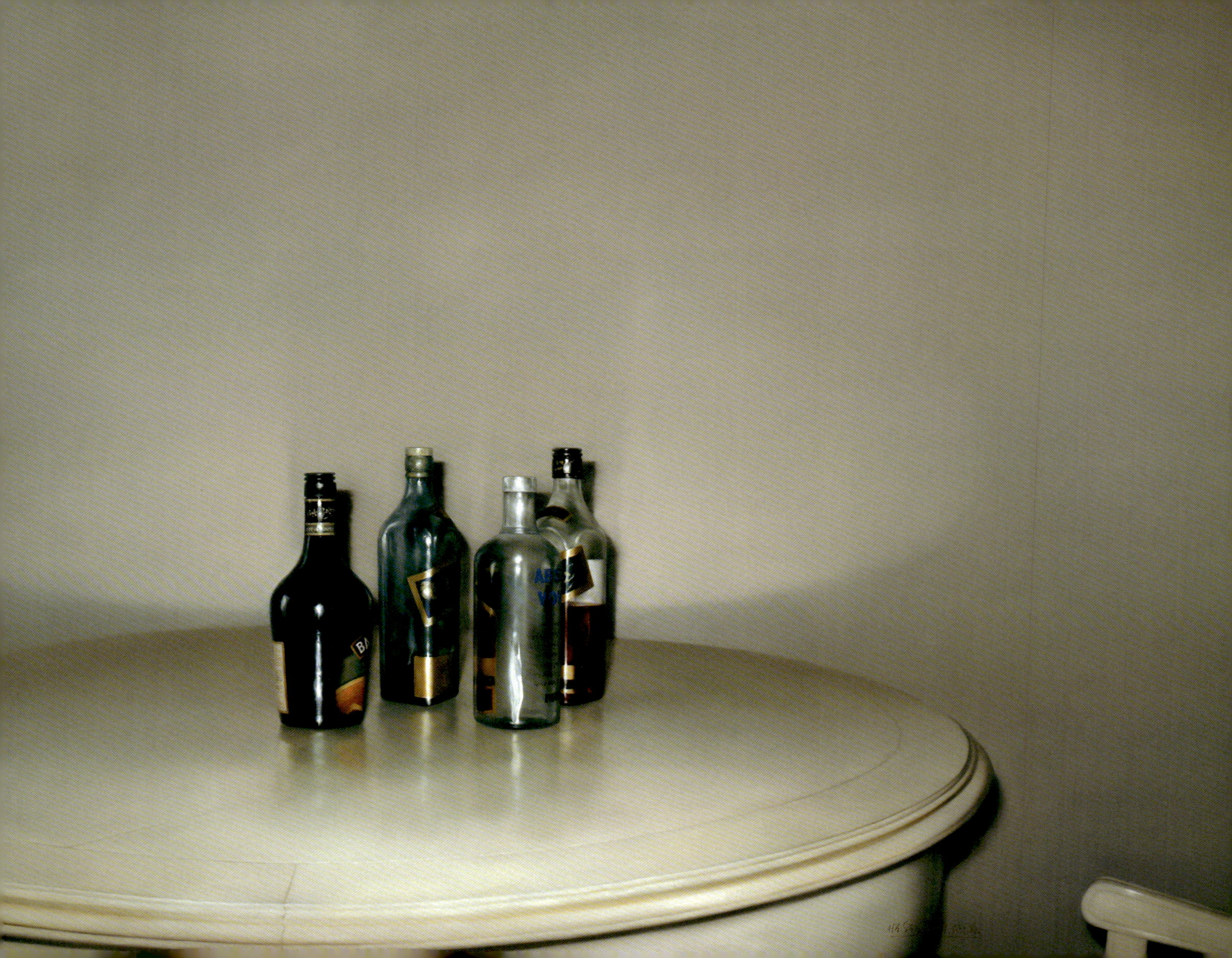

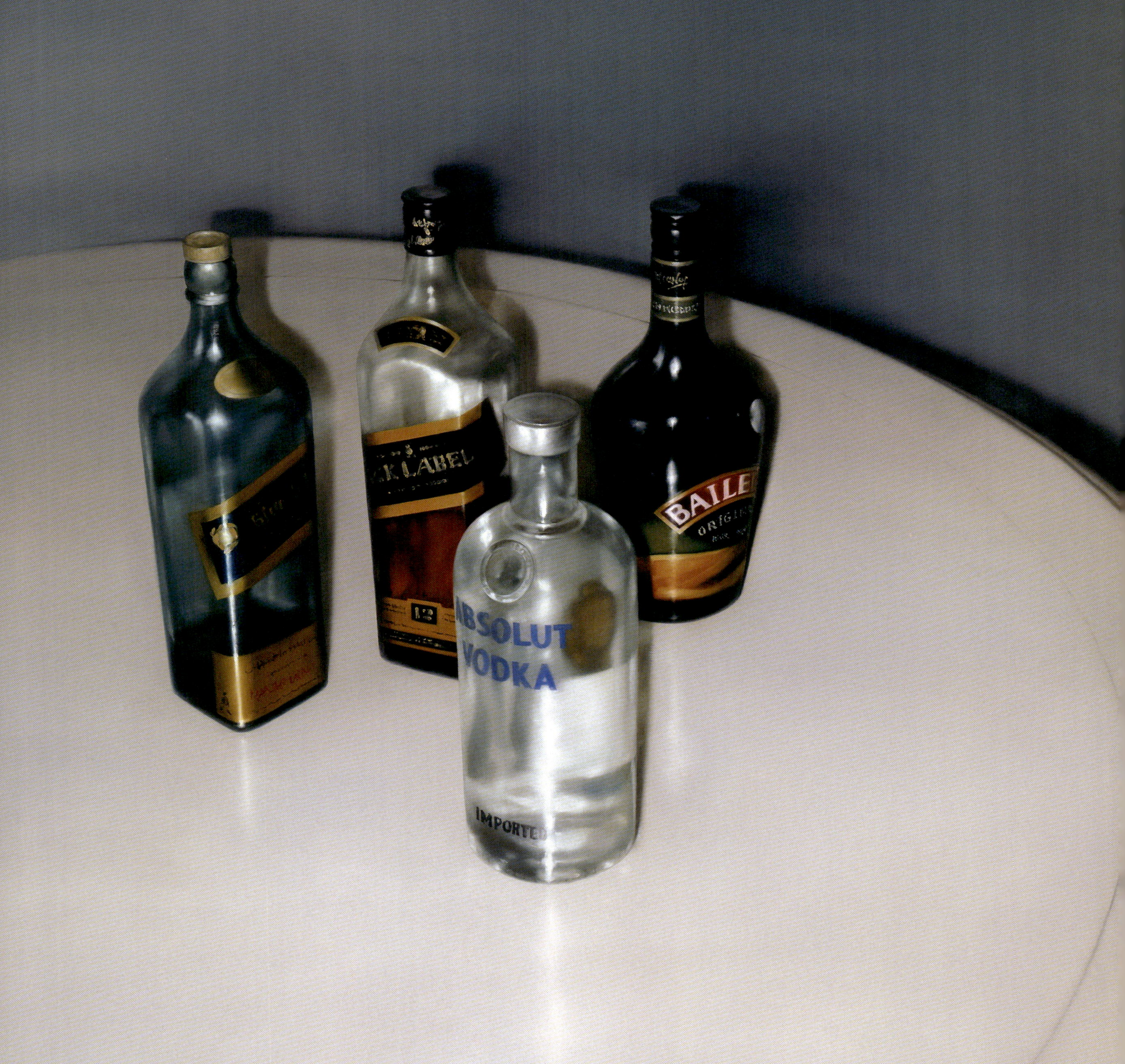

BLACK LABEL
BAILEYS
ORIGINAL
ABSOLUT
VODKA
IMPORTED

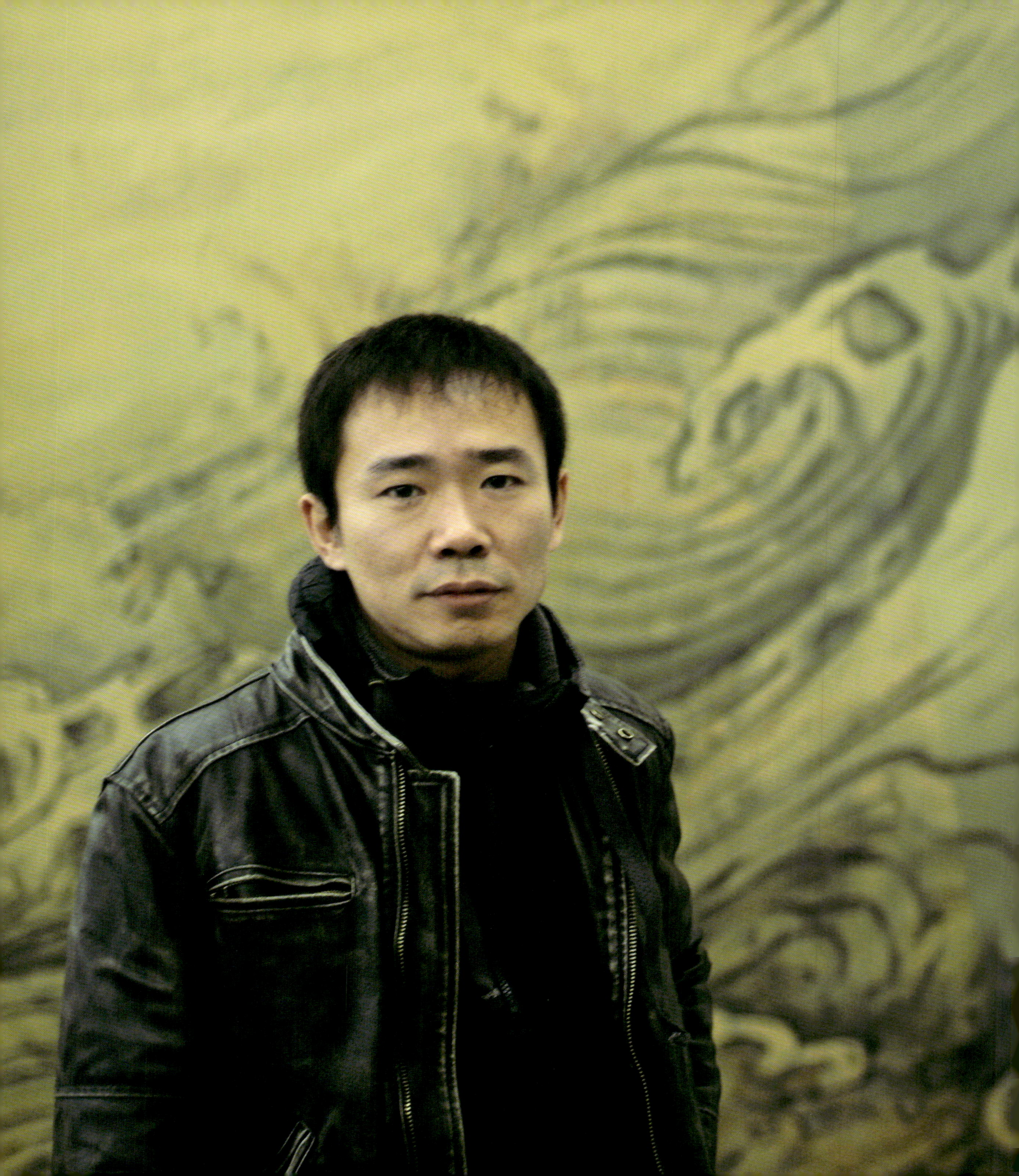

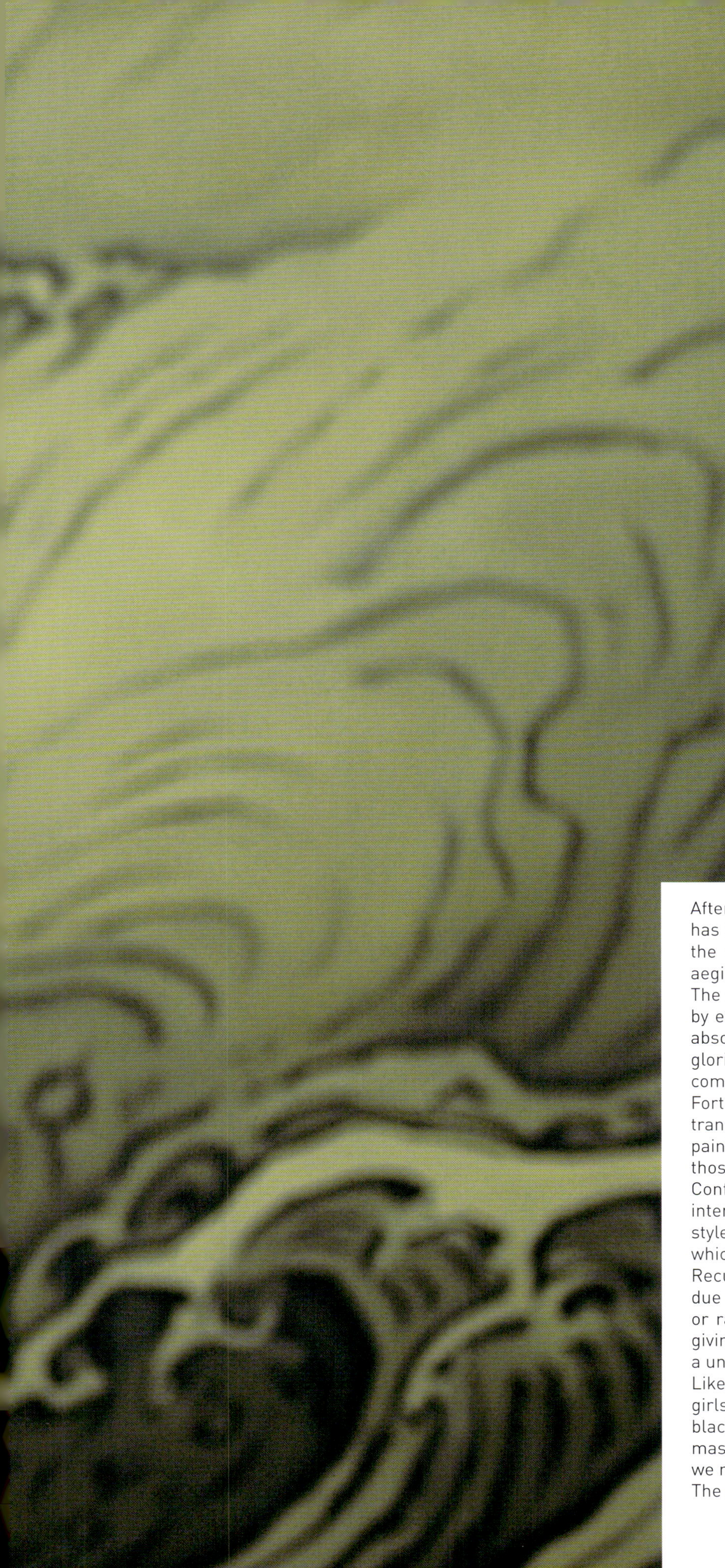

JOURNEY TO THE EAST
Eleonora Battiston

After a few decades of gazes and ambitions aimed at that West which has been the cradle of contemporary art, many Chinese artists have felt the need to return to their own past, hidden and forgotten under the aegis of China's development and modernization.

The history of China is a cyclical history of destruction and rebirth caused by empires and tolitarian regimes which, in order to impose their own absolutism, have repeatedly sought to burn and erase the remains of a glorious past, flourishing and at times threatening in so far as a term of comparison.

Fortunately, however, art has often been the treasure-trove of traditions transmitted and bequeathed, from one hand to the next, from one paintbrush to the other. So why then do Chinese artists have to ignore those millennia of ink paintings, ceramics and Buddhist, Taoist and Confucian iconographies that are part of their own DNA? Being international artists does not necessarily mean levelling techniques, styles and subjects typical of that – firstly – European and American art, which loves oil on canvas and man as the centre of the representation.

Recuperating one's own past would be easy if the obligation of originality, due to every artist, did not impose itself. He Sen was able to do this, or rather take possession of famous works by others, recreating and giving them back to the public with personality and subjectivity through a unique creative process that cannot be imitated.

Like in his previous and most famous works – the so-called "Smoking girls" – he started with photos of models to create his portraits mainly in black and white; now he is inspired by the photos of well-known Chinese masterpieces published in Art History books to elaborate his works – if we may call them such – "of landscape".

The most interesting aspect is surely the technique, or rather the formal aspect: painted in part with a brush and a spatula, He Sen's canvases transmit a perception of material and style alternation that focuses the attention on the brushstrokes and composition structure, leaving the content of the scene to the side for a moment. The act of painting – with thick layers created with a spatula and able to make the work three-dimensional and with diluted brushstrokes that call to mind the effect of ink – is central to the work and research of this artist.

Equally fascinating are the subjects, well-known and the source of pride for the Chinese and lesser known but enchanting for a foreign public.

The main body of works in this series inspired by tradition consists in two genres typical of Chinese painting: "landscape" and "flowers and birds". Both subjects portray what in China is the main source of artistic inspiration and poetical exalting: Nature.

At times human presence is hinted at, often a wise man or hermit isolated in a natural context of which these men constitute one of the many elements. Man's fragility and melancholy are lost in the vigour of a nature that is strong and powerful also for the clear-cut and aggressive features with which he is depicted, oftentimes sharp and pointy.

One of the main masters He Sen refers to is Xu Wei, a painter from the Ming period, often defined as the "founder of modern Chinese painting" and affected by a manic-depressive disorder that led him to kill one of his wives, to prison and to madness. Restlessness and genius brought about a revolution in aesthetical canons and greater expression in Chinese art. His work inspired artists of later years, also known for their extravagance, eccentricity and individualism, such as Zhu Da (Bada Shanren), prodigious painter from the Qing period famous for his decided brushstrokes and ability to render an image with few lines, an evident ability adopted by He Sen in the painting entitled *Medlar and Bird*. They say he descended from a prince of the Ming dynasty, a time that witnessed the flourishing of the arts and the need to recuperate a national identity following the Mongol domination during the Yuan period. Therefore, we see another parallel of a China that, in a few moments of its History, reclaims its own autonomy, a liberation from foreign dominion which at first enriches with its influences and then ends up being too restrictive. Besides, how can one lose sight of and ignore a History that is so centrist and full of pride like Chinese history?

That of He Sen is a sort of neo-classicism: he refers to the "classics", to the canonical works of his own country which he sums up and gives new life to.

A culture that wants to be aware of itself and its own traditions feels sooner or later the need to reclaim something that escaped and which is part of its "genetic heritage". He Sen had momentarily lost sight of a past which now returns because it is impossible to forget one's own roots. The artist follows the warning of the modernist poet Ezra Pound in "Make it New", and thanks to this he is able to express himself and renew himself in turn.

Another group of works with more colourful, though with nuanced, shades and clearly outlined contours regards the character of "the Monkey". The Monkey King, Sun Wukong is one of the most well-known characters in Chinese literature, from the *Journey to the West*, a classic in Chinese literature also composed during the Ming period which narrates the mythical journey of the Buddhist monk Xuanzang sent by Bodhisattva Guanyin to India to recuperate important Buddhist texts. Three disciples accompany him along his adventures: the monkey, the pig Zhu Bajie and the river ogre Sha Wujing. The monkey, compared to the monk, represents according to some scholars "the restless instability of genius" and his adventures, somewhere between comical and didactic, have inspired cartoons, theatrical works and artists of all kinds.

He Sen reproposes him in various scenes, like during a revolt or on a peach tree (a tree that according to the story has magical powers), all absorbed in carefully observing the horizon of his next adventure. These images emanate a sense of adventure, of freedom and search that have always incited man to discover new worlds and artistic and cultural treasures. Thus, accompanied by the artist, with his free boldness and desire to experiment, we as well allow ourselves to be carried away in this "journey to the east" amidst the paintings and images of Nature and distant characters, in the times and settings of a mythical and legendary China.

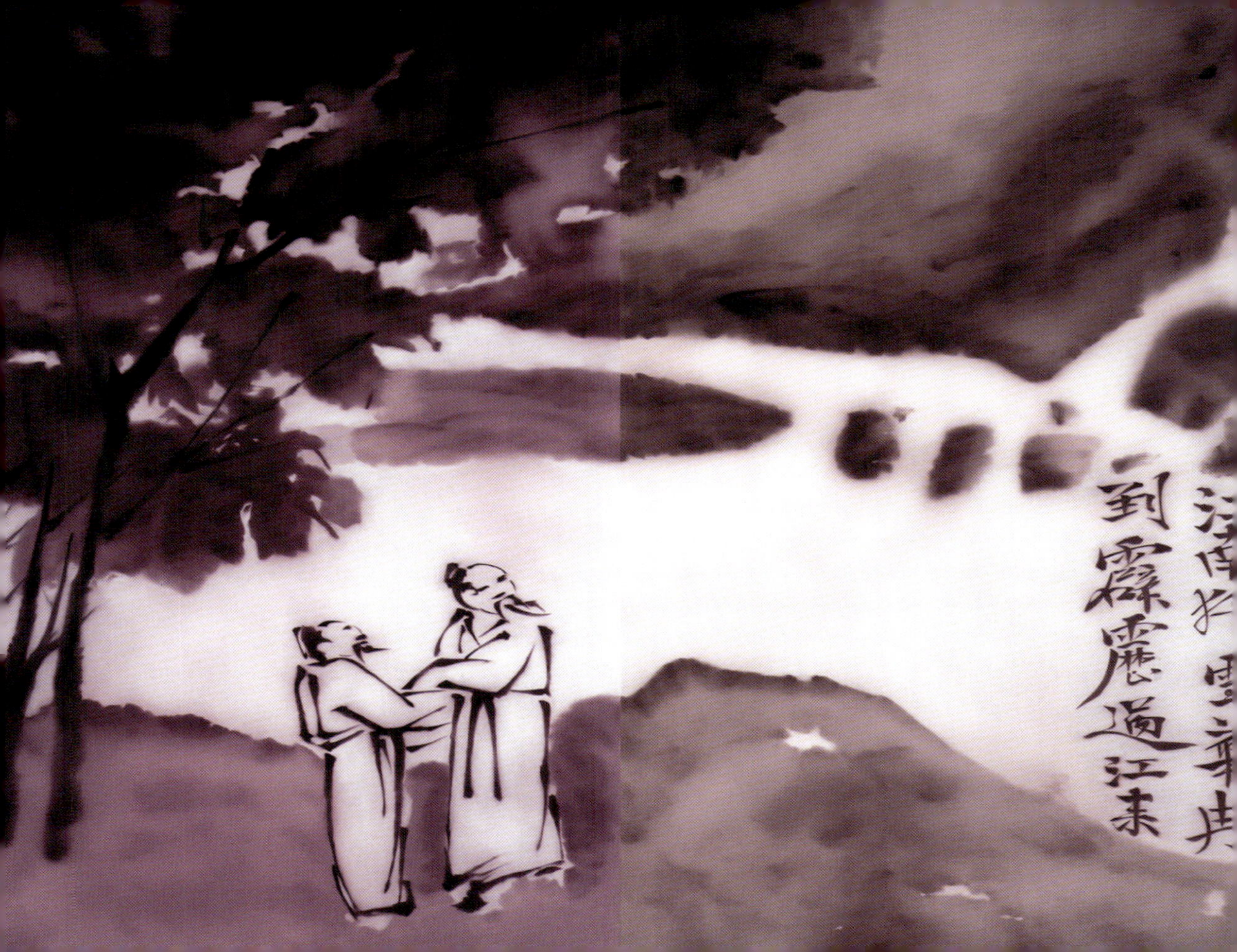
到霖霽遍江来

VIAGGIO VERSO EST
Eleonora Battiston

Dopo alcuni decenni di sguardi e ambizioni rivolti a quell'Occidente che è stato culla dell'arte contemporanea, molti artisti cinesi hanno sentito l'esigenza di ritornare ad un proprio passato da tempo nascosto e dimenticato sotto l'egida dello sviluppo e della modernizzazione della Cina.

La storia della Cina è una storia ciclica di distruzioni e rinascite causate da imperi e regimi totalitari che, per imporre il proprio assolutismo, hanno cercato di bruciare e cancellare più volte le vestigia di un passato glorioso, fiorente e a volte minaccioso in quanto termine di paragone.

Fortunatamente però l'arte è stata spesso lo scrigno di tradizioni trasmesse e tramandate di mano in mano e di pennello in pennello. Perchè quindi gli artisti cinesi devono ignorare quei millenni di pittura ad inchiostro, ceramiche e iconografie buddiste, taoiste e confuciane che fanno parte del proprio DNA? Essere artisti internazionali non vuole per forza dire uniformarsi a tecniche, stili e soggetti tipici di quell'arte Europea prima e Americana poi amante degli oli su tela e dell'uomo sempre al centro della figurazione.

Recuperare un proprio passato sarebbe facile se non s'imponesse l'obbligo, dovuto da ogni artista, dell'originalità. Questo è riuscito a fare He Sen, ossia appropriarsi di famose opere altrui ricreandole e restituendole al pubblico con personalità e soggettività proprie attraverso un processo creativo unico ed inimitabile.

Come nelle sue opere precedenti e più famose – le cosiddette "Smoking girls" – partiva da fotografie di modelle per creare i suoi ritratti prevalentemente in bianco e nero; così ora prende spunto da fotografie di noti capolavori cinesi pubblicati sui libri di Storia dell'Arte per elaborare le sue opere – se così possiamo chiamarle – "di paesaggio".

L'aspetto più interessante è sicuramente la tecnica, ovvero l'aspetto formale: dipinte in parte a pennello ed in parte a spatola, le tele di He Sen trasmettono una percezione di alternanza materica e stilistica che concentra l'attenzione sulle pennellate e sulla struttura compositiva, lasciando per un attimo da parte il contenuto delle scene. L'azione del dipingere - sia con spessi strati resi a paletta e capaci di rendere l'opera tridimensionale, sia con pennellate diluite che ricordano l'effetto dell'inchiostro - è centrale nel lavoro e nella ricerca di questo artista.

Altrettanto affascinanti sono però i soggetti, conosciuti e fonte di orgoglio per i cinesi, meno noti e anche per questo incantevoli per un pubblico straniero.

Il corpo principale di lavori di questa serie ispirata alla tradizione è costituito da due noti generi tipici della pittura cinese: i "paesaggi" e i "fiori ed uccelli". Entrambi i soggetti ritraggono quella che in Cina è la fonte primaria di ispirazione artistica ed esaltazione poetica: la Natura.

A volte si accenna alla presenza umana, spesso un saggio o un'eremita isolati in un contesto naturale di cui questi uomini costituiscono uno dei tanti elementi che lo compongono. La fragilità e la malinconia dell'uomo si perdono nel vigore di una natura che è forte e potente anche per la nettezza e l'aggressività dei tratti con cui è raffigurata, spezzo aguzzi e spigolosi.

Uno dei principali maestri a cui He Sen si rifà è Xu Wei, pittore di epoca Ming, spesso definito il "capostipite della pittura cinese moderna" e affetto da un bipolarismo che lo portò all'omicidio di una delle mogli, al carcere e alla follia. Irrequietezza e genio portano ad un rivoluzionamento dei canoni estetici ed ad un maggiore espressionismo nell'arte cinese. La sua arte ispirò artisti successivi anch'essi noti per la loro stravaganza, eccentrici ed individualisti come Zhu Da (Bada Shanren), pittore prodigio di epoca Qing famoso per le sue pennellate decise e la capacità di rendere un immagine con pochi tratti, capacità evidente e ripresa da He Sen nel quadro intitolato *Nespola ed uccello*. Di lui si dice che discendeva da un principe Ming, dinastia che vide il rifiorire delle arti e la necessità di recuperare una propria identità nazionale in seguito alla trascorsa dominazione mongola del periodo Yuan. Pertanto si affaccia un altro parallelo di una Cina che, in alcuni momenti della sua Storia, rivendica una propria autonomia, una liberazione da un giogo straniero che prima arricchisce con le sue influenze e poi risulta troppo stretto. Del resto come si può perdere di vista ed ignorare una Storia così centrista e piena d'orgoglio come quella cinese?

Quello di He Sen è una sorta di Neo-classicismo: egli si rifà ai "classici", alle opere canoniche del proprio paese che lui sintetizza ridandogli nuova vita.

Una cultura che vuole essere consapevole di se stessa e della propria

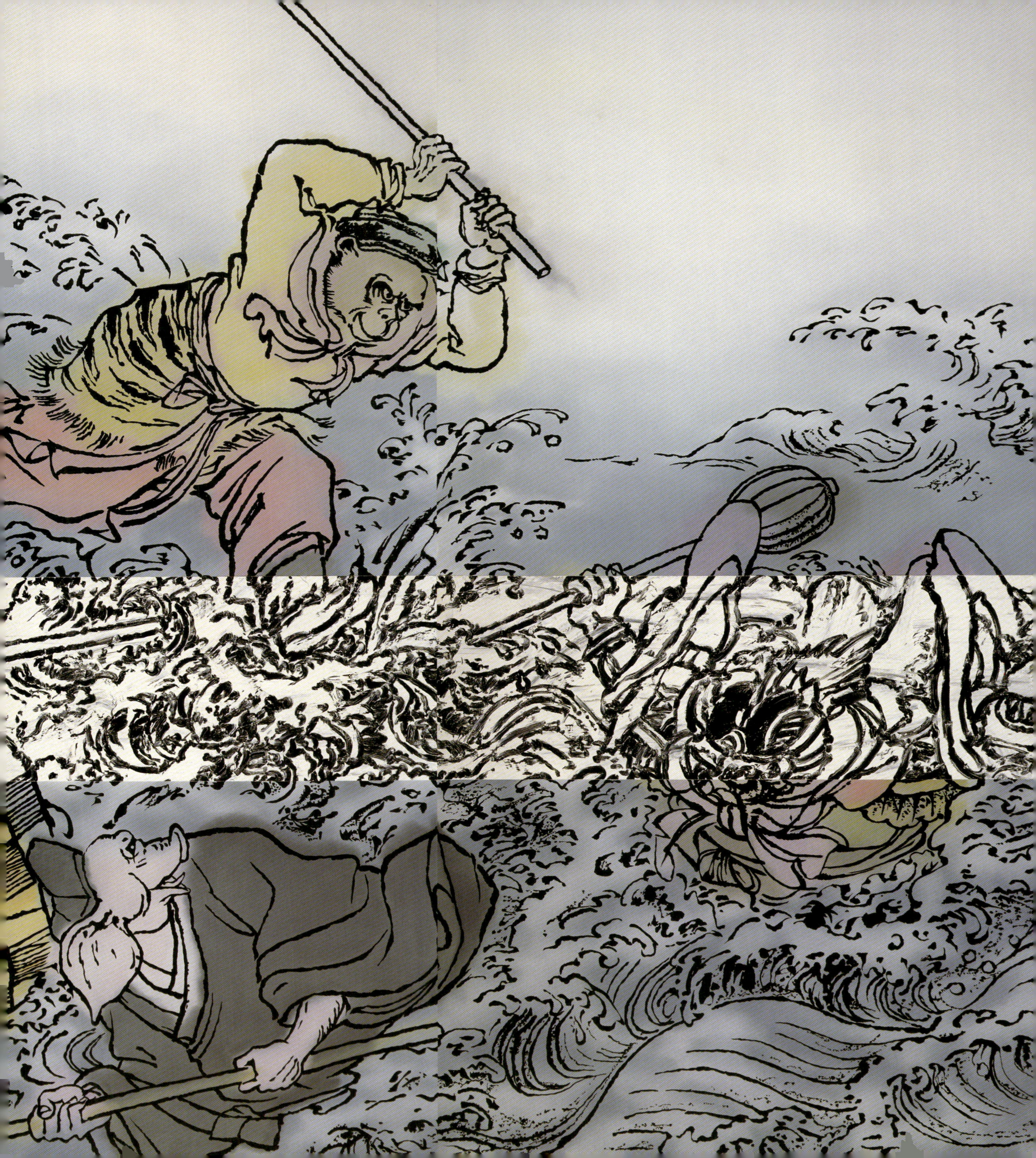

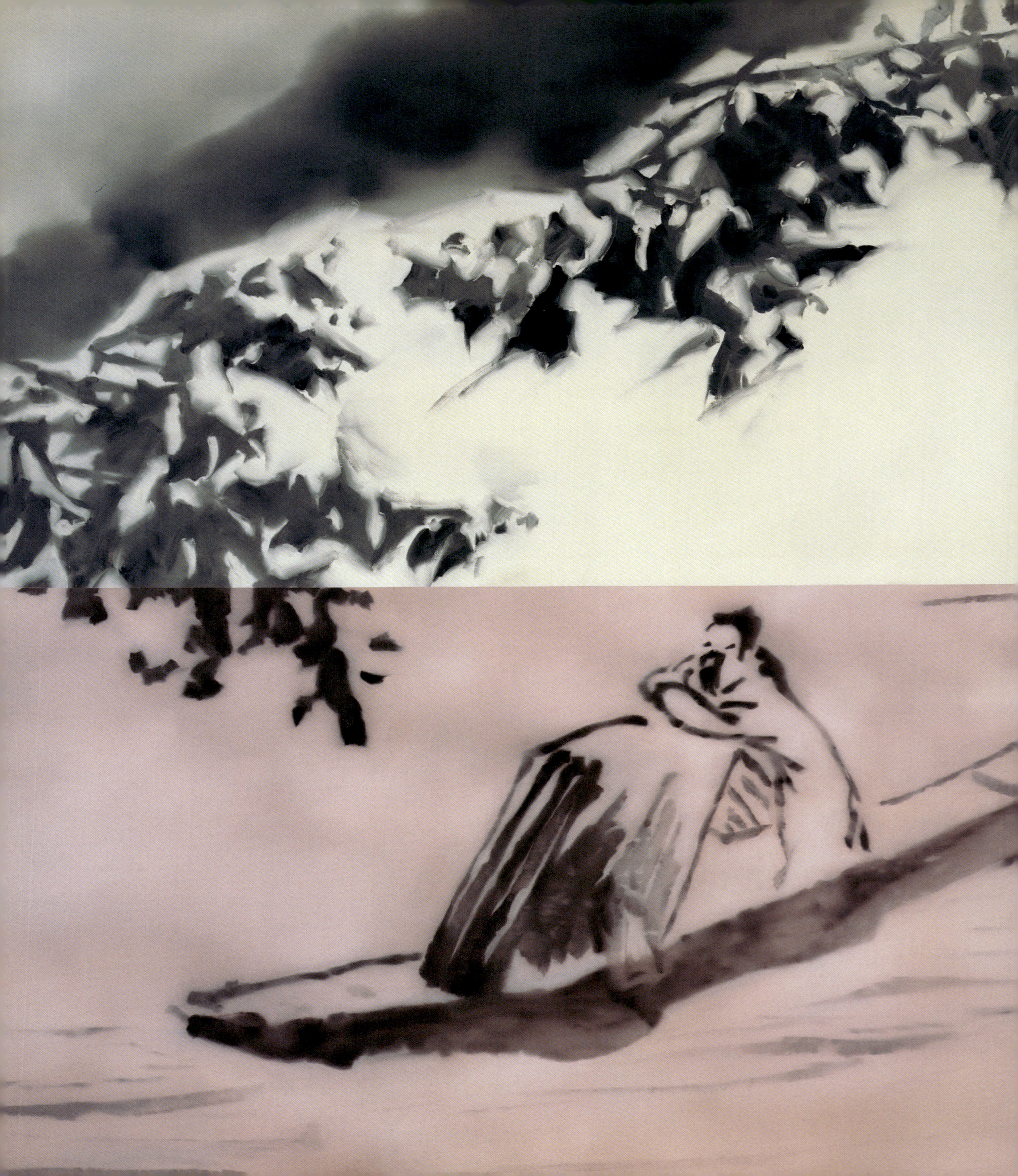

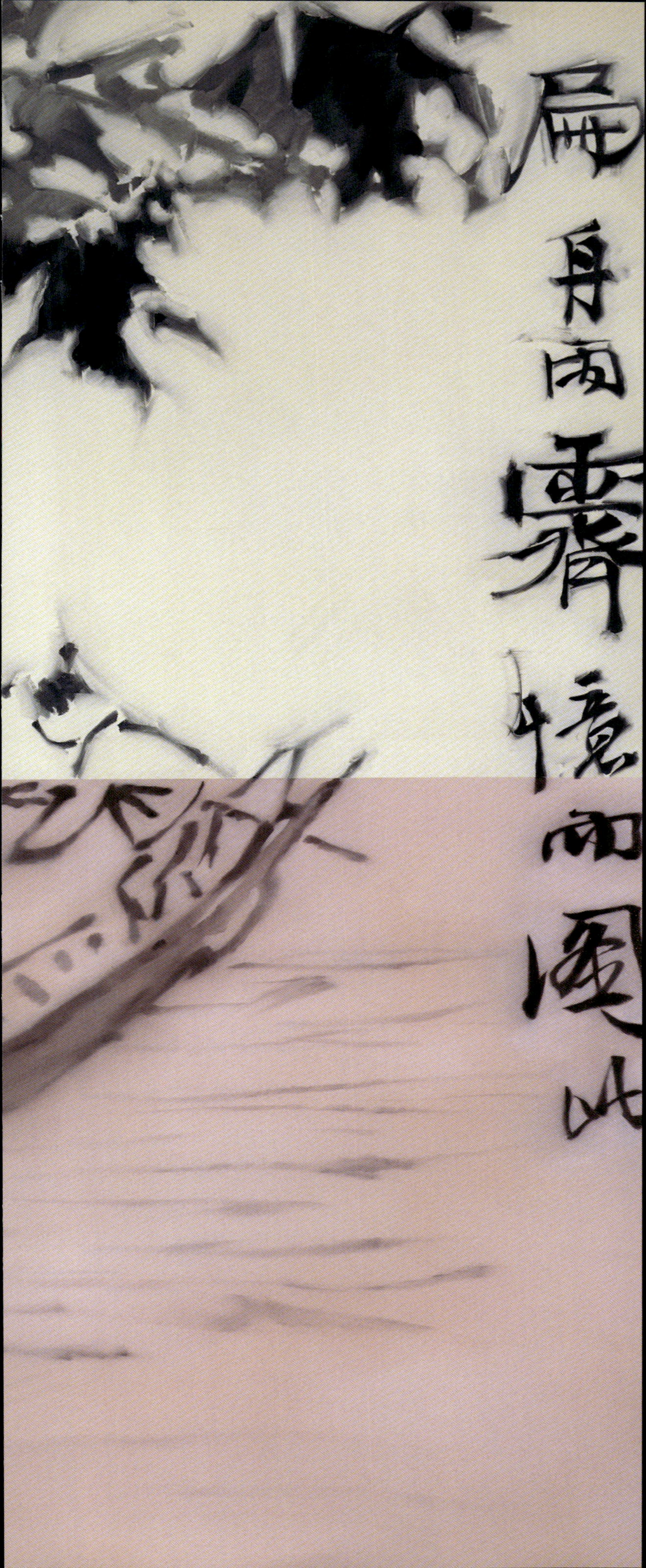

tradizione, sente prima o poi la necessità di riappropriarsi di un qualcosa che le è sfuggito e che fa parte del suo "patrimonio genetico". He Sen aveva momentaneamente perso di vista un passato che ora ritorna perché è impossibile dimenticare le proprie radici. L'artista segue il monito del poeta modernista Ezra Pound "Make it New" e grazie a ciò riesce ad esprimere se stesso e a rinnovarsi a sua volta.

Un altro gruppo di lavori più colorati seppure con tonalità sfumate, e con i contorni delle immagini nettamente tracciati, sono quelli relativi al personaggio de "Lo Scimmiotto". Il Re delle scimmie Sun Wukong è uno dei personaggi più noti della tradizione letteraria cinese. Si tratta di uno dei personaggi del *Viaggio in Occidente*, un classico della letteratura Cinese composto anch'esso in epoca Ming, che racconta del mitico viaggio del monaco buddista Xuanzang mandato dal Bodhisattva Guanyin in India per recuperare importanti testi Buddisti. In queste avventure è accompagnato dai tre discepoli: lo Scimmiotto appunto, il maiale Zhu Bajie e il demone fluviale Sha Wujing. Lo scimmiotto, paragonato al monaco, rappresenta secondo alcuni studiosi "l'irrequieta instabilità del genio" e le sue avventure, tra il comico ed il didascalico, hanno ispirato cartoni animati, opere teatrali ed artisti di vario genere.

He Sen lo ripropone in diverse scene come durante una battaglia di ribellione o su un albero di pesco (pianta che secondo il romanzo ha poteri magici) intento a scrutare l'orizzonte della sua prossima avventura. Queste immagini emanano appunto un senso di avventura, di libertà e di ricerca che da sempre spingono l'uomo alla scoperta di nuovi mondi e di tesori artistici e culturali. Così, accompagnati dall'artista, col suo libero ardire e la sua voglia di sperimentare, anche noi ci lasciamo trasportare in questo "viaggio ad oriente" tra i quadri e le immagini di una Natura e di personaggi lontani, nei tempi e negli scenari di una Cina mitica e leggendaria.

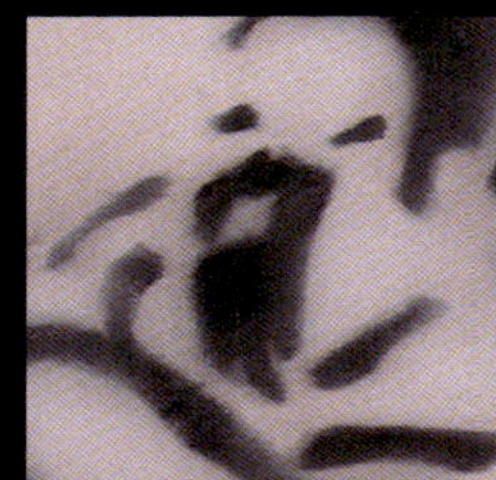

**Xu Wei No. 1
of landscape
and figure series**
oil on canvas
200x250 cm
2008

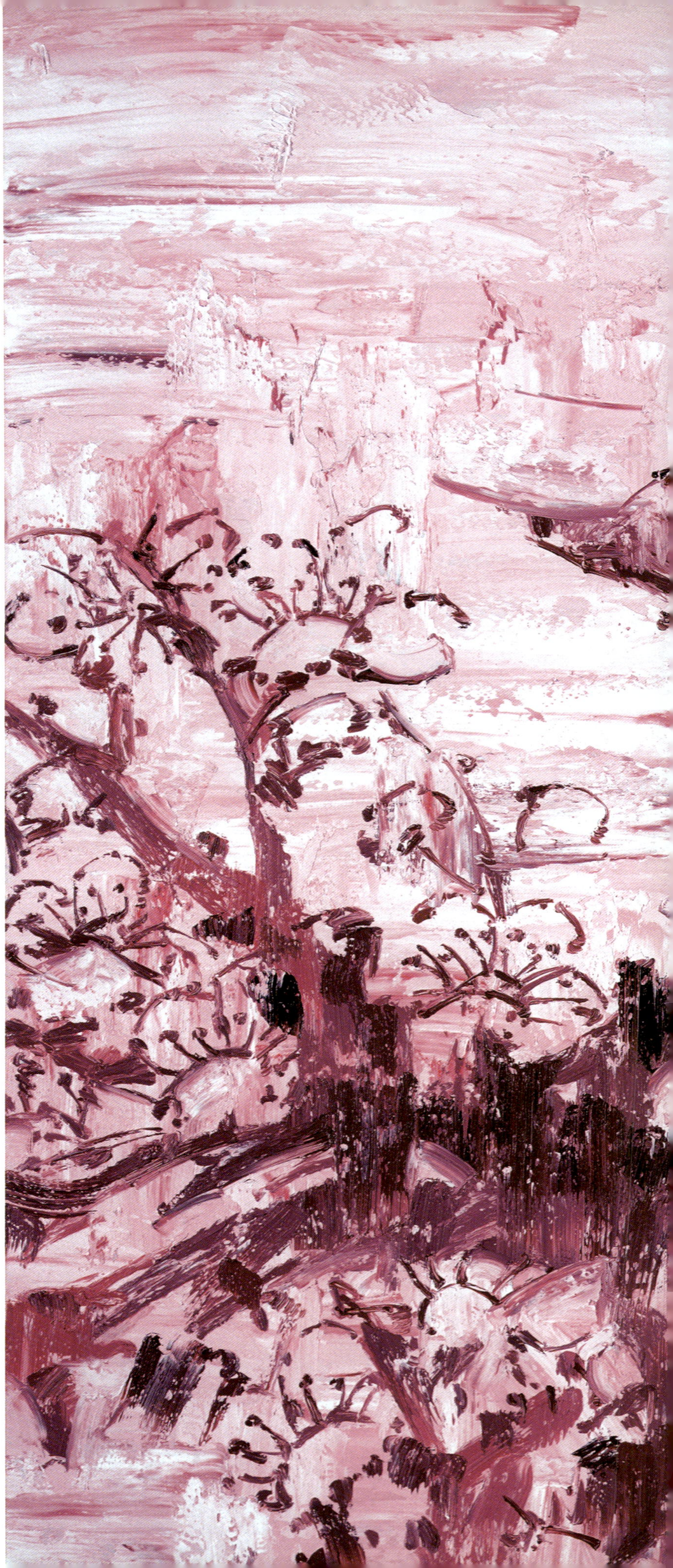

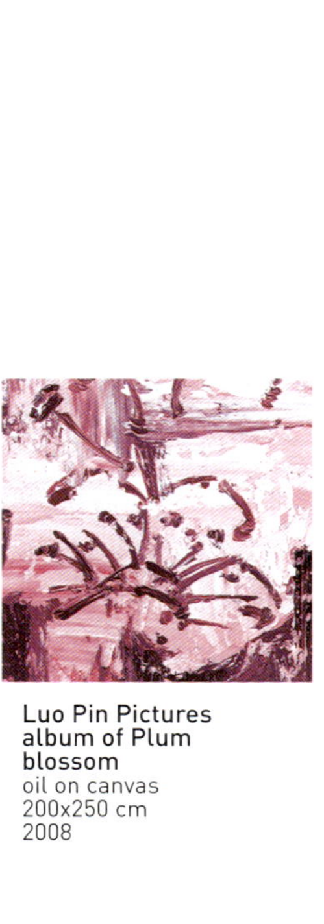

Luo Pin Pictures
album of Plum
blossom
oil on canvas
200x250 cm
2008

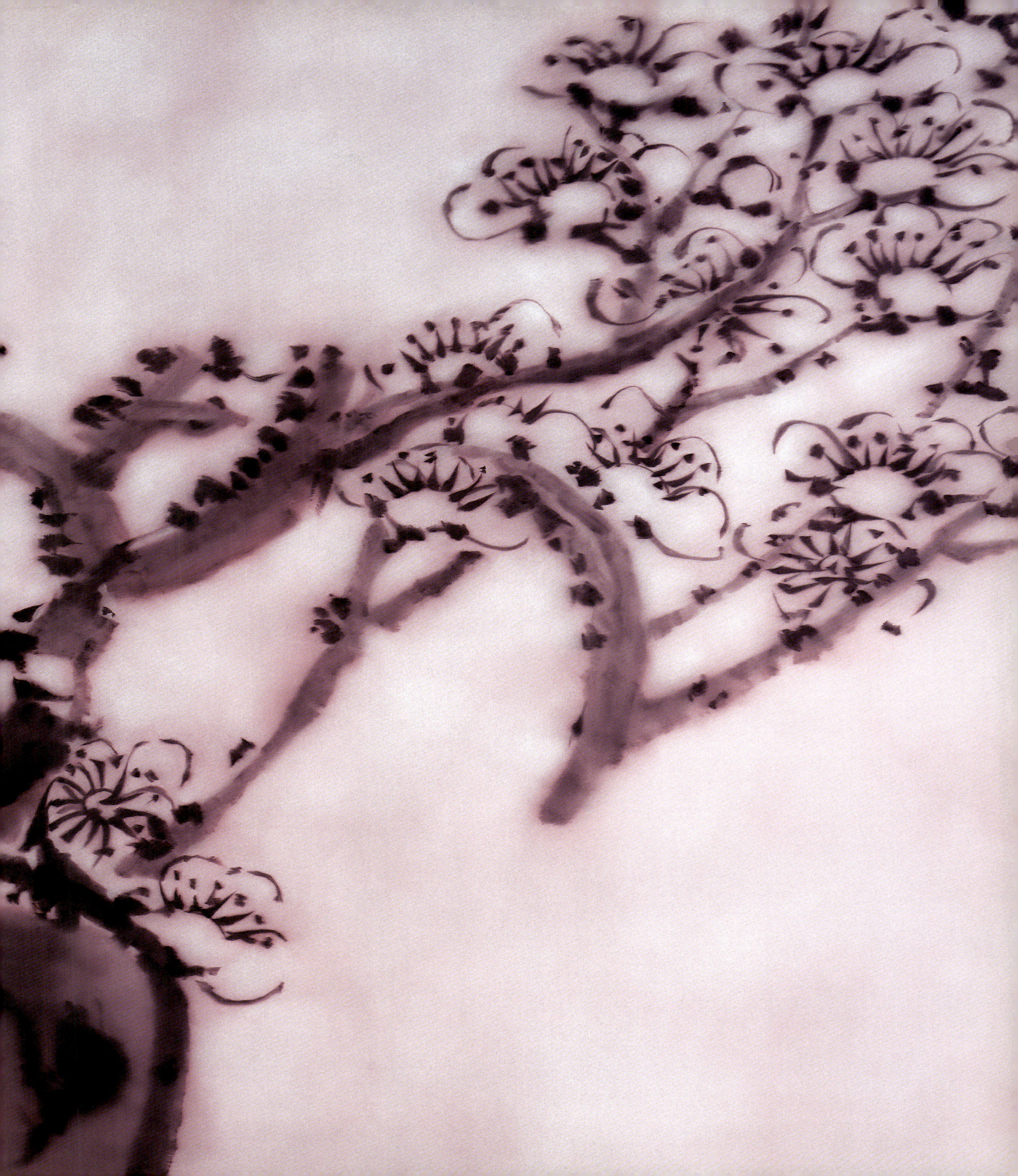

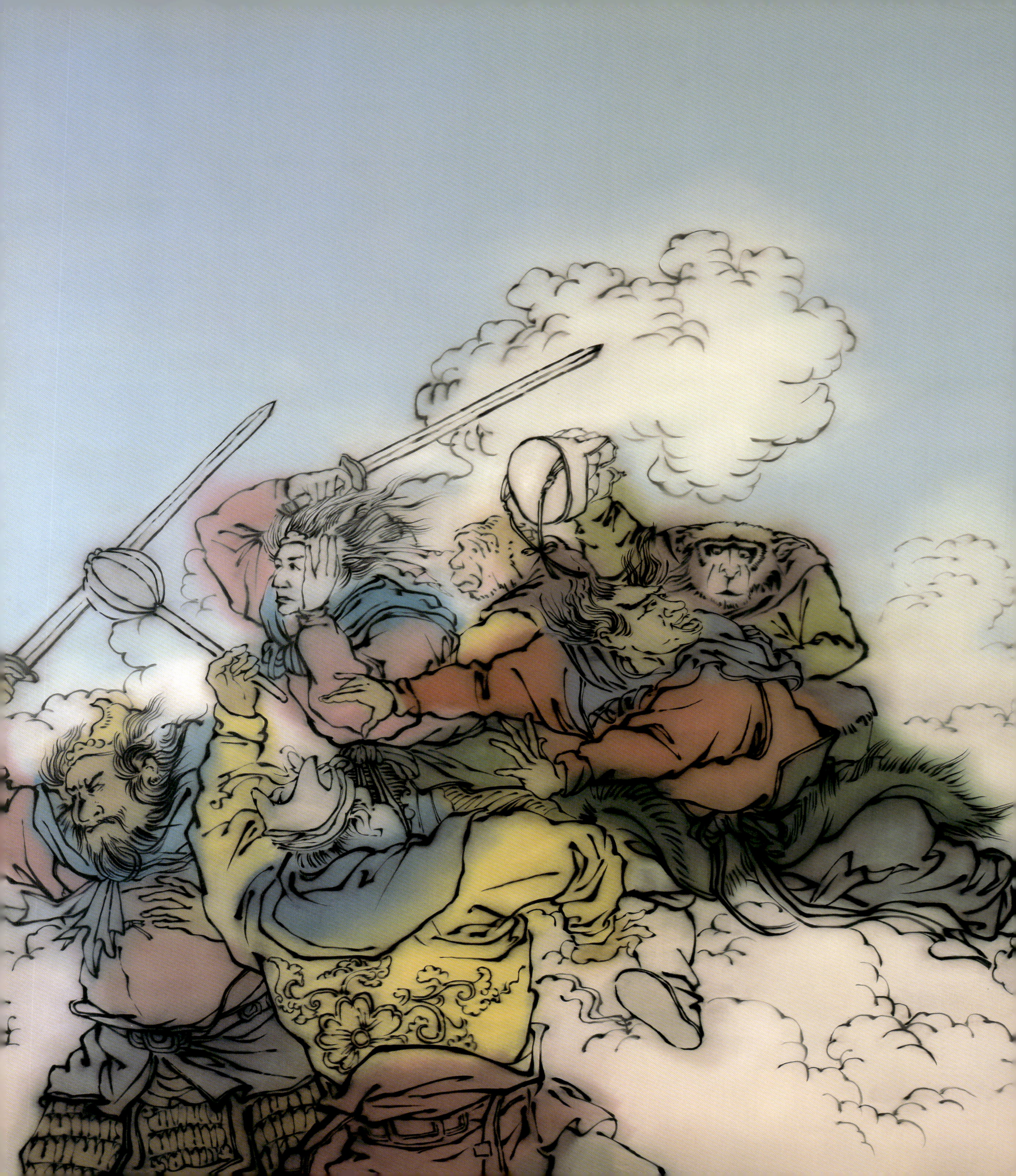

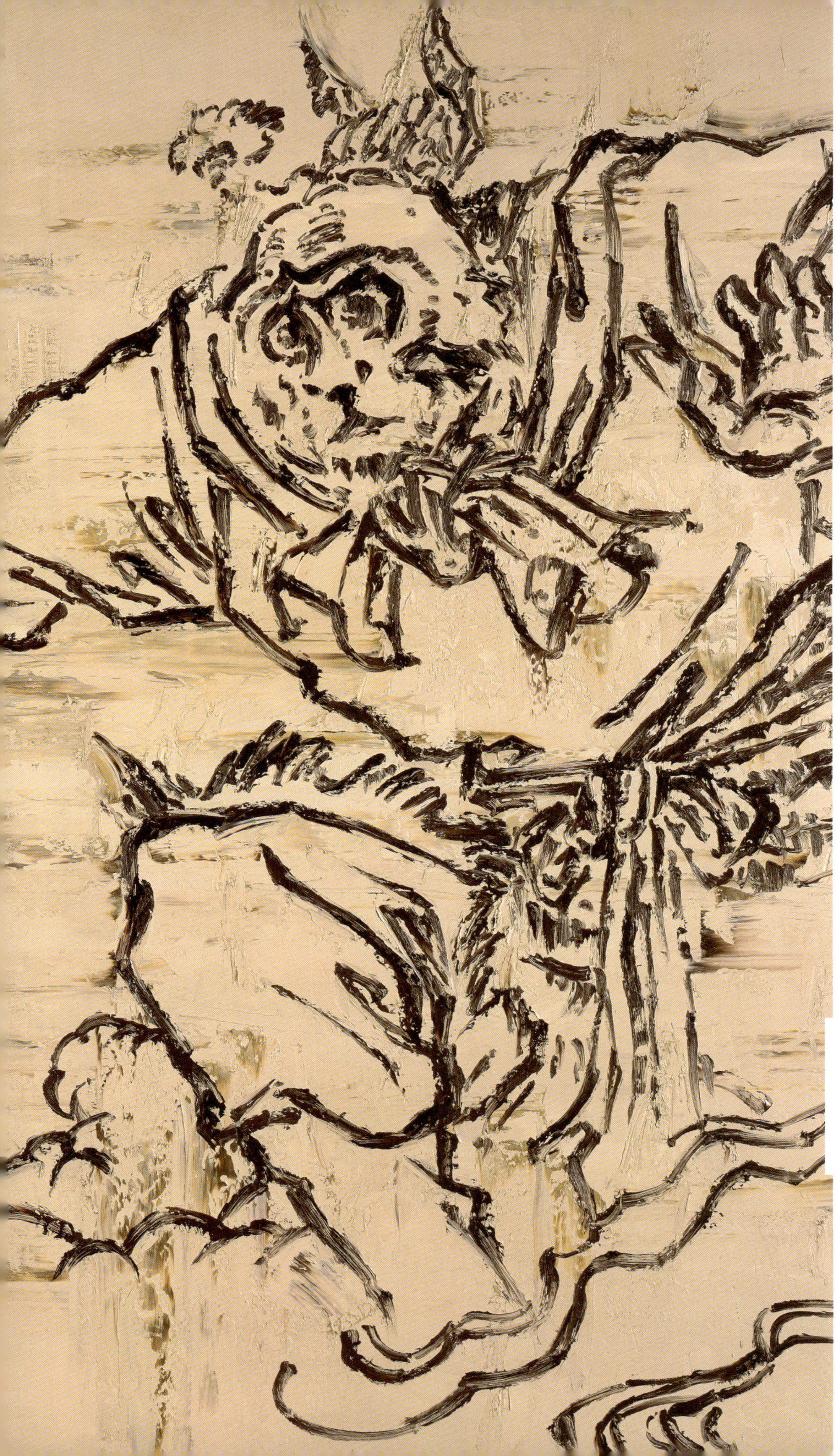

Rebellious
Monkey King
oil on canvas
300x400 cm
2008

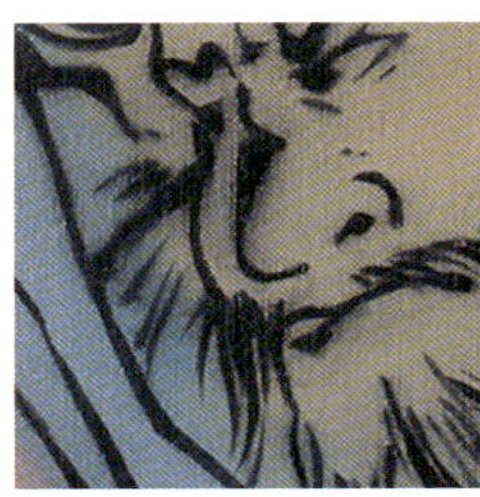

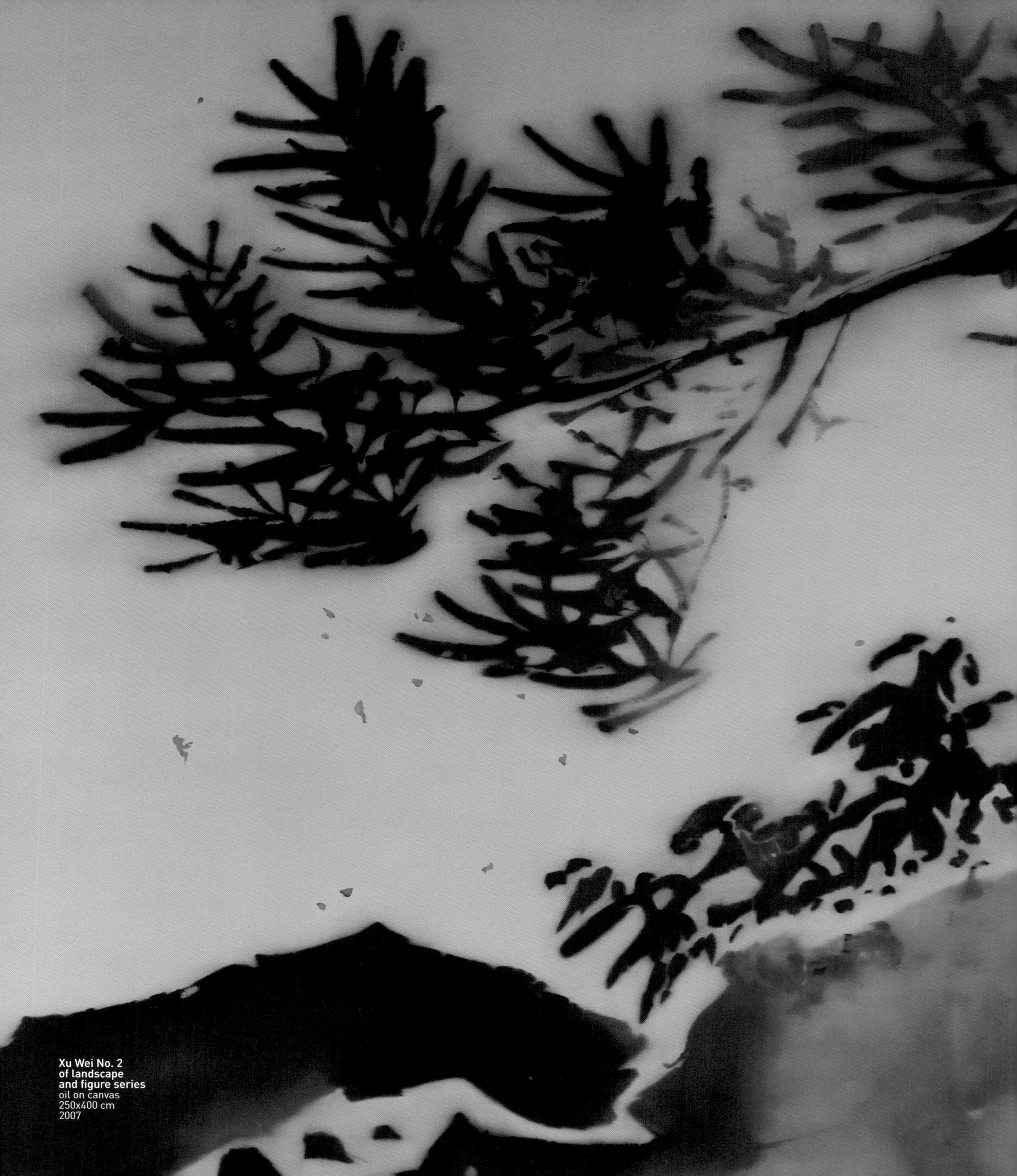

Xu Wei No. 2
of landscape
and figure series
oil on canvas
250x400 cm
2007

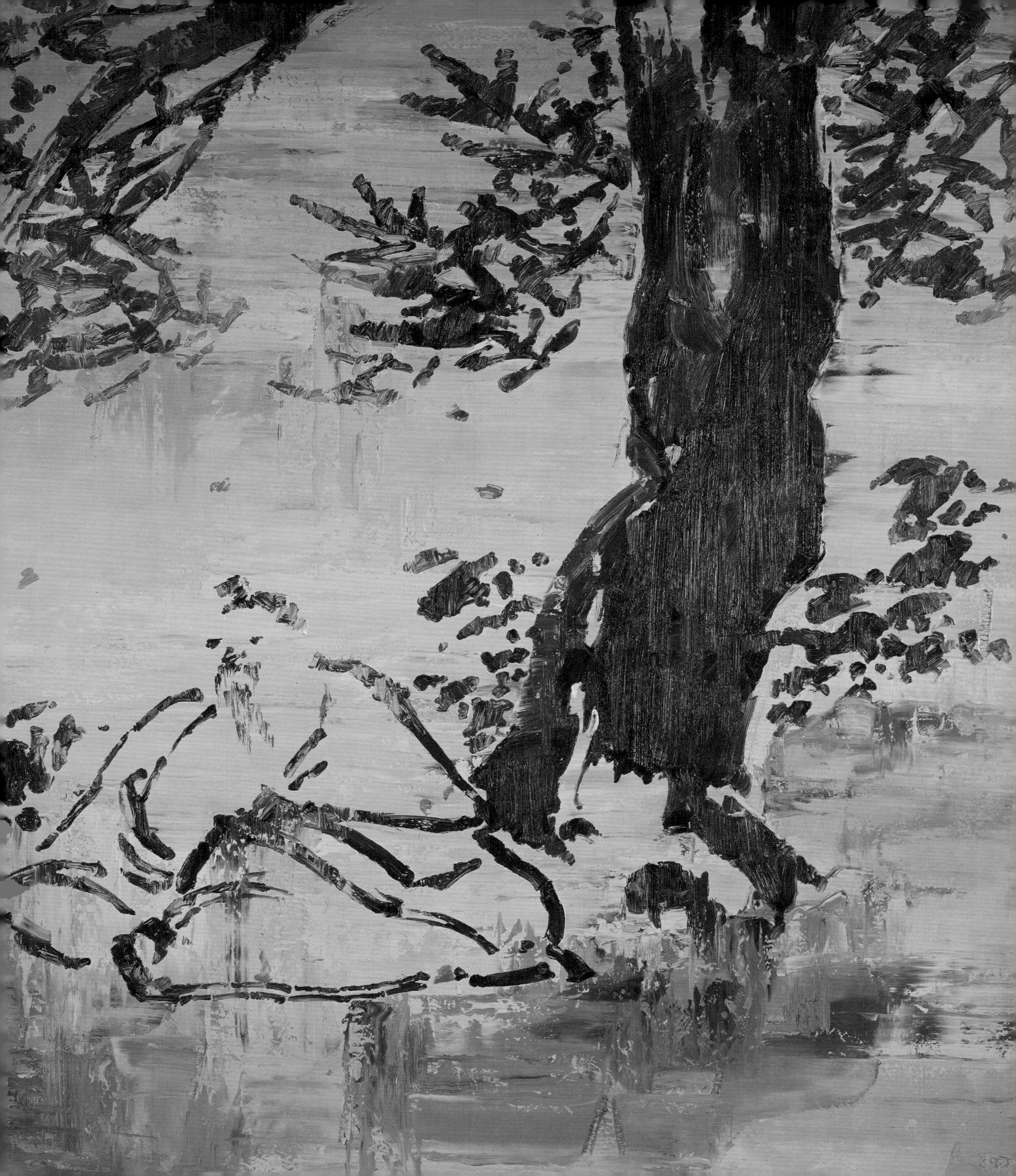

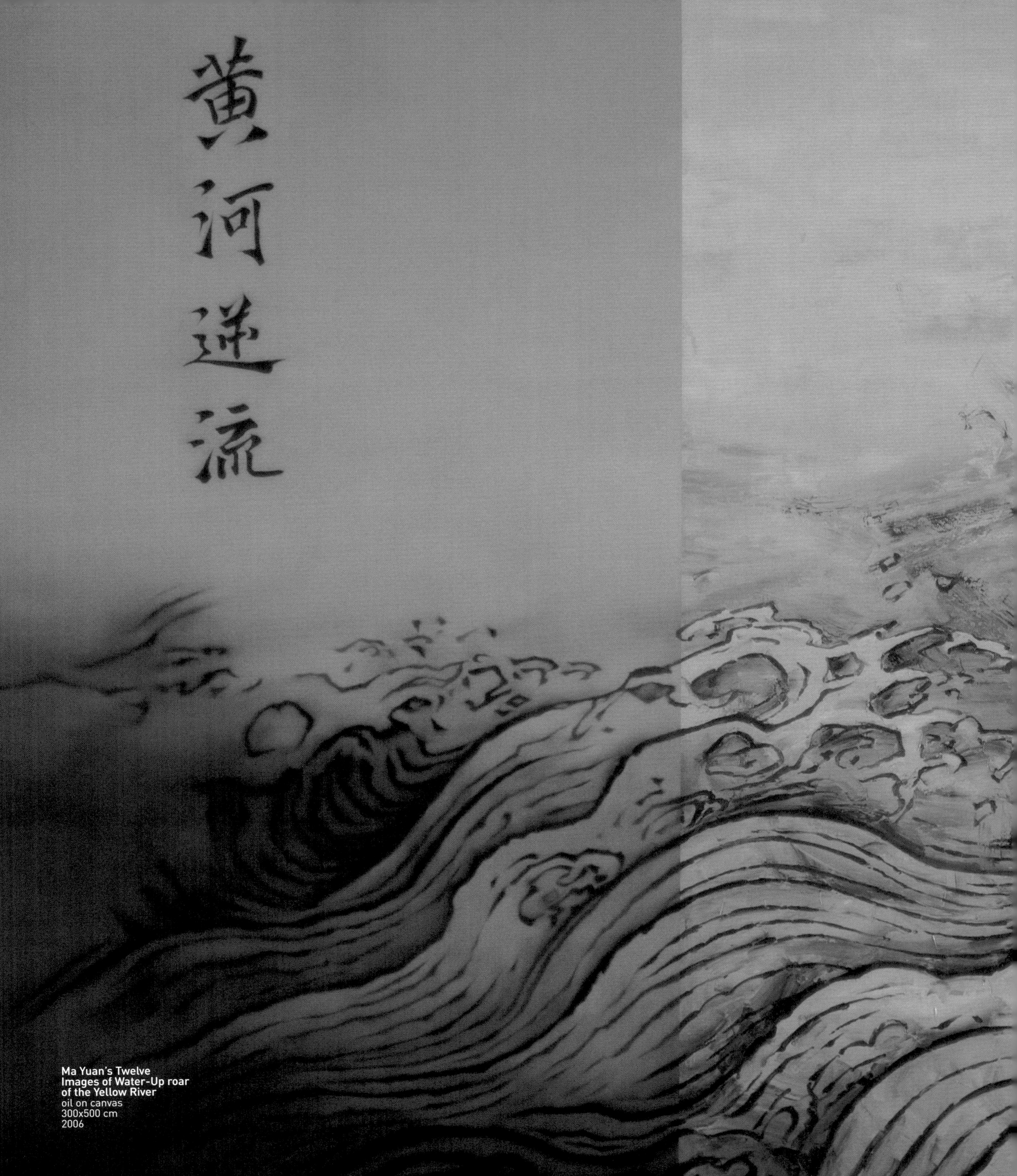

Ma Yuan's Twelve
Images of Water-Up roar
of the Yellow River
oil on canvas
300x500 cm
2006

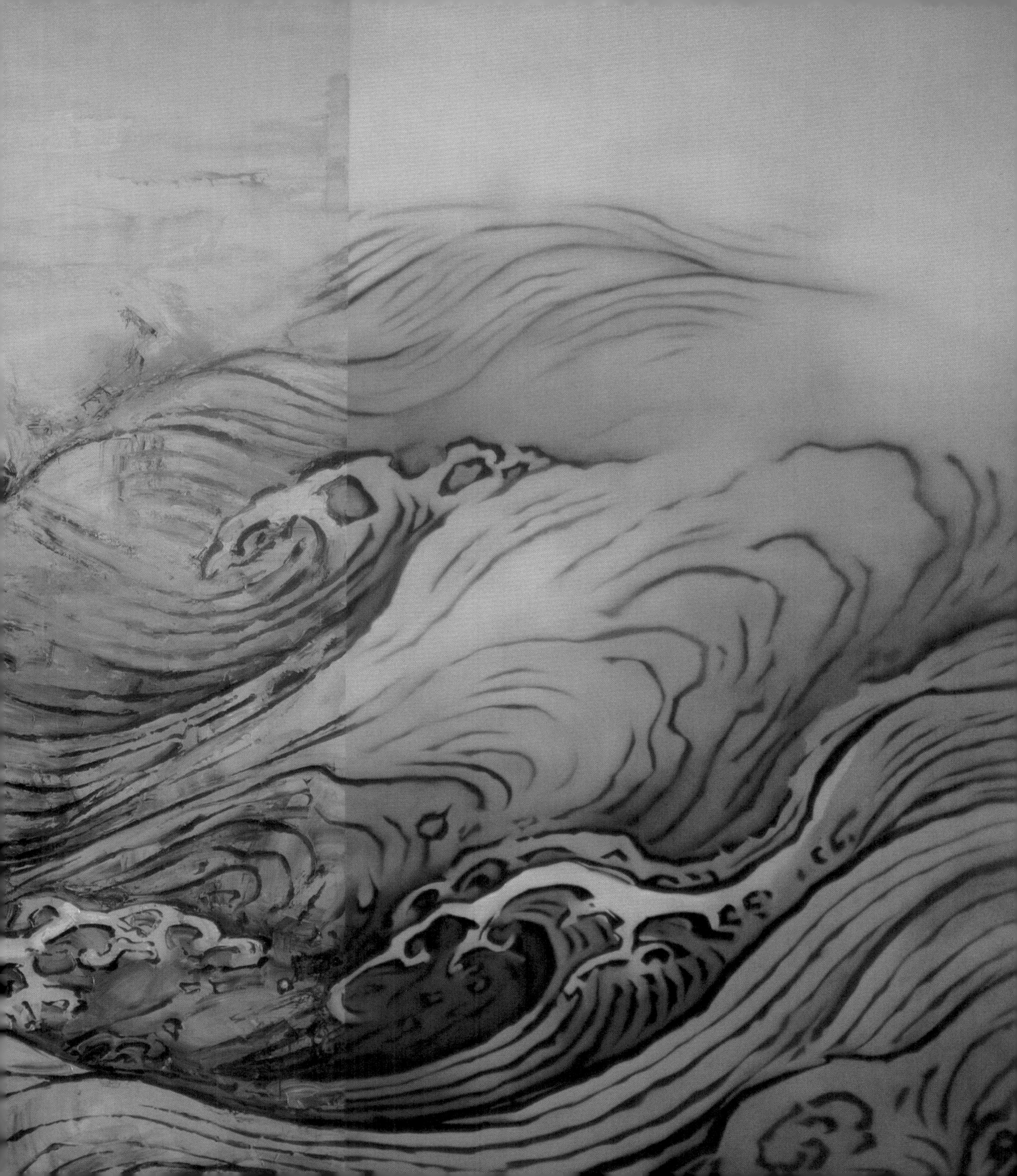

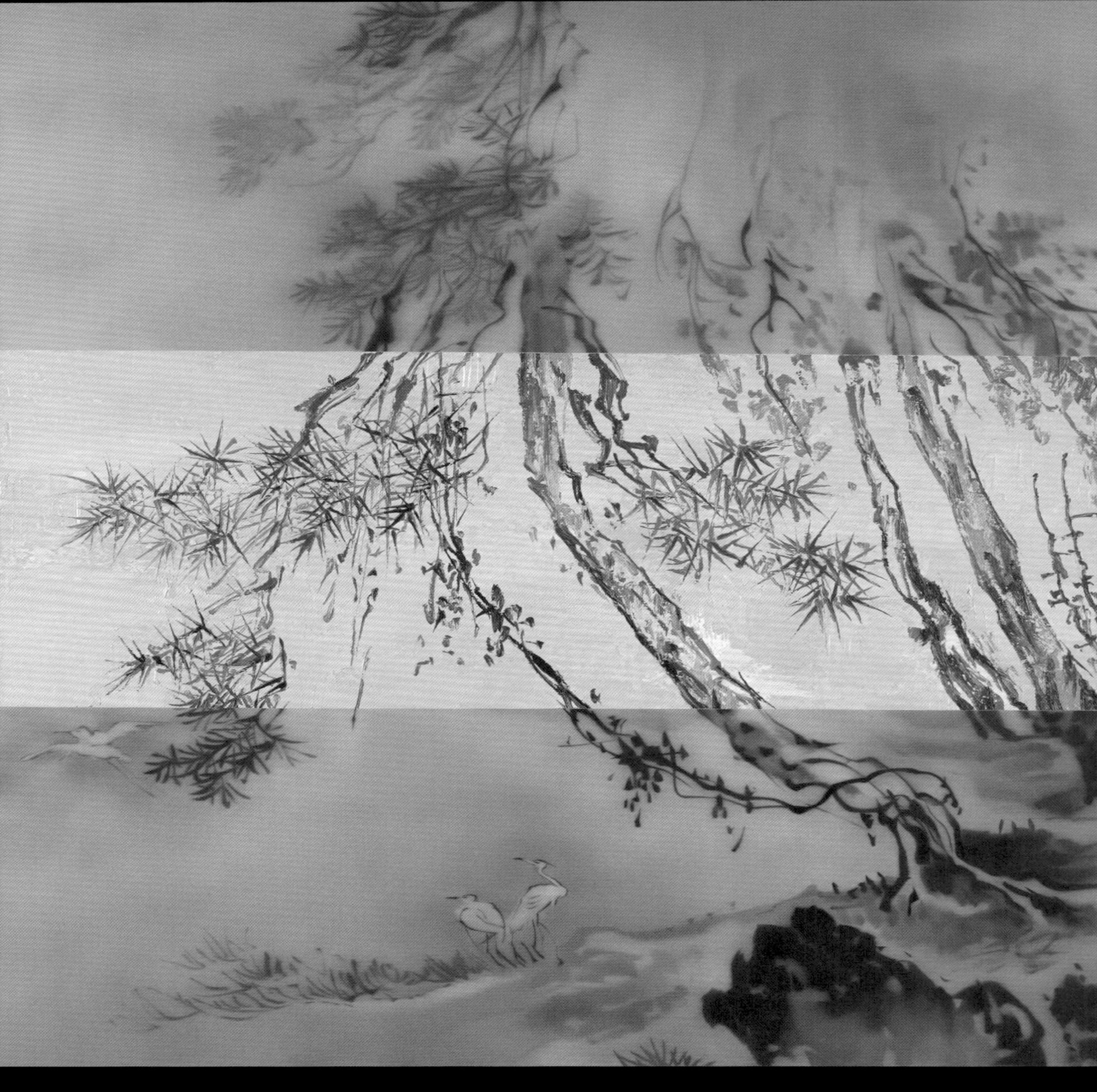

Daijin Scenery
oil on canvas
300x300 cm
2008

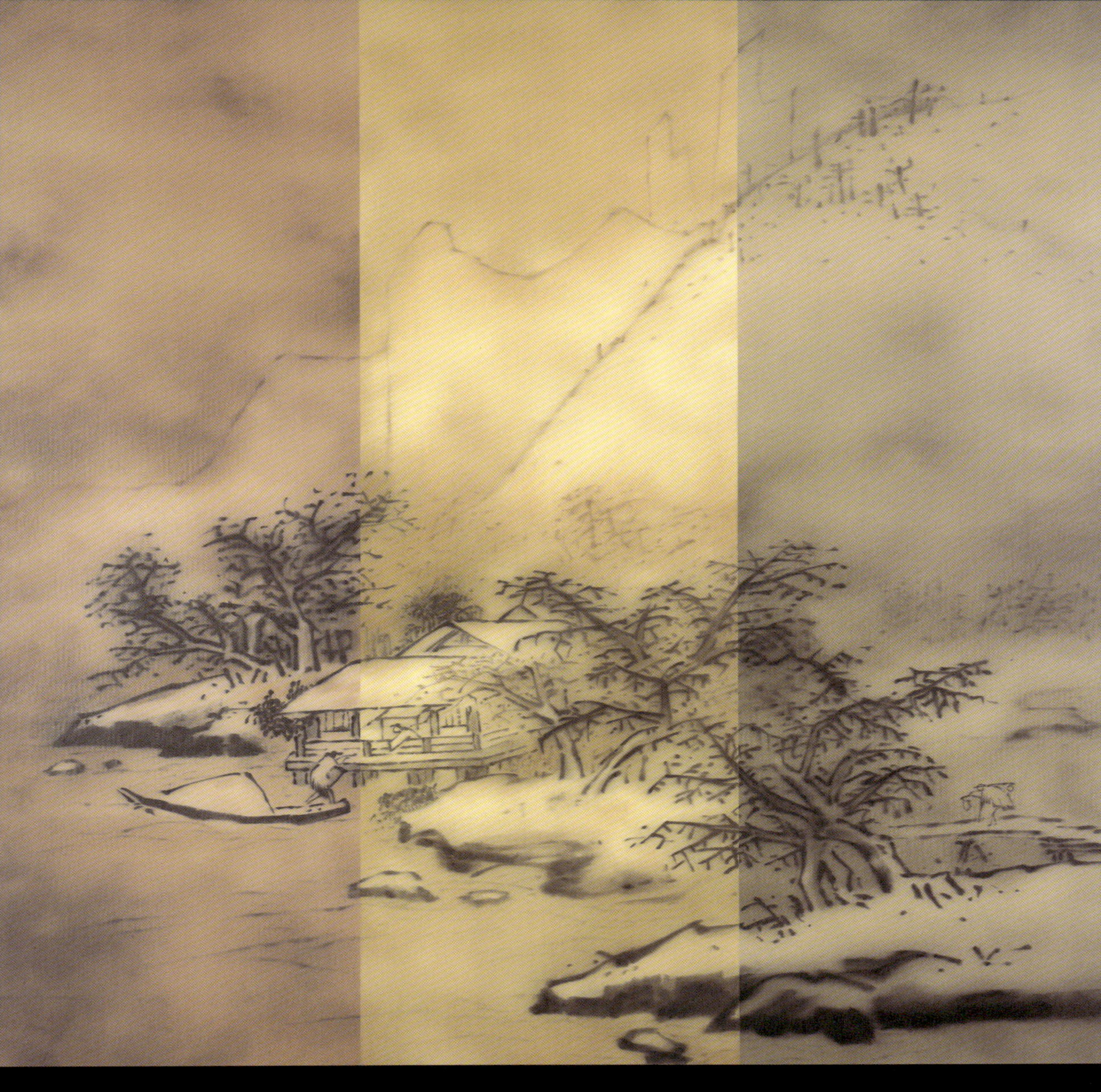

Li Dong. The image
of sell the fish in snow
oil on canvas
300x300 cm

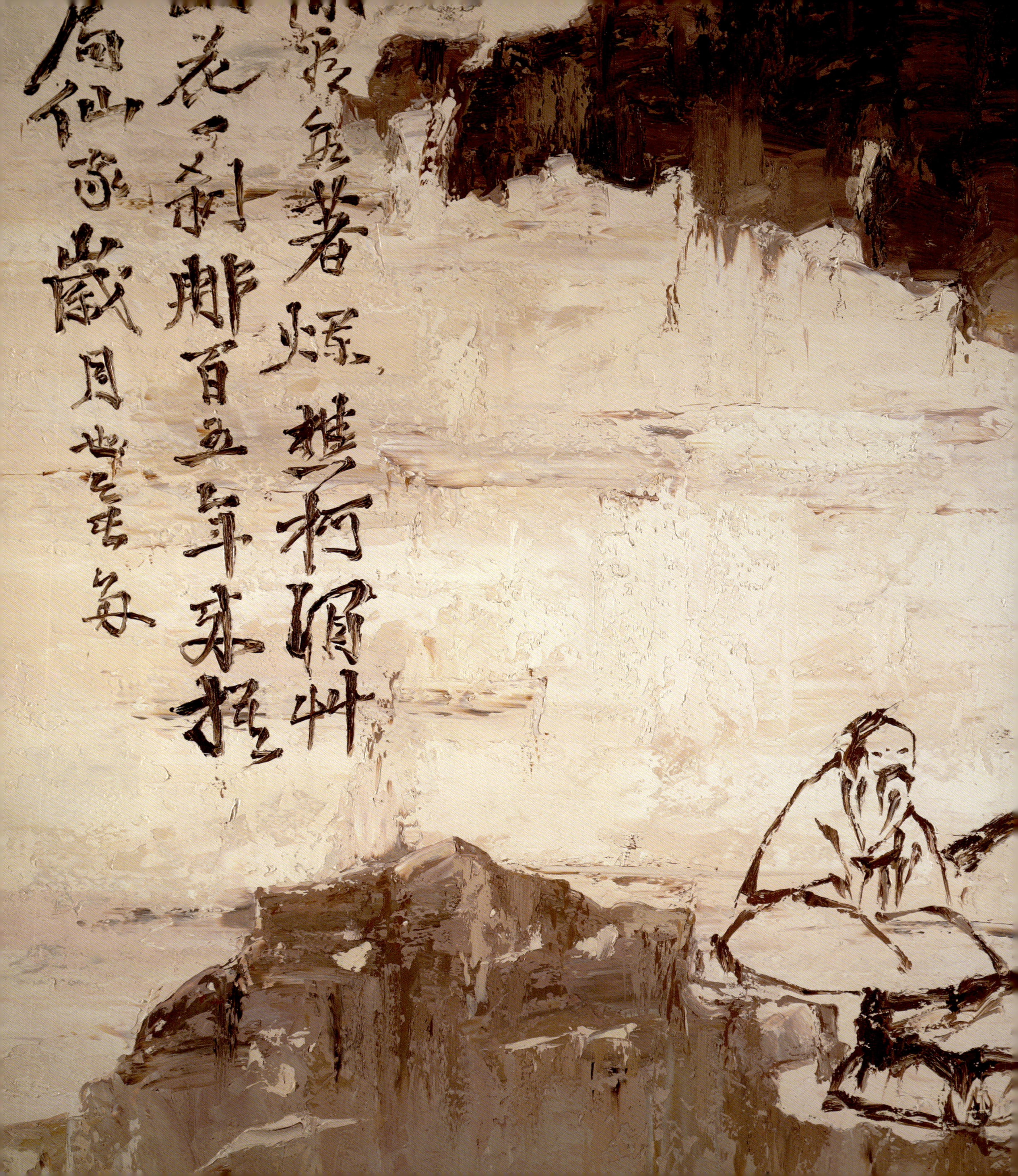

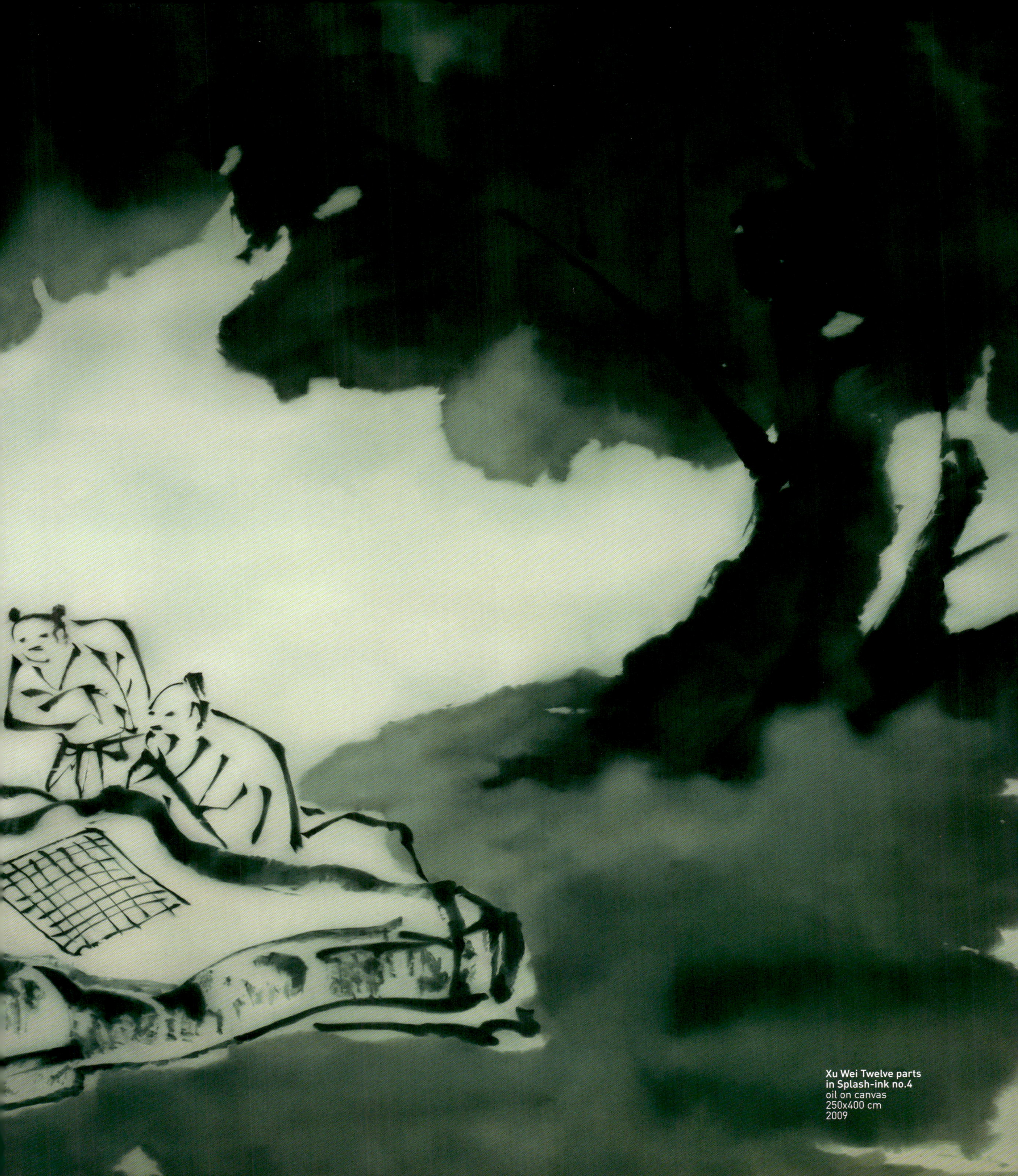

Xu Wei Twelve parts
in Splash-ink no.4
oil on canvas
250x400 cm
2009

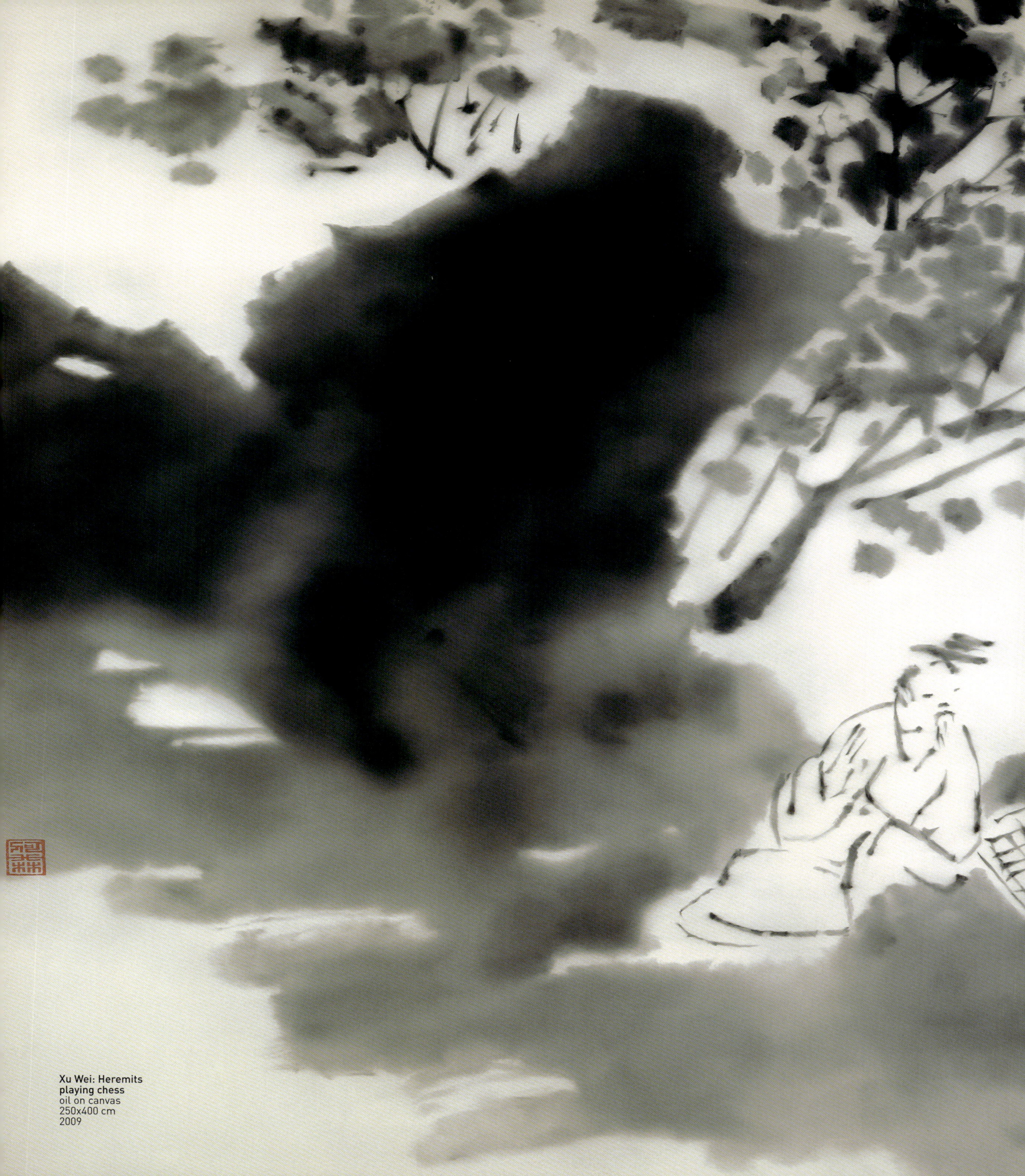

Xu Wei: Heremits
playing chess
oil on canvas
250x400 cm
2009

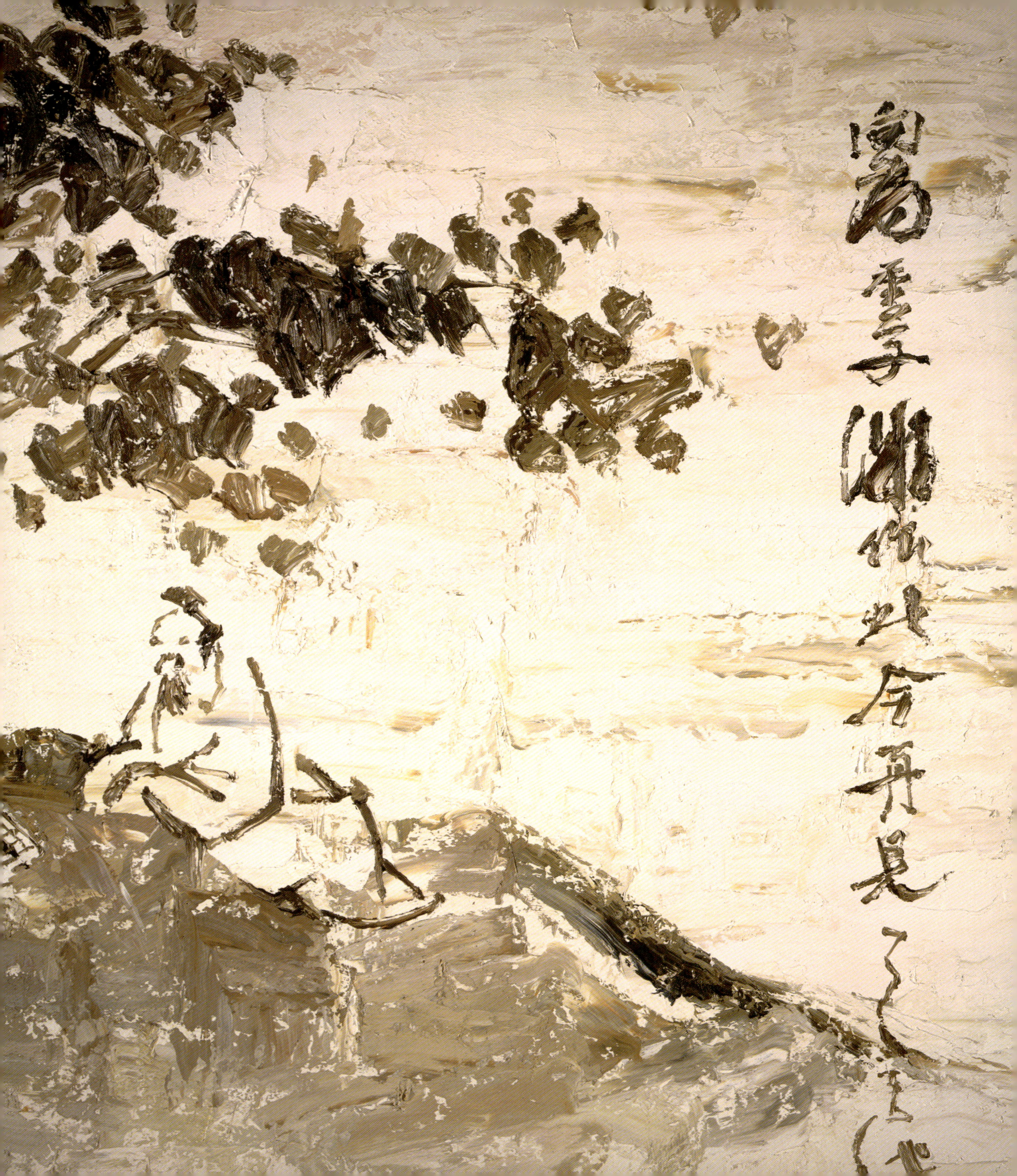

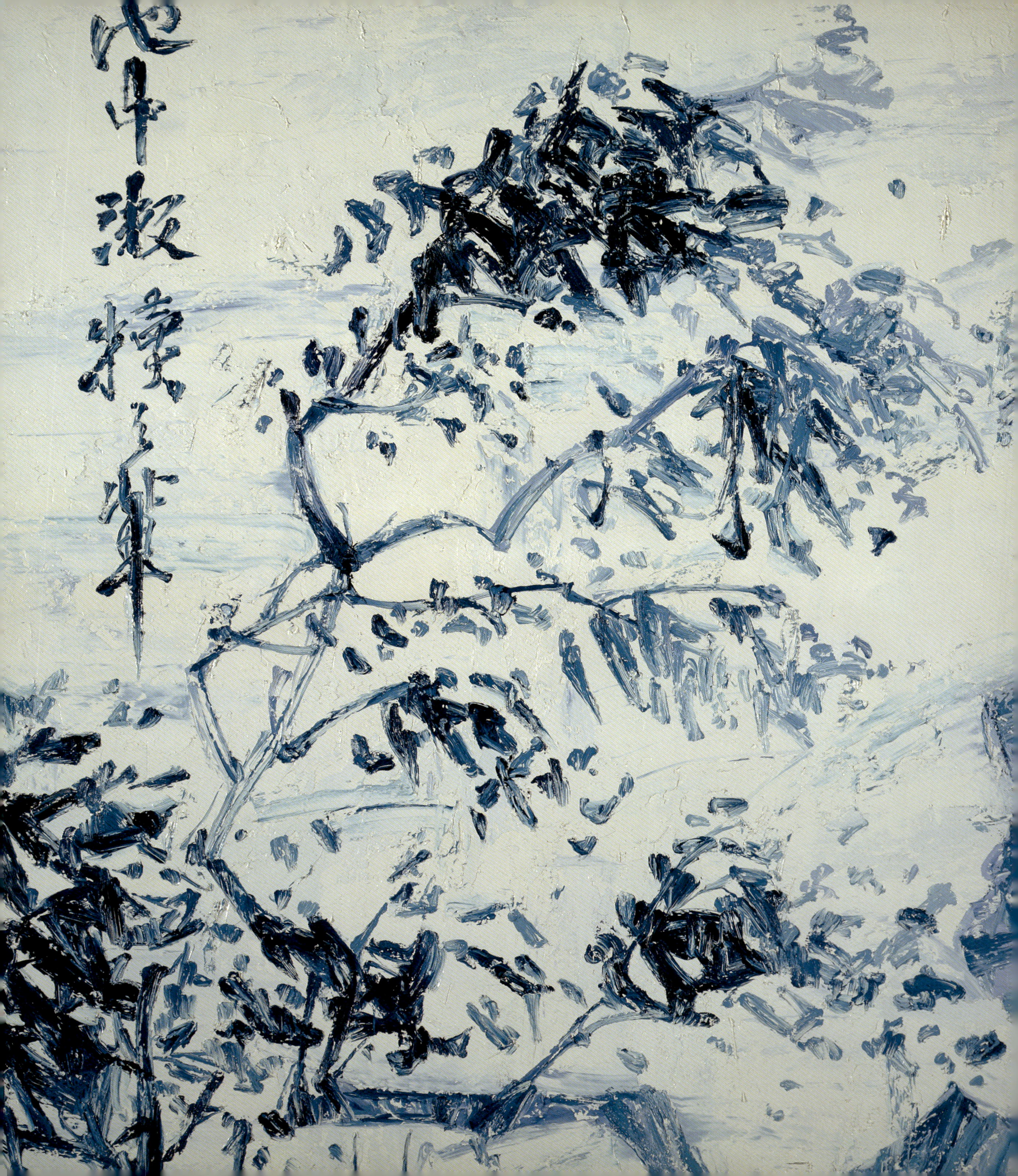

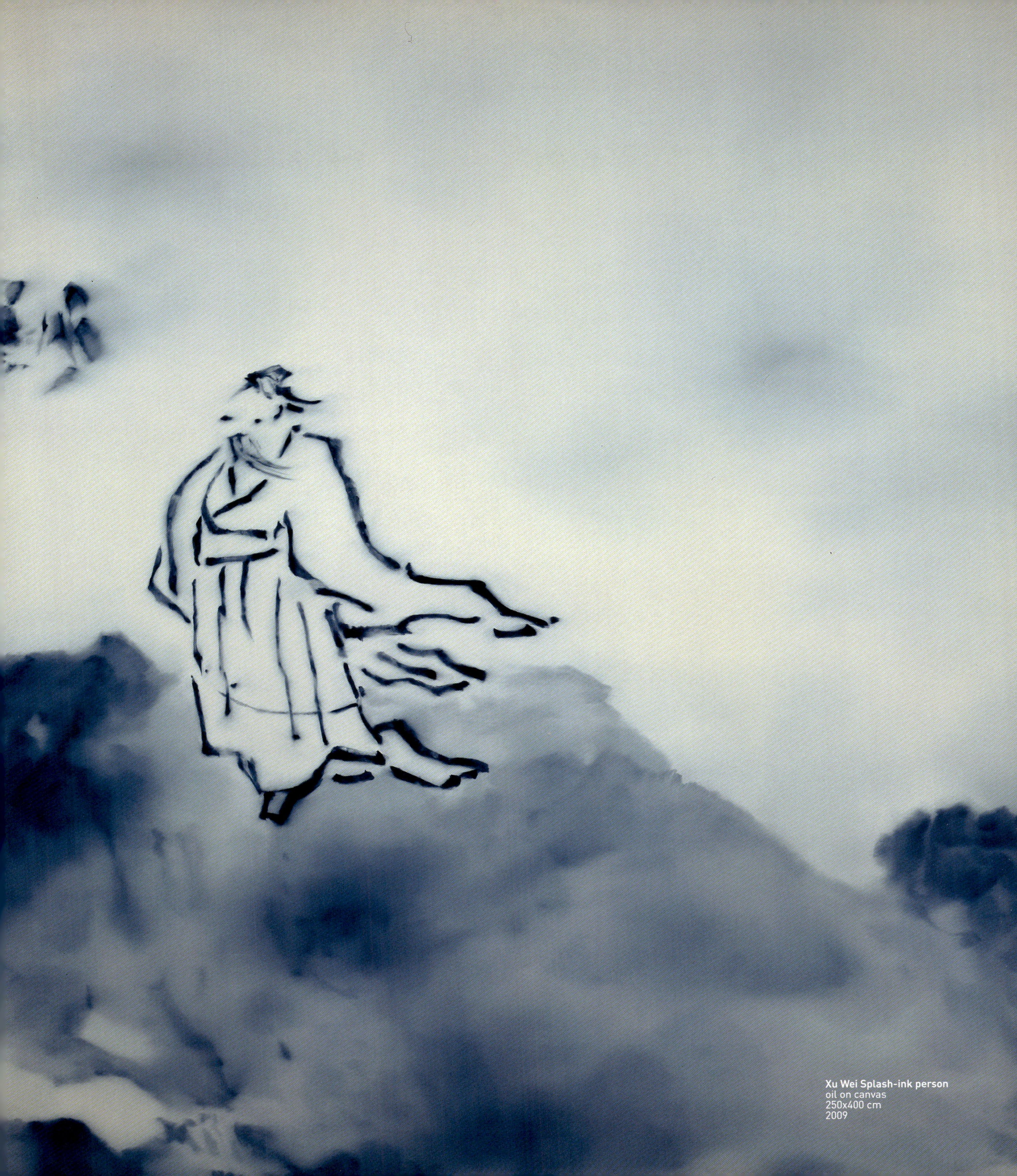

Xu Wei Splash-ink person
oil on canvas
250x400 cm
2009

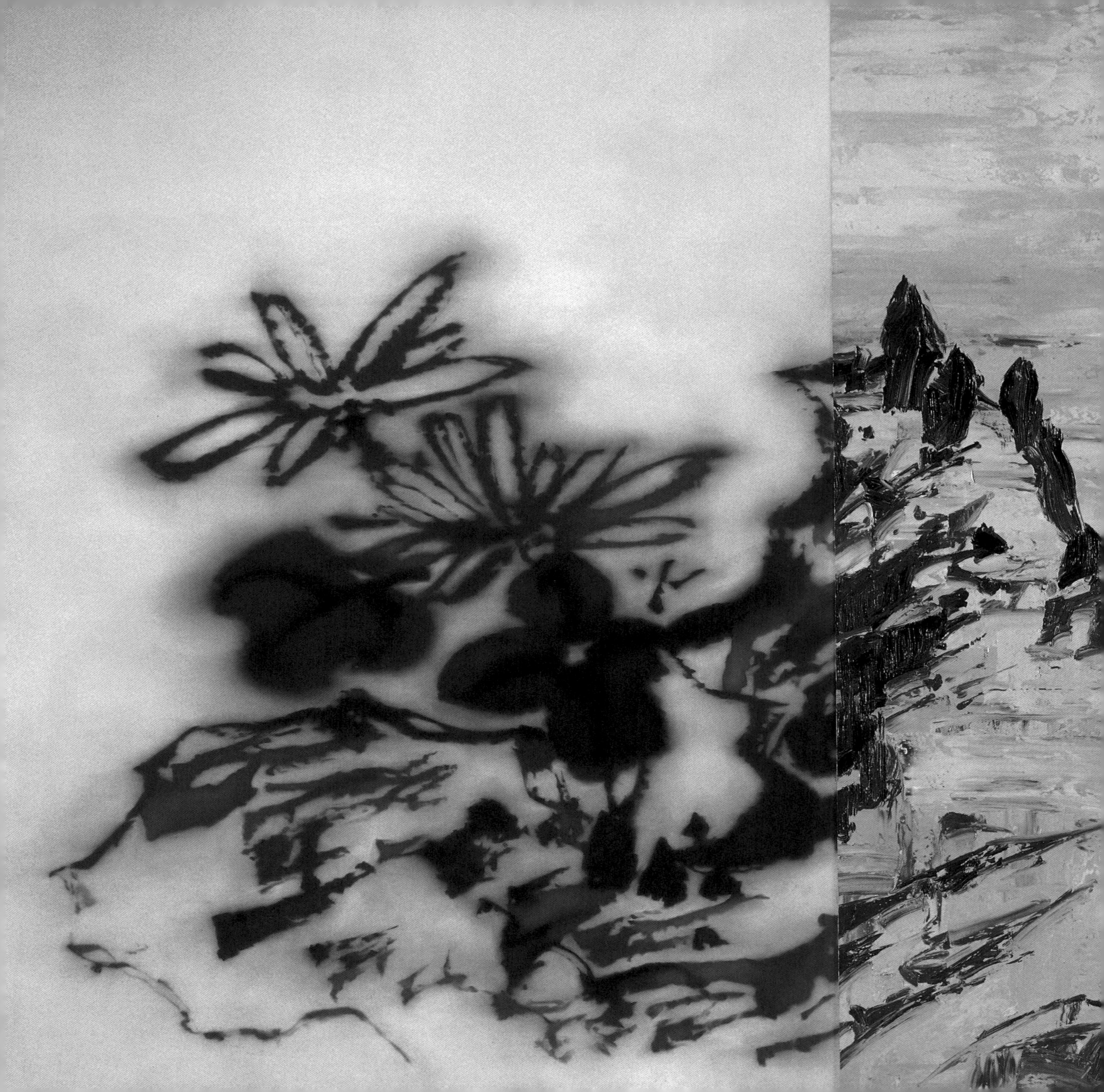

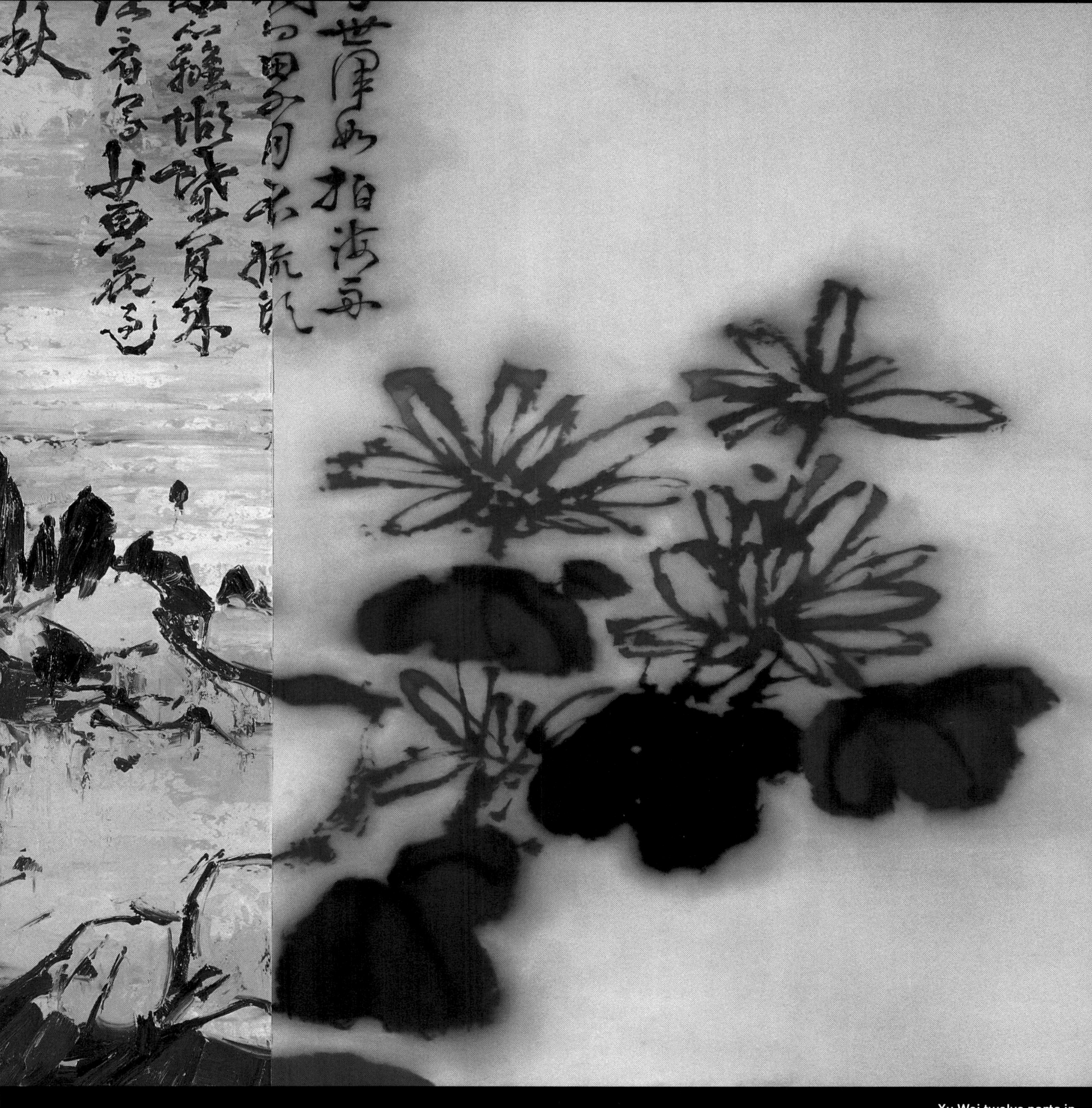

Xu Wei twelve parts in
Splash-Ink No. 7
oil on canvas
200x400 cm
2007

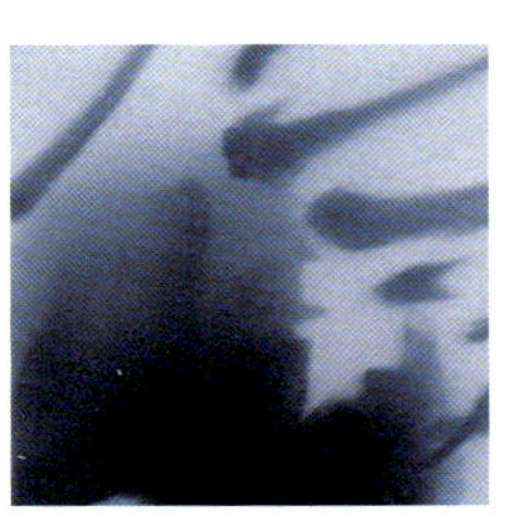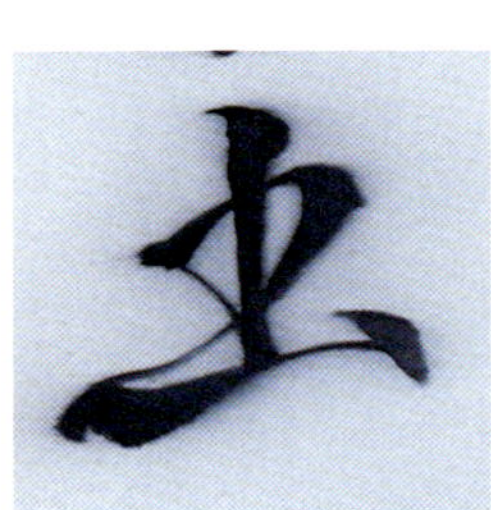

Xu Wei No. 2
of Flower series
in ink
oil on canvas
200x250 cm
2007

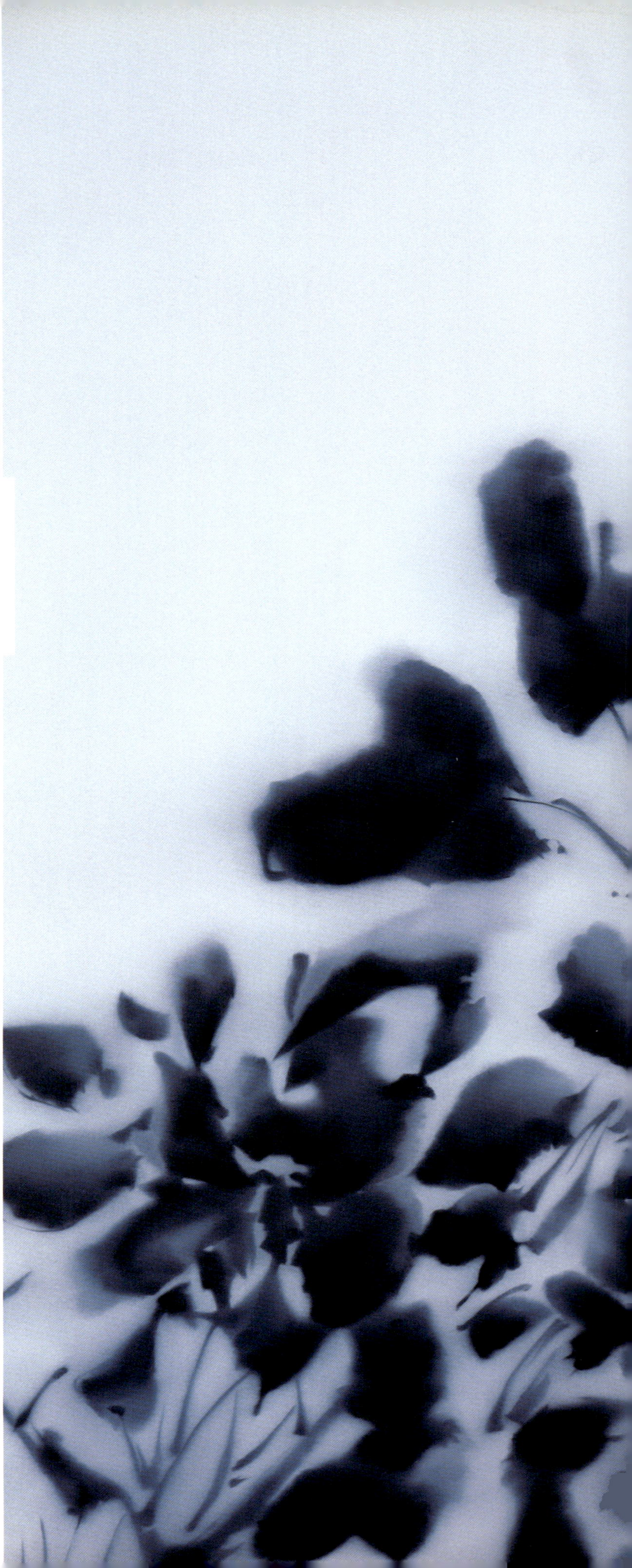

松指梁白好呢入流淇園一公

珊十隊裹虫珊瑚玉班

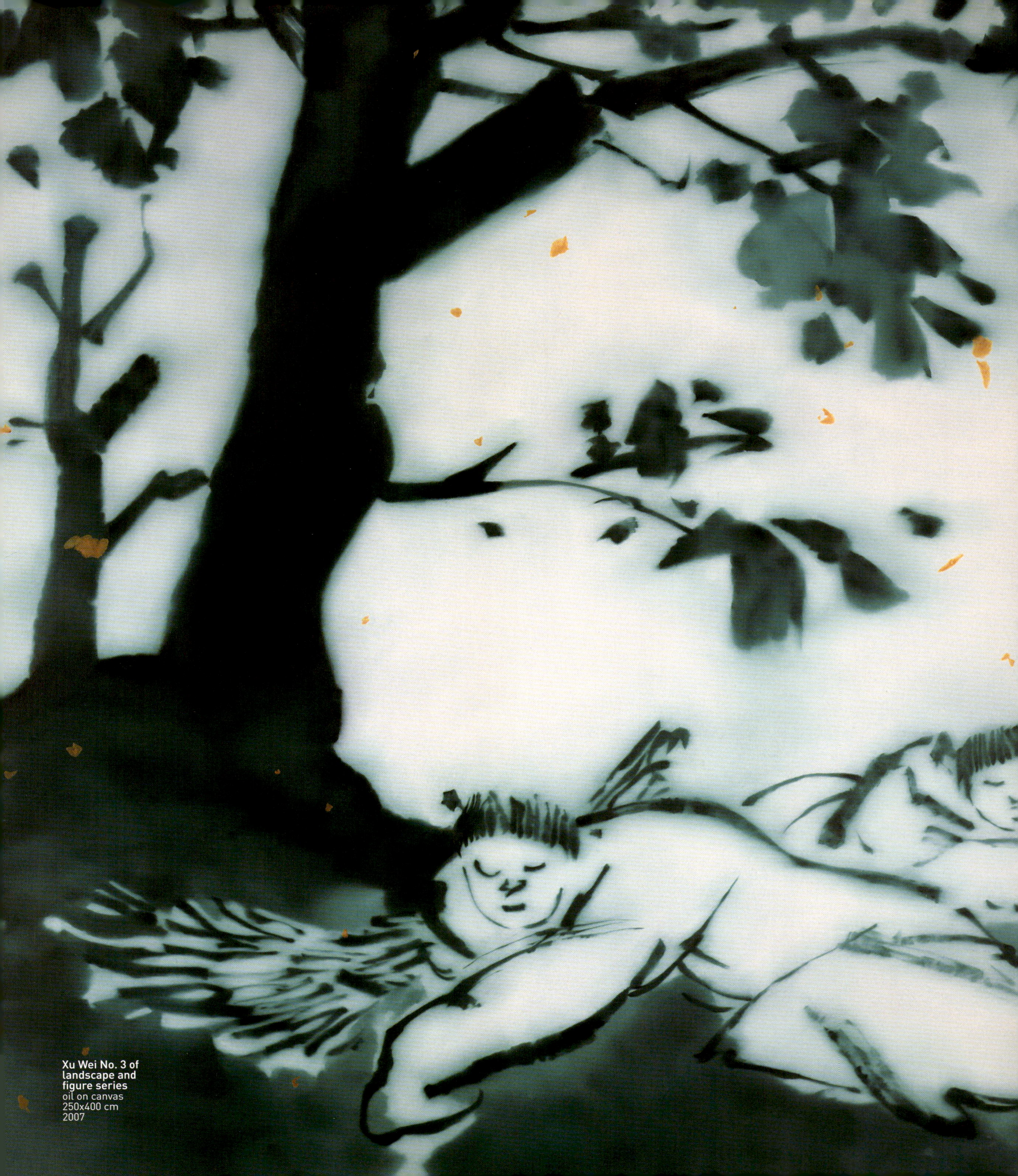

Xu Wei No. 3 of
landscape and
figure series
oil on canvas
250x400 cm
2007

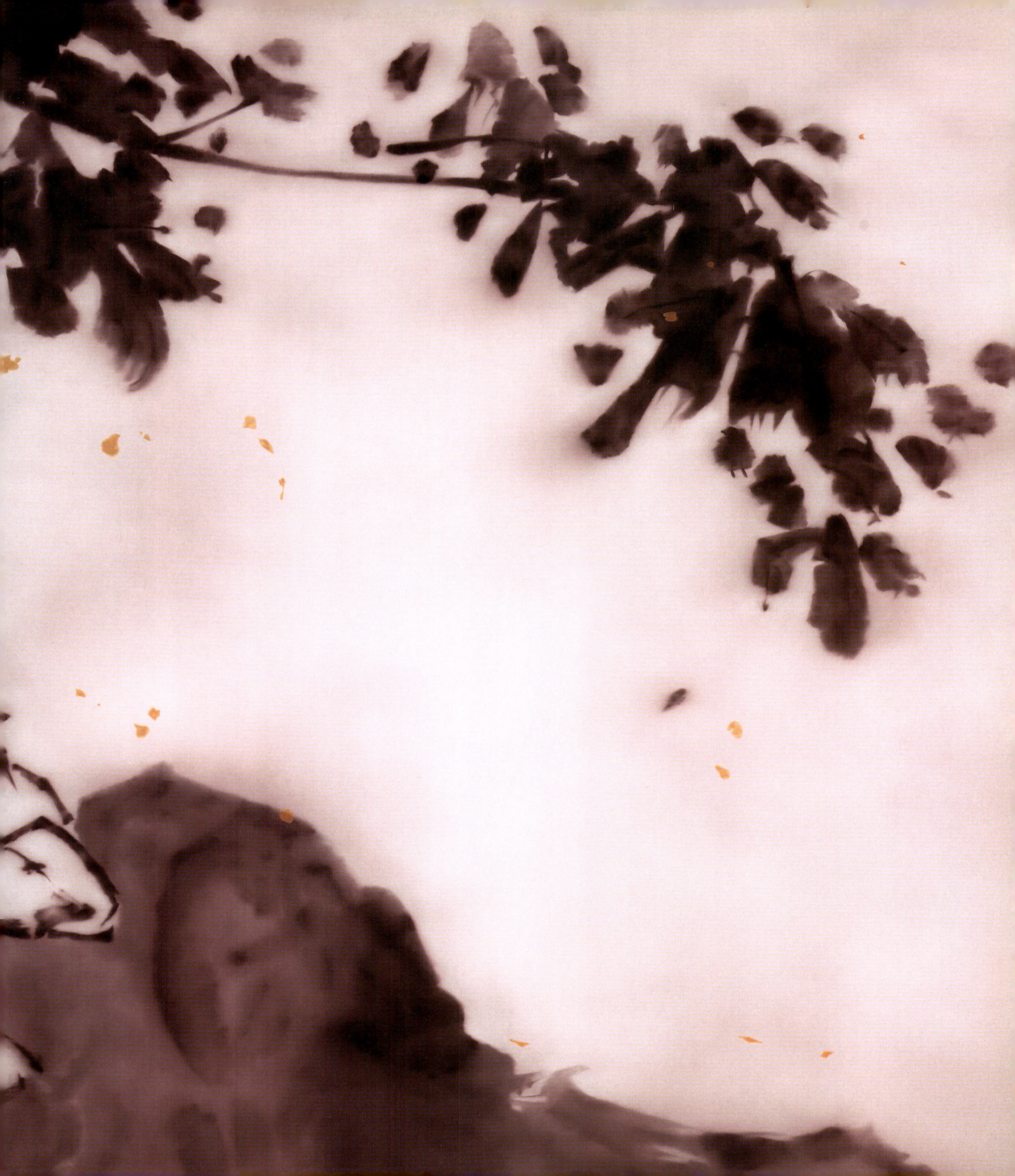

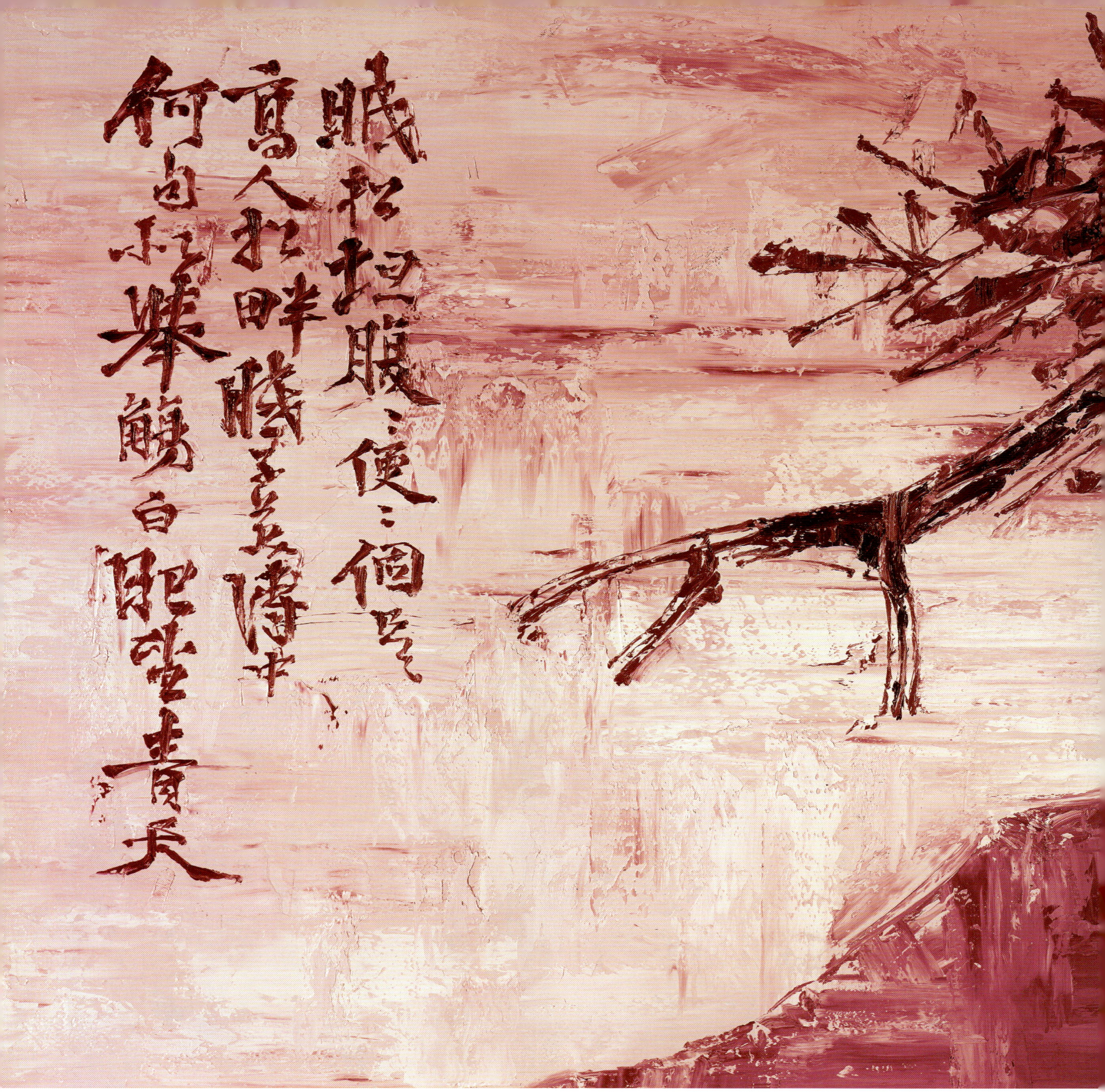

**Xu Wei twelve parts
in Splash-ink No.9**
oil on canvas
200x400 cm
2007

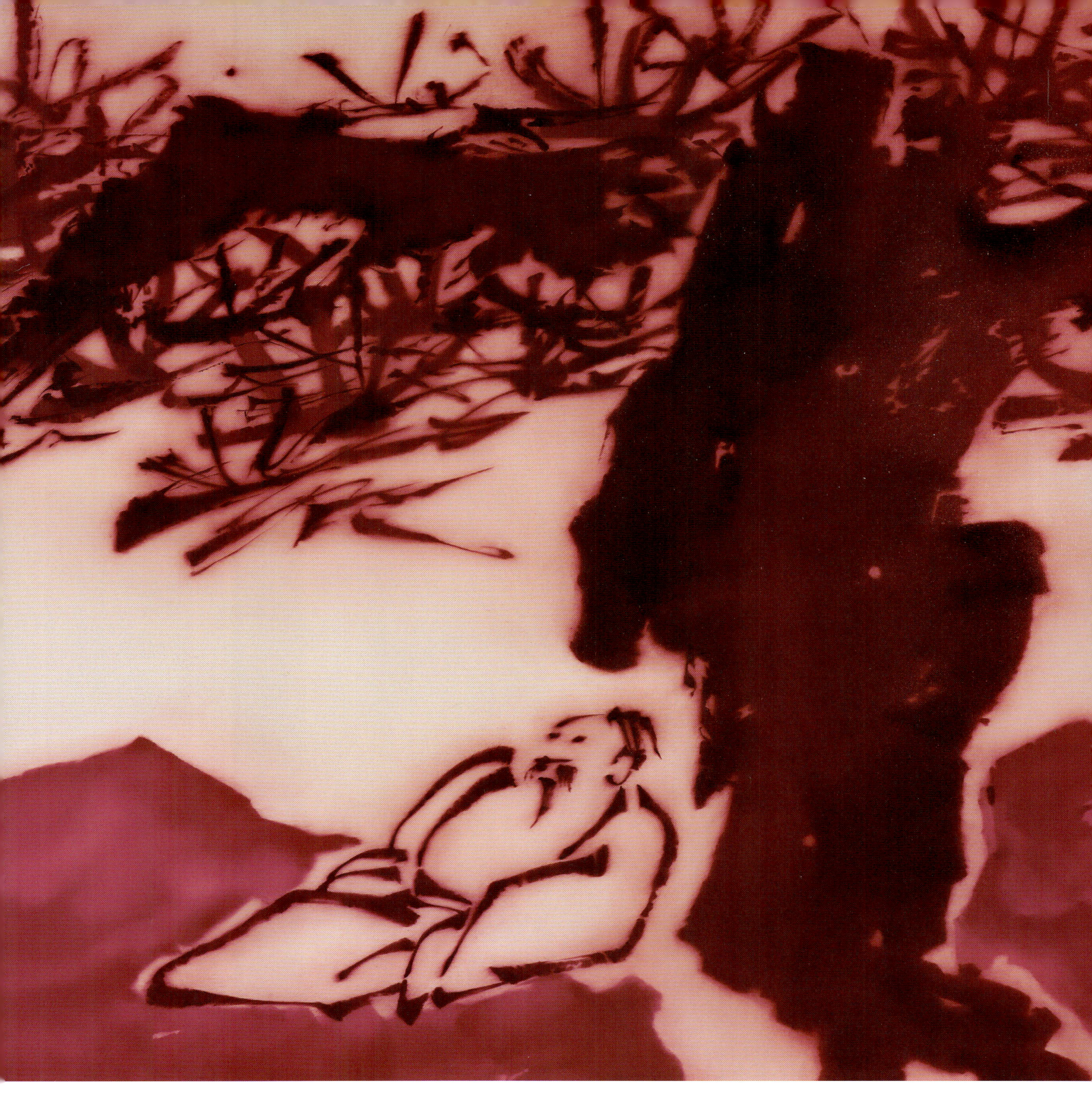

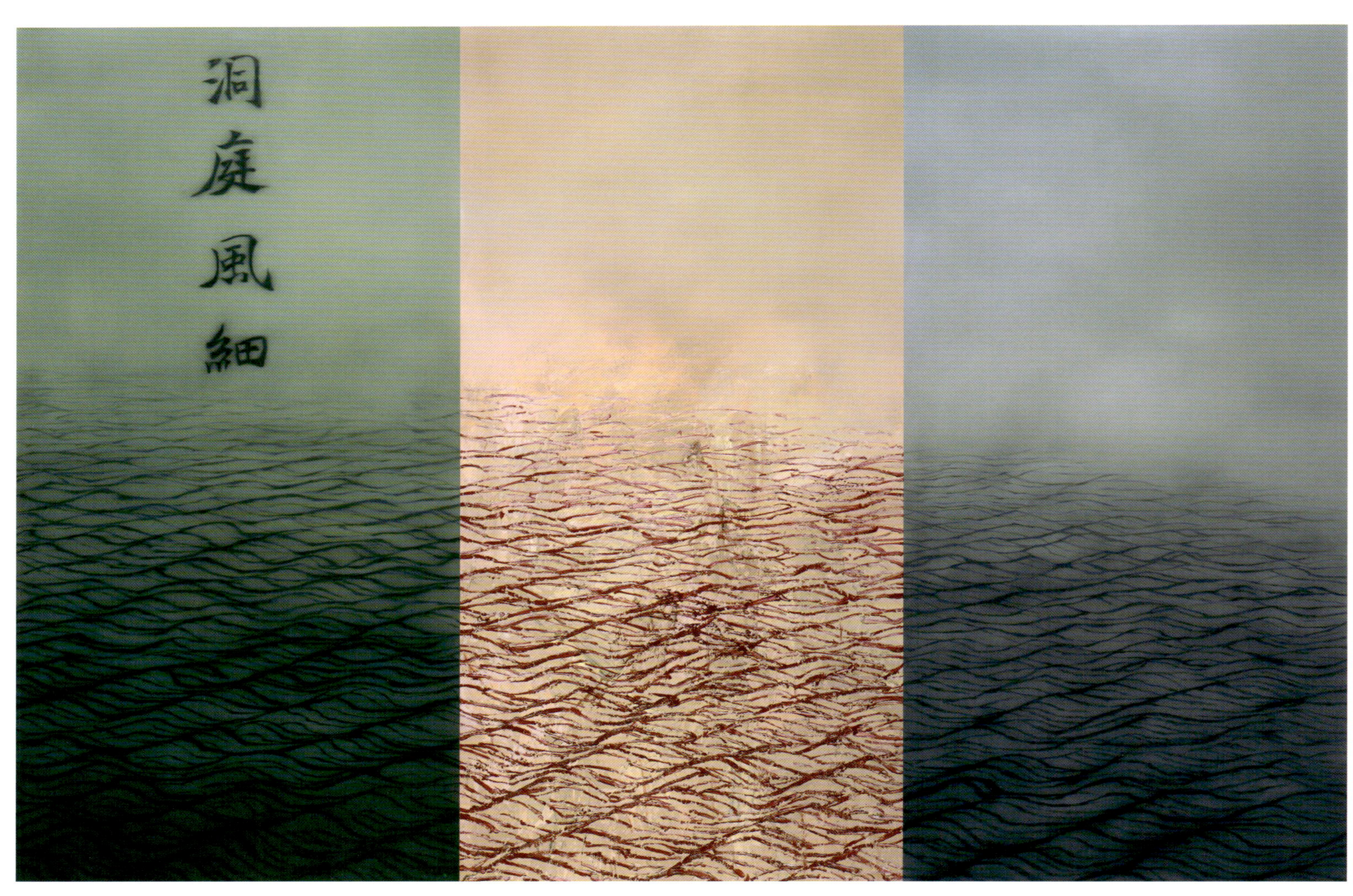

Ma Yuan Rippling
Lake in Mist
oil on canvas
400x600 cm
2009

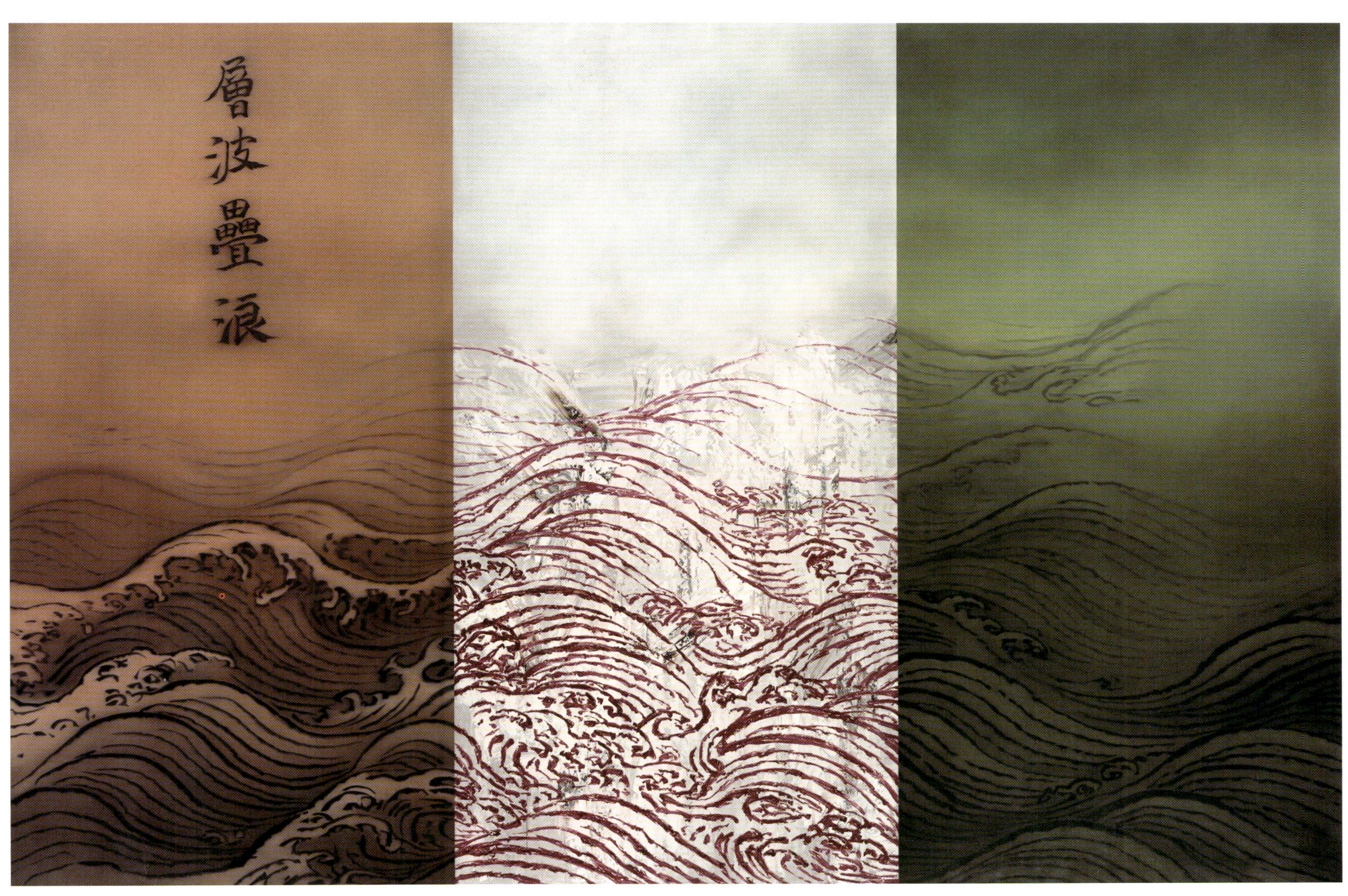

Ma Yuan's Twelve
Images of water–
Waves rolling one
higher than another
oil on canvas
400x600 cm
2008

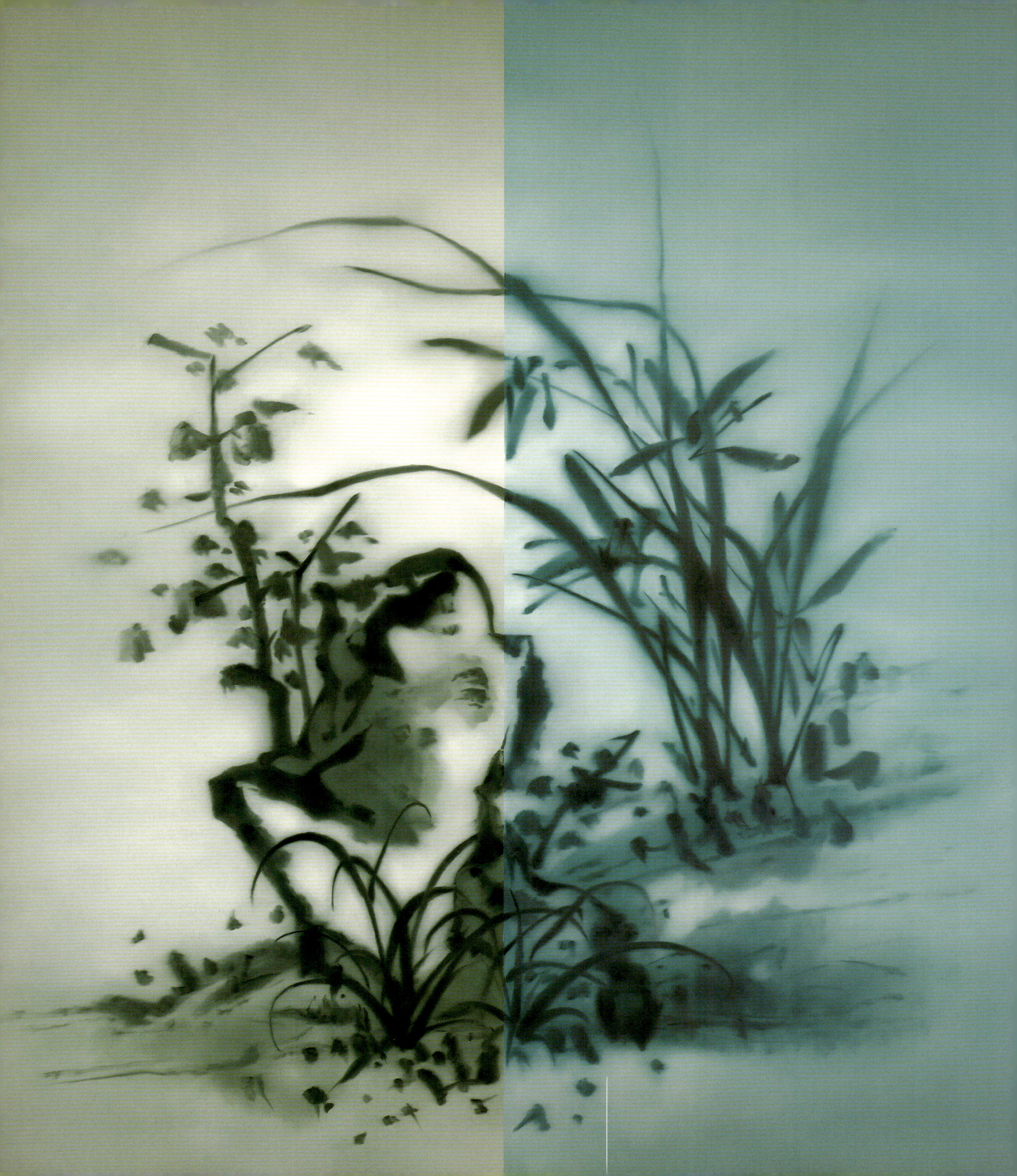

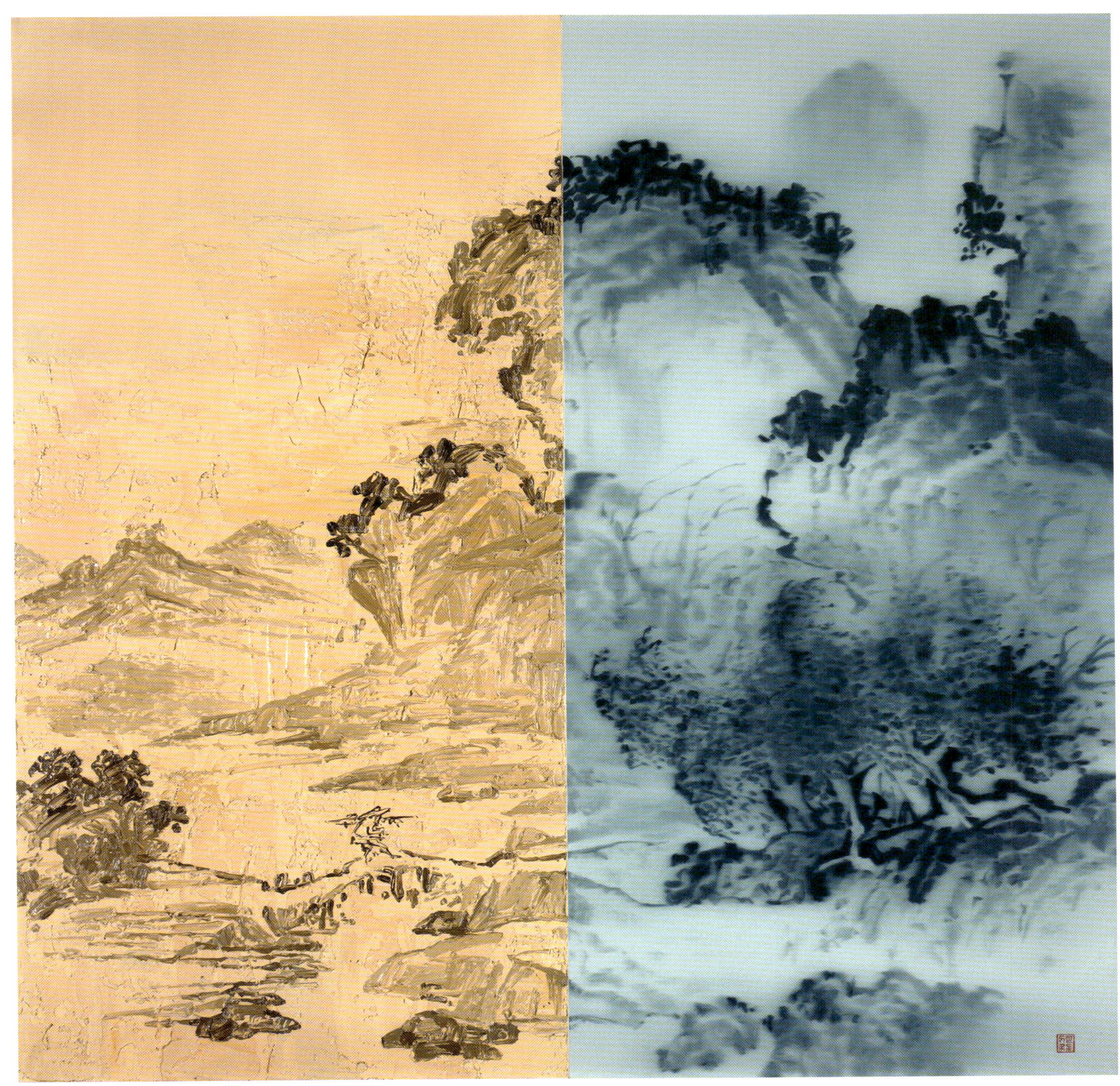

Zhu Sheng Bamboo
and Orchids
oil on canvas
250x200 cm
2008

Landscape in mist
oil on canvas
200x200 cm
2009

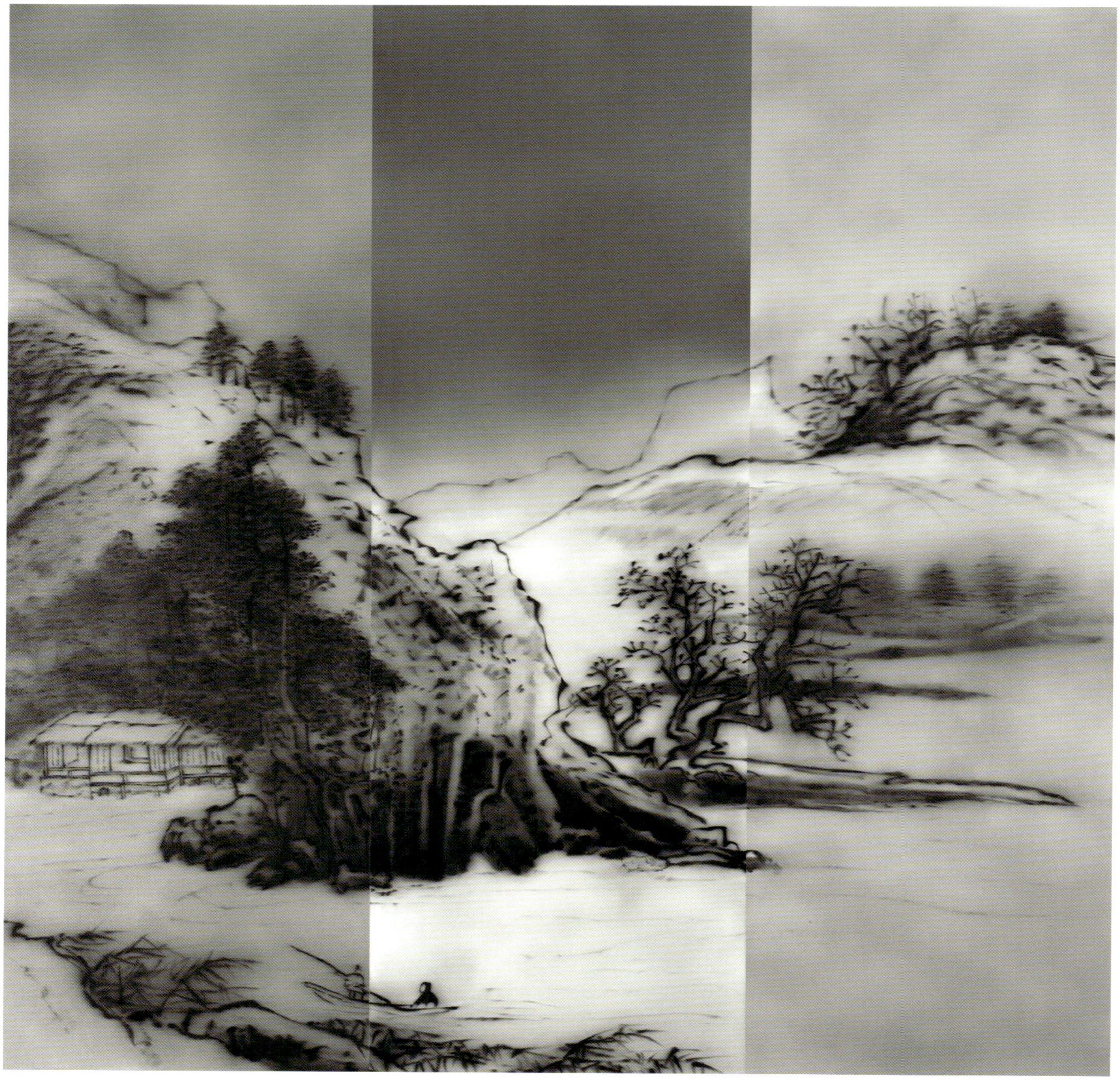

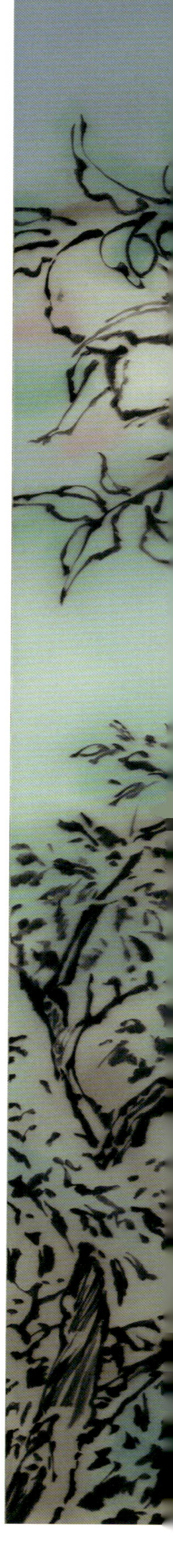

Anonym. The image of
Boating in snow
oil on canvas
300x300 cm
2008

**Monkey king on
the peach tree**
(diptych)
oil on canvas
200x200 cm
2010

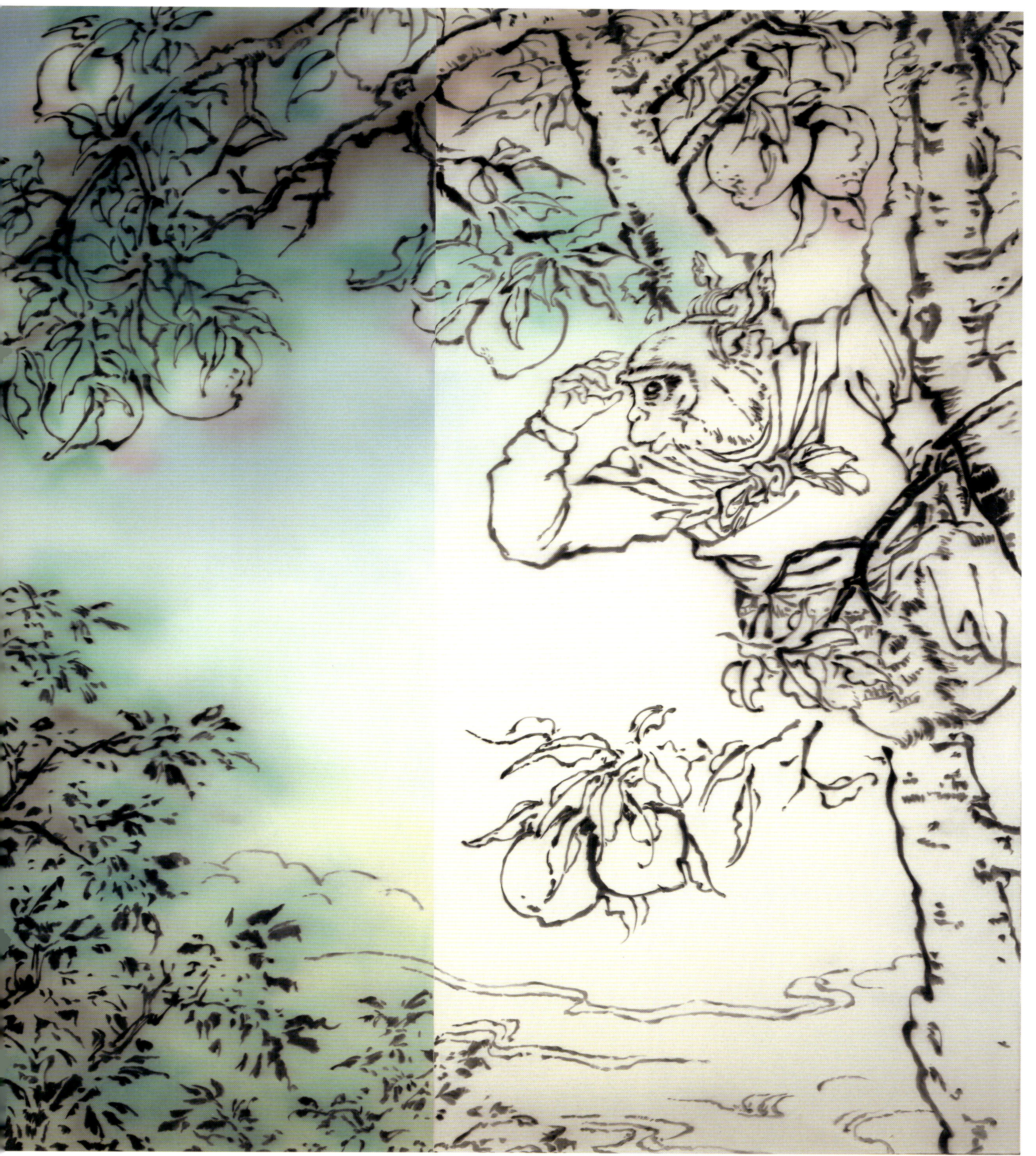

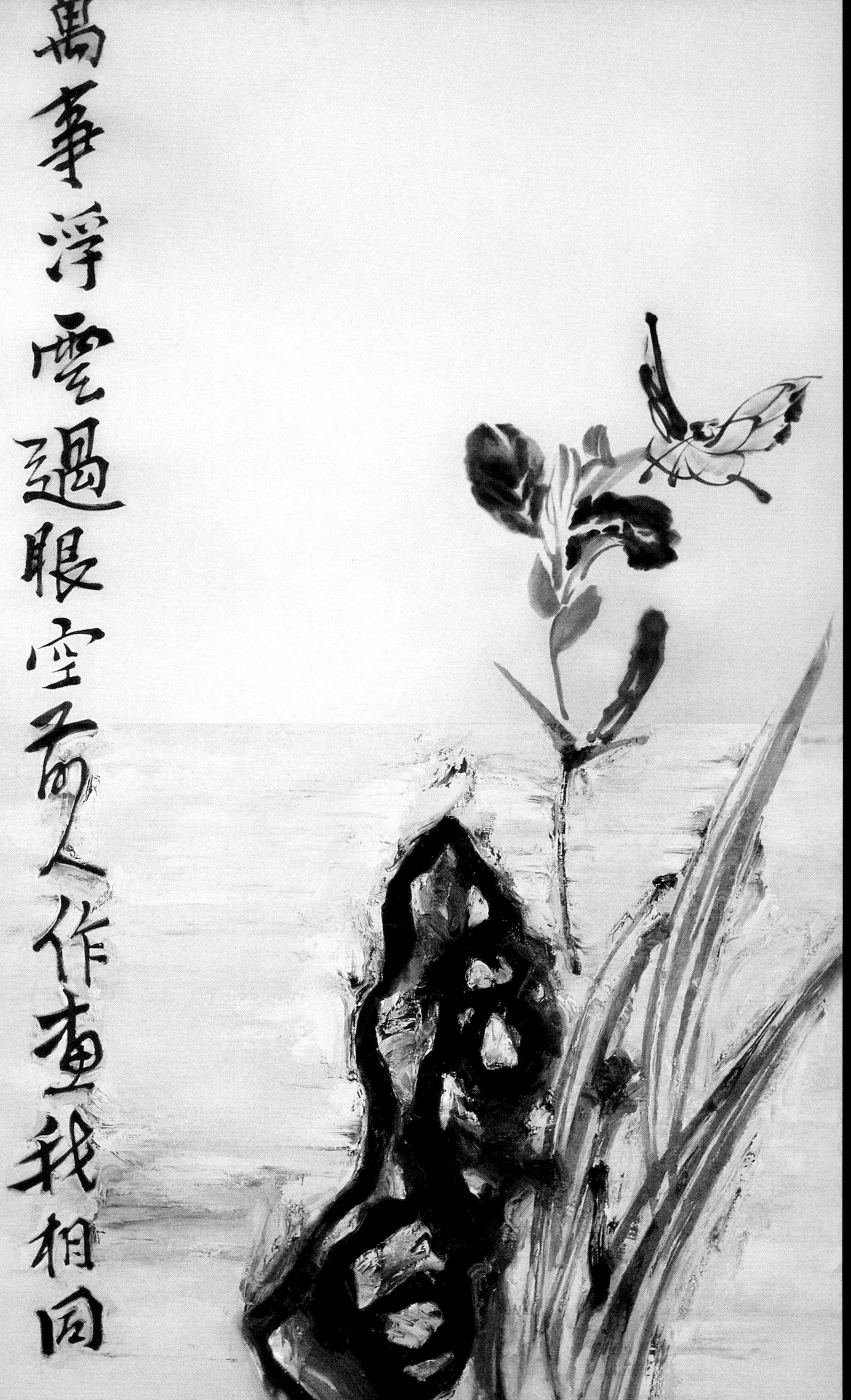

Li Shan miscellaneous
oil on canvas
350x210 cm
2006

Xu Wei three friends
oil on canvas
400x250 cm
2007

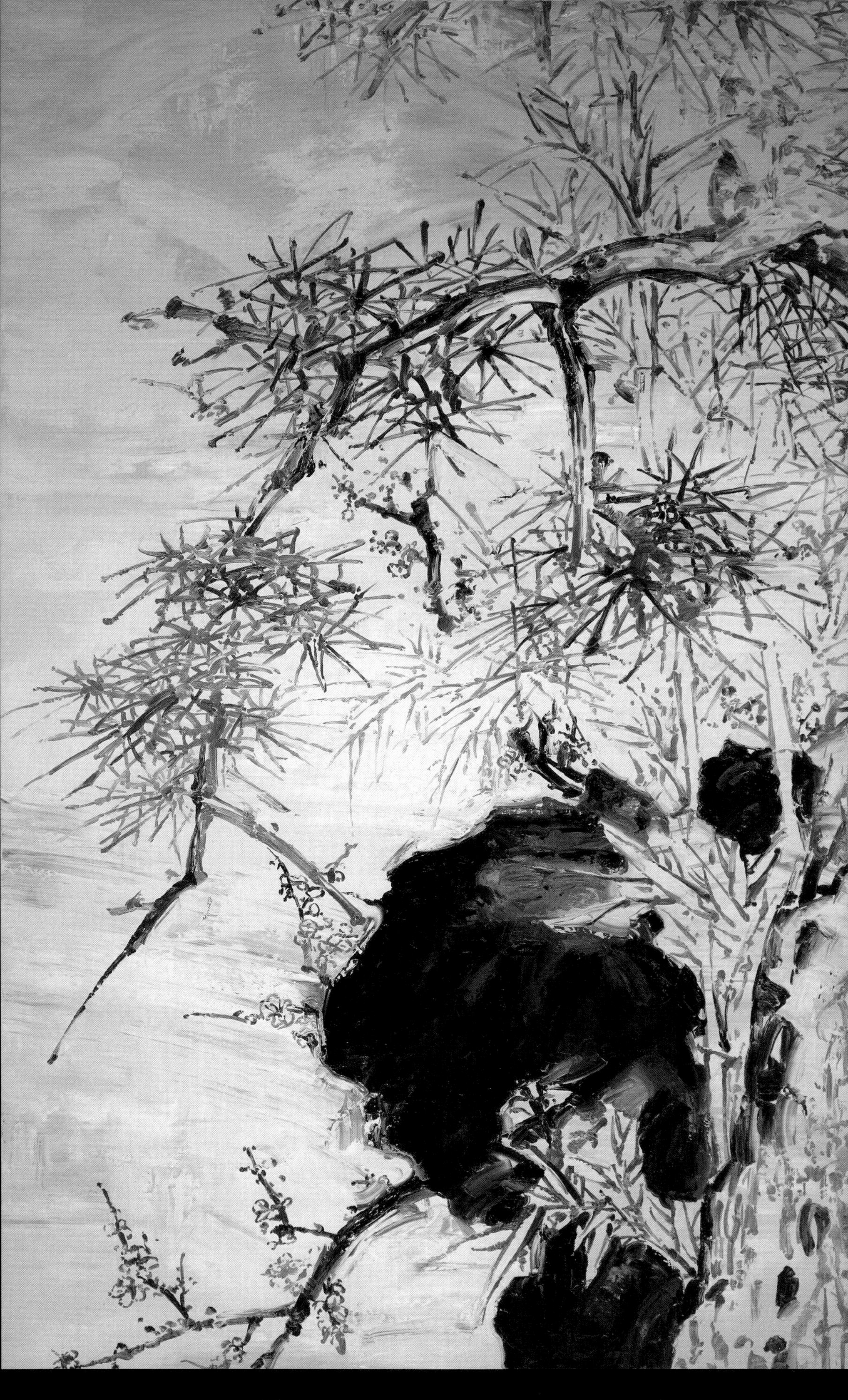

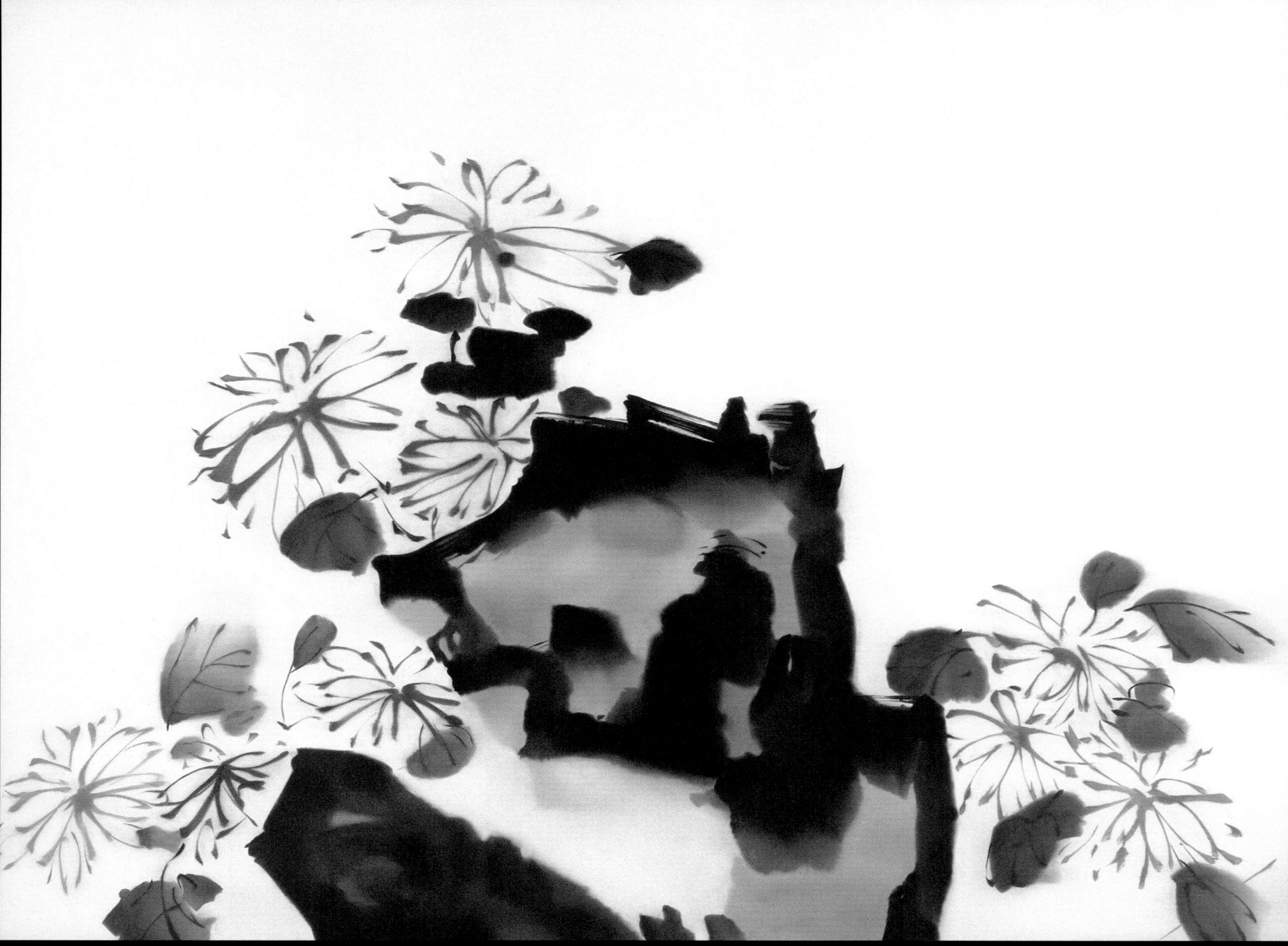

**Xu Wei chrysanthemum
and stone**
oil on canvas
150x200 cm
2007

**Wang Fu.The image
of The ink bamboo**
oil on canvas
400x200 cm
2008

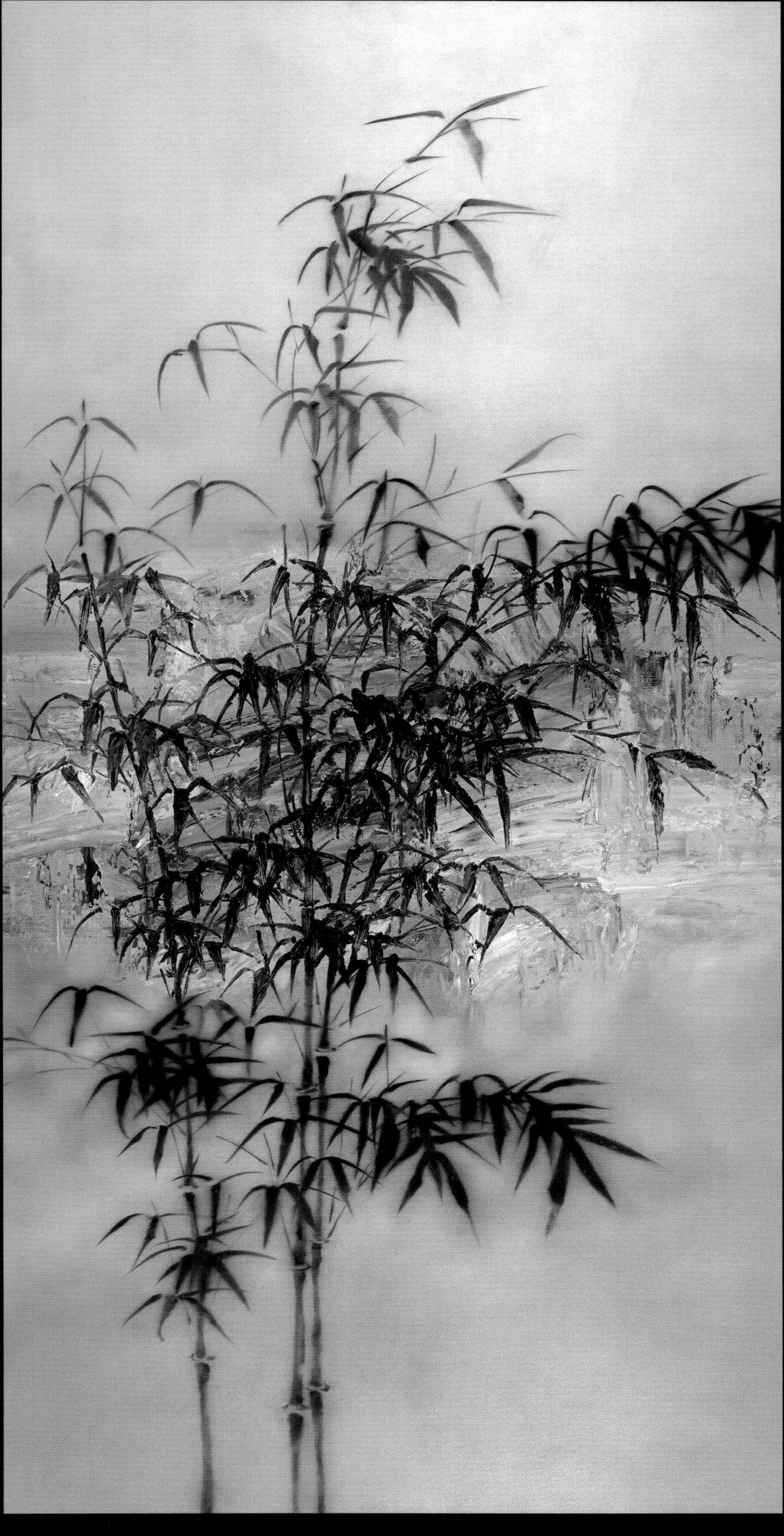

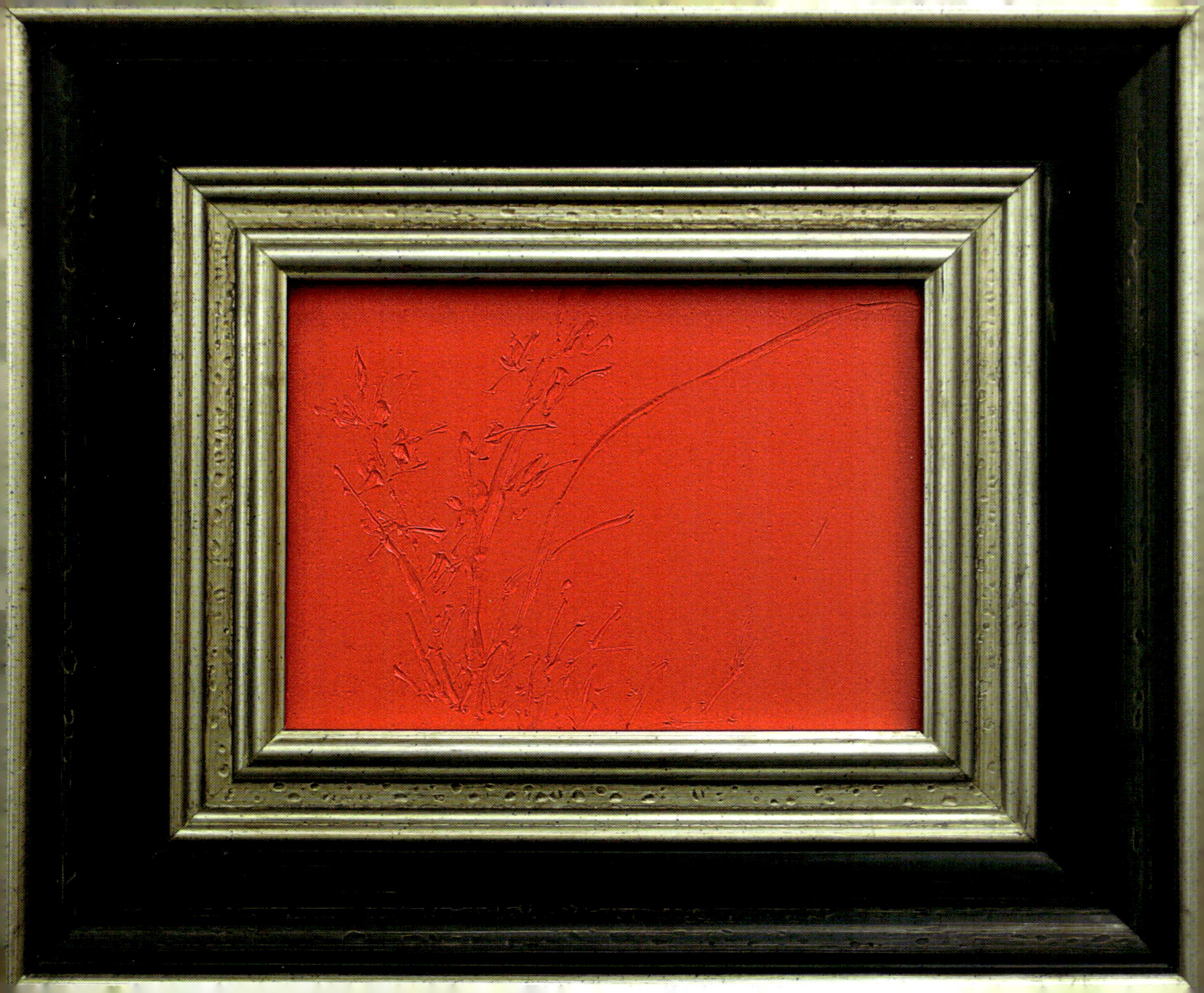

INTERVIEW FOR THE CATALOGUE FOR THE CHINESE PAVILION AT THE 53RD VENICE BIENNIAL

Lu Hao

Lu Hao: In late 1998, you started a series of works featuring young girls. Why did you do it? Was it because of market forces or the so-called youth perplexity?

He Sen: Although there was an "Art Market" magazine even back in 1992 or 1993, but for those in the know, there was barely any art market to speak of in 1998. Youth perplexity is a term employed by some literary youths. In fact, I did it simply for technical reasons and for the effect that would entail. It is a bit boring to talk about it now: images in the "Stack" series are painted to protrude out of the flat background. Many people said to me that something was missing from the background and the subject. So, to link them up, I did many experiments such as applying the flare effect. I used to paint purely with a painting knife. But to paint the flare effect, I took up the brush again. The effect was gradually enlarged and my painting grew thinner and softer (it had been rather thick). Eventually, I started drawing with brushes. Then I realized that the soft effect would apply very well to painting girls. In continuation with past practice, the girls in those paintings still had no eyes. Of course, the loss of eyes due to glaring light could also be explained from many literary and sociological angles.

Lu Hao: Your earlier works are known for depicting disoriented and confused urban girls. Why did you later turn to copying, transplanting, appropriating and altering the classical works of traditional Chinese master painters on canvas?

He Sen: On seeing my new works, most people find it hard to understand why I have turned to subjects that had nothing to do with female themes. They feel that the turn was abrupt or there was no continuation. In the 18 years as a professional artist, I painted a number of objects and carried out many kinds of experiments. Changes were many and vastly different. I have never been trapped in something in which I had to make numerous adjustments. Of course, changes are a double-edged sword. But I am someone who easily get bored. I have faith in my ability and hope to challenge myself at all time. This has nothing to do with external factors. I do not want to be known only for a particular motif. I like to be known as an artist whose artistic direction and aesthetics are accepted. Apart from the "Stage" series, most of my previous works have something in common, i.e. escapism: self-abandonment in the face of harsh realities, something negative and illusionary.

It took me a long time to start using traditional Chinese imagery in my paintings. The preparation was long and I thought about many issues. For me, to paint is a way to escape. Therefore, why did I not try to paint with a technique that is completely secluded from reality? Chinese art today is in principle a reflection of sociology. It is too close to reality and too far from art. Art's being close to reality has

its own merits but I am very tired of it. Whenever you open an art catalogue in China, people come into view: people in reality, people in society bearing all kind of societal marks. Apart from these, what imagination do we have?

Most of the fundamental elements in contemporary Chinese art came from the west, including things artists learned as art students, which was Western culture. It appeared to be a standard but I don't think that it is a big problem. From the traditional angle, the West is objective and three-dimensional, while China is subjective and horizontal. The difference of expression and observation stems from differences in culture, worldview and mindset. Why are we bending closer together now? At the end of the day, it is a question of cultural rights.

To grapple with reality, traditional Chinese artists painted with an attitude that is far detached from reality. I am touched by their works and feel that the same attitude is in my genes. I use traditional imagery and do not want to change it. I only want to use it as a foundation, to paint what is felt and what I feel today. It also fits very well with my desire to flee from reality. It also goes well with my passion for painting and my exploration of painting per se. That is, to paint for the sake of painting.

Lu Hao: What do you make of the so-called first-rate artists?

He Sen: I don't know when the term came to be used. I don't know where to draw the line. Other people say that you categorize them by their auction prices. But I think that that approach is too partial. It is true that the vast majority of top selling artists have illustrious academic achievement and standard, which can not be gained overnight. Influence determines the price. But high prices are also the result of good business strategy. Still, it is easier and more understandable for non-artists to measure success with money.

Lu Hao: You are one of the most favored artists on the market in recent years. Some people think that contemporary Chinese art market is a big bubble. Are you part of the bubble?

He Sen: Economic overheating and recession lead to fluctuations in every field. Everyone is affected to a certain degree. Right now, there are not that many people spending at the bars and the restaurants. Can you therefore say that the restaurants were in a bubble when they were crammed with customers? My career is relatively stable. It is normal.

LuHao: What expectations do you have for the Chinese Pavilion of the 53rd Venice Biennial?

HeSen: Of course, I hope that will be the best China exhibition ever.

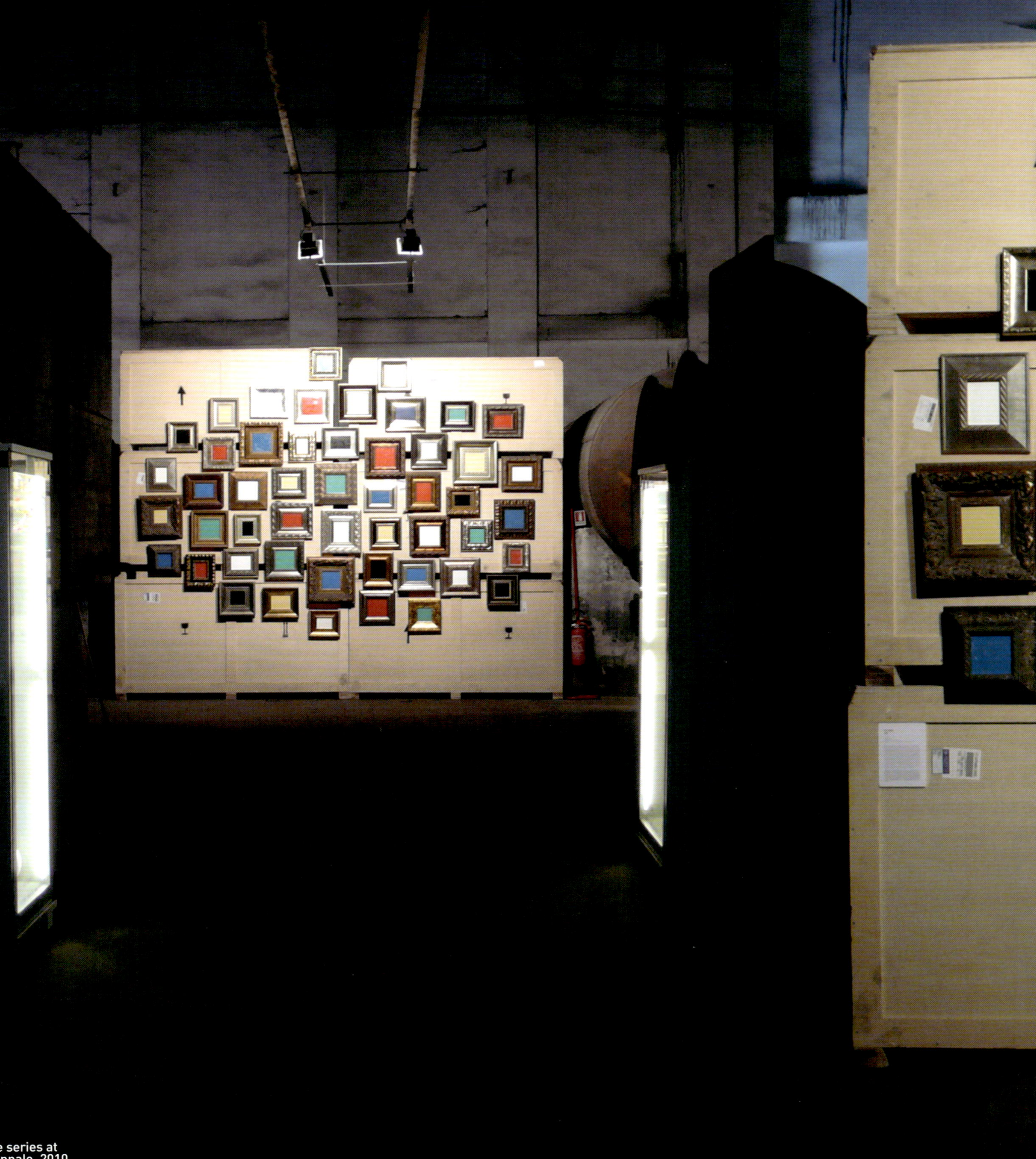

...e series at
...nnale, 2010

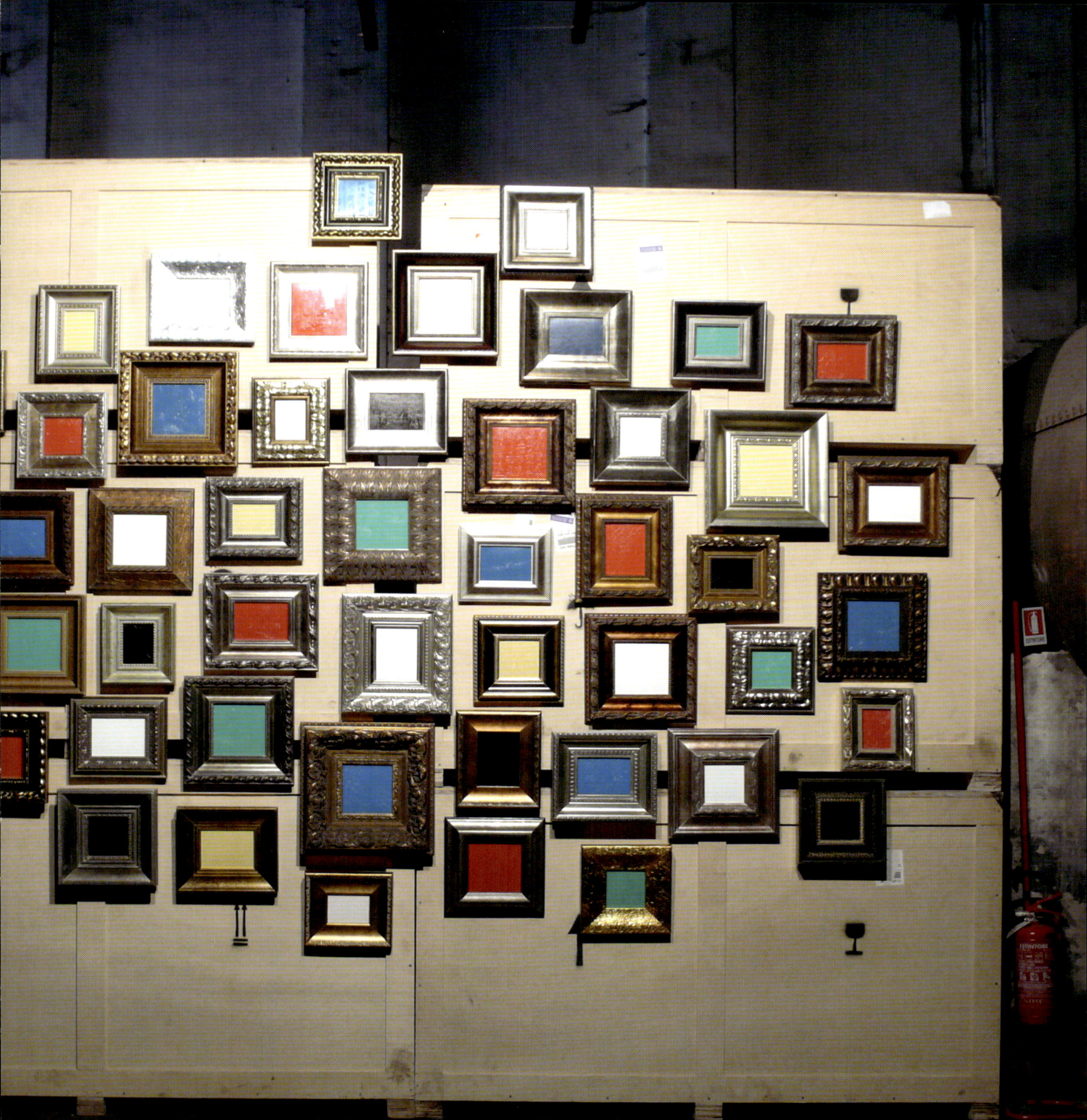

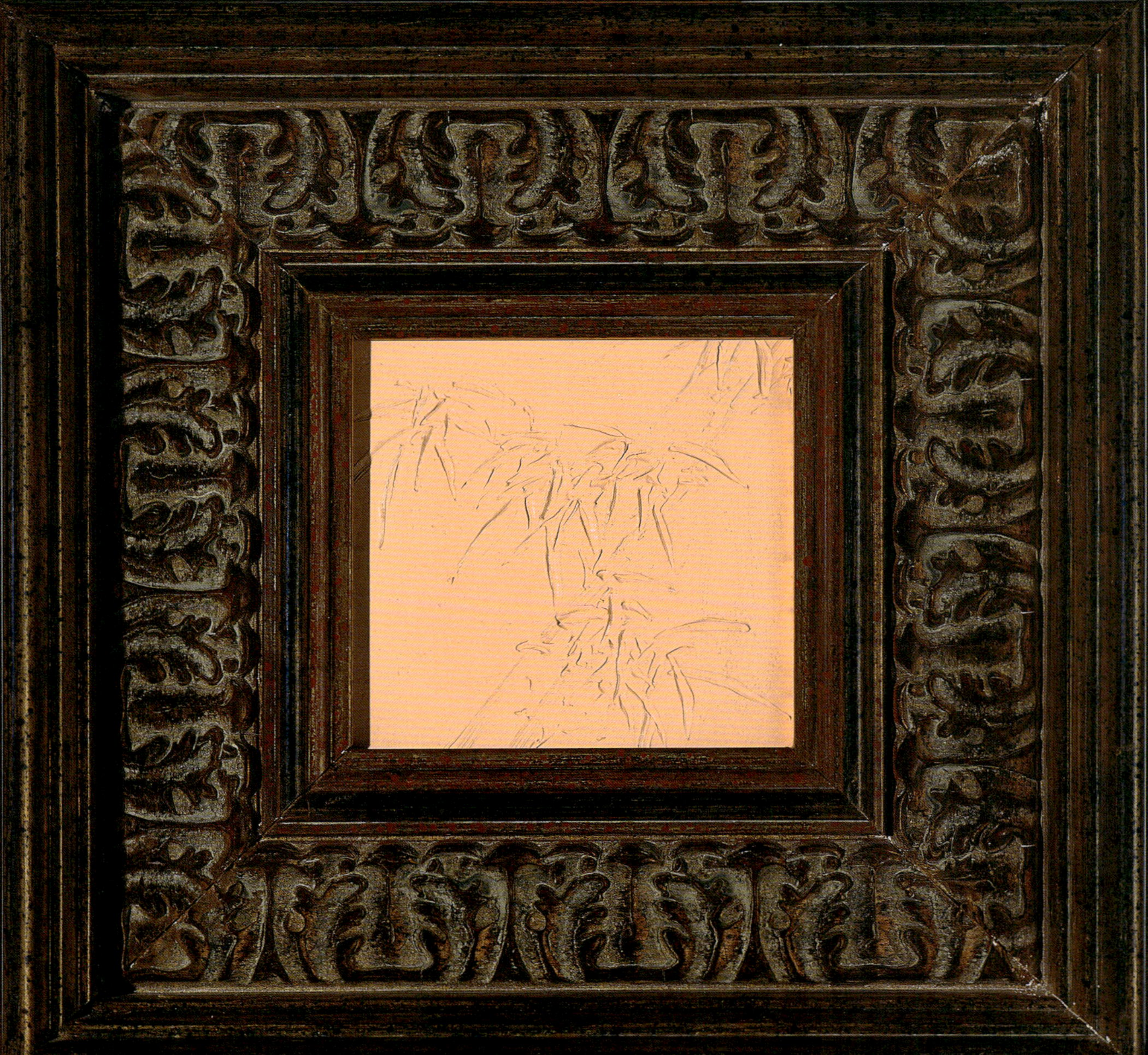

INTERVISTA PER IL CATALOGO DEL PADIGLIONE CINA ALLA 53ᴵᴹᴬ BIENNALE DI VENEZIA

Lu Hao

Lu Hao: Alla fine del 1998, hai cominciato una serie di lavori in cui comparivano delle ragazzine. Perché? È stato per una logica di mercato o per approfondire la cosiddetta perplessità della giovinezza?
He Sen: È vero che già nel 1992 o 1993 circolava una rivista intitolata "Art Market", ma di fatto nel 1998 non esisteva ancora un vero e proprio "mercato dell'arte". L'idea di una perplessità della giovinezza viene impiegata da alcuni giovani autori letterari. Io l'ho fatto solo per motivi tecnici e per l'effetto che mi avrebbe permesso di ottenere. È un po' noioso parlarne adesso: le immagini della serie "Stack" sono dipinte in modo che sporgano dallo sfondo piatto. Molti mi dissero che avevano l'impressione che mancasse qualcosa nello sfondo e nel soggetto. Così, per legarli, tentai diversi esperimenti, uno dei quali fu utilizzare l'effetto sfumato. Prima dipingevo soltanto con una spatola. Ma per creare l'effetto sfumato ripresi a usare il pennello. Gradualmente questo metodo ha preso piede nel mio modo di dipingere e la mia pittura è diventata più liquida e morbida (prima era piuttosto densa). A un certo punto ho cominciato anche a disegnare col pennello. Poi mi sono reso conto che quell'effetto morbido avrebbe funzionato benissimo per dipingere ragazze. Coerentemente con i miei lavori precedenti, le ragazze in quei dipinti non avevano ancora gli occhi. Ovviamente, la perdita degli occhi a causa di una luce abbagliante si può spiegare anche da molti punti di vista letterari e sociologici.

Lu Hao: Sei noto per aver ritratto ragazze disorientate e confuse. Perché, in seguito, hai cominciato a copiare, trapiantare, ad appropriarti e alterare le opere classiche dei pittori tradizionali cinesi?
He Sen: Vedendo i miei nuovi lavori, la maggior parte della gente trova difficile capire perché mi sia rivolto a soggetti che non hanno niente a che vedere con temi femminili. Il cambiamento è sembrato brusco, come se non ci fosse la minima continuità. Nei miei diciotto anni da artista professionista, ho dipinto un gran numero di soggetti e condotto tanti esperimenti diversi. I cambiamenti sono stati tanti ed estremamente diversi. Non mi sono mai lasciato intrappolare in qualcosa in cui dovessi allontanarmi troppo da me. È chiaro che i cambiamenti sono un'arma a doppio taglio. Ma io sono uno che si annoia facilmente. Ho fiducia nelle mie capacità e spero di mettermi sempre alla prova. I fattori esterni non c'entrano niente. Non voglio essere conosciuto soltanto per un soggetto particolare. Vorrei essere conosciuto per una direzione artistica e un'estetica identificabili. A parte la serie degli "Stage", la maggior parte dei miei precedenti lavori ha un comune denominatore: per esempio l'evasione dalla realtà, l'abbandonarsi di fronte a una realtà troppo dura, qualcosa di negativo e illusorio.
Mi ci è voluto molto tempo per cominciare a usare immagini tradizionali cinesi nei miei quadri. La preparazione è stata lunga e ho tenuto conto di molte problematiche diverse. Per me, dipingere è un modo di evadere. Quindi perché non provare a dipingere con una tecnica che sia completamente staccata dalla realtà? L'arte cinese oggi è, in principio, un riflesso della siocologia. È troppo vicina alla realtà e

troppo lontana dall'arte. Certo, il fatto che l'arte sia vicina alla realtà ha i suoi meriti, ma ormai mi ha stancato. Ogni volta che apro un catalogo d'arte in Cina, vedo gente: gente calata nella realtà, gente immersa nella società contrassegnata da identificatori sociali di ogni tipo. Se si mettono da parte queste cose, cosa rimane della nostra immaginazione?
La maggior parte degli elementi fondamentali dell'arte cinese contemporanea viene dall'Occidente, comprese le nozioni che gli artisti hanno appreso da studenti, ovvero la cultura occidentale. Questa cultura si poneva come un modello, ma non credo che sia questo il problema. Dal punto di vista della tradizione, l'Occidente è obiettivo e tridimensionale, mentre la Cina è soggettiva e orizzontale. La differenza d'espressione e di osservazione nasce dalle differenze culturali, dalla diversa visione del mondo e dalla mentalità. Perché ci avviciniamo di più oggi? Tutto sommato, è una questione di diritti culturali.
Per cimentarsi con la realtà, gli artisti tradizionali cinesi dipingevano con un atteggiamento che era lungi dall'esserne distaccato. I loro lavori mi toccano e sento di avere nei miei geni lo stesso atteggiamento. Io uso l'immaginario tradizionale e non voglio cambiarlo. Voglio solo usarlo come base, dipingere quello che si sente e che sento oggi. Questo si adatta benissimo anche al mio desiderio di sfuggire dalla realtà. E si accorda bene con la mia passione per la pittura e per l'esplorazione della pittura in quanto tale. Ovvero, dipingere per dipingere.

Lu Hao: Cosa ne pensi dei cosiddetti artisti di prima classe?
He Sen: Non so quando si è cominciato a usare questo termine. Non so dove si possa tracciare la linea di demarcazione. Alcuni dicono che la si stabilisce in base ai prezzi di vendita alle aste. Ma mi sembra un approccio troppo parziale. È vero che la maggiore parte degli artisti più quotati hanno un curriculum accademico illustre, che non si ottiene certo dal giorno alla notte. La capacità di influenzare le opinioni determina il prezzo. Ma i prezzi alti sono anche il risultato di una buona strategia di mercato. Comunque, è più facile e più comprensibile per chi non è un artista quantificare il successo in termini di denaro.

Lu Hao: Negli ultimi anni sei stato uno degli artisti più favoriti del mercato. C'è chi ritiene che il mercato d'arte cinese contemporaneo sia solo una grossa bolla. Tu fai parte della bolla?
He Sen: Il surriscaldamento economico e la recessione determinano delle fluttuazioni, in ogni campo. Ne siamo tutti colpiti, chi più chi meno. In questo periodo, non sono molti a spendere soldi nei locali notturni o nei ristoranti. Si può dire per questo che quando invece sono stipati di avventori, i ristoranti siano una bolla? La mia carriera è relativamente stabile. È normale.

Lu Hao: Cosa ti aspetti per il Padiglione Cinese della 53ᴵᴹᴬ Biennale di Venezia?
He Sen: Ovviamente spero che sia la miglior esposizione della Cina di tutti i tempi.

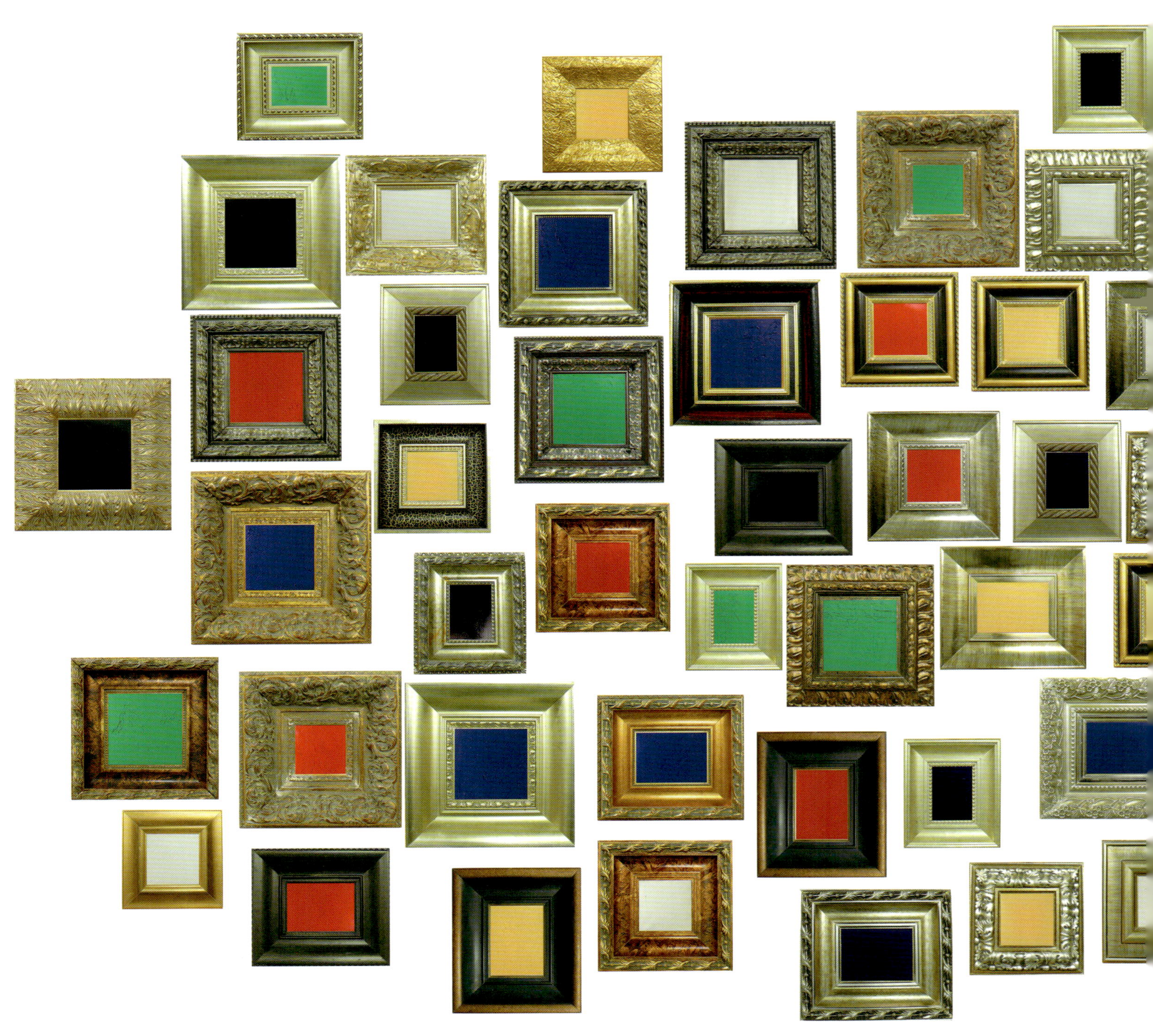

Landscape Series
Painting on canvas,
old frame
variable dimension
2009

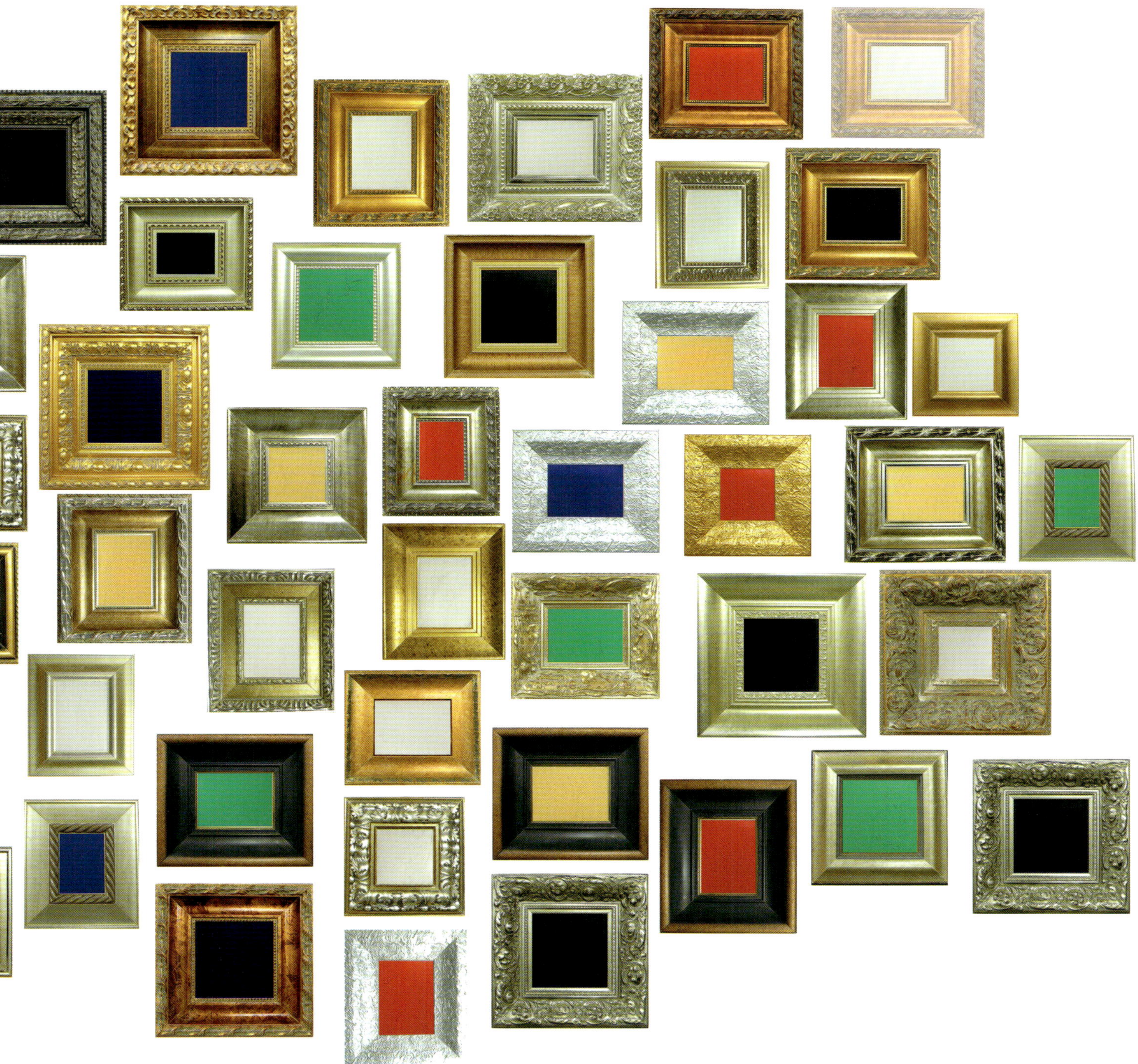

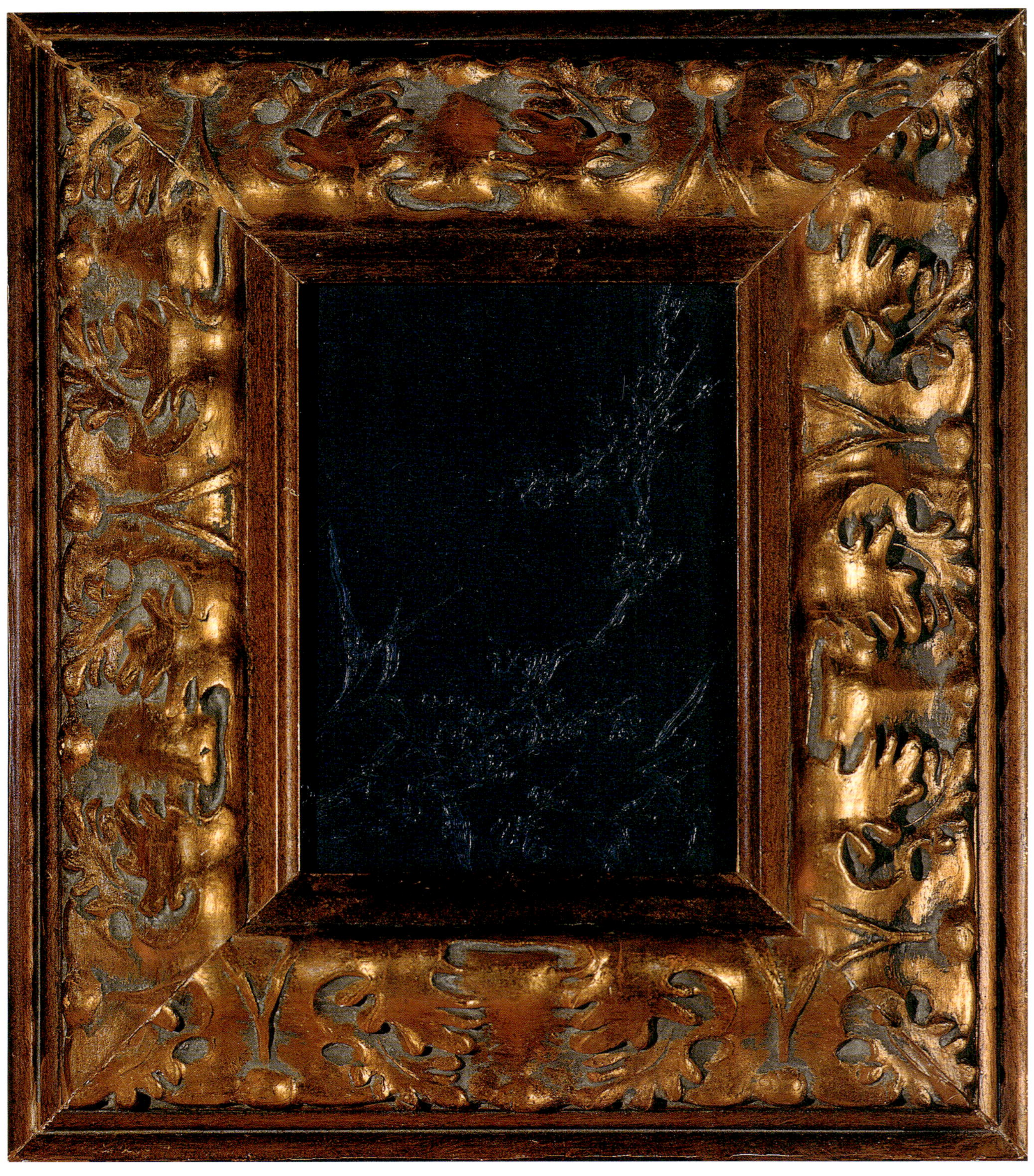

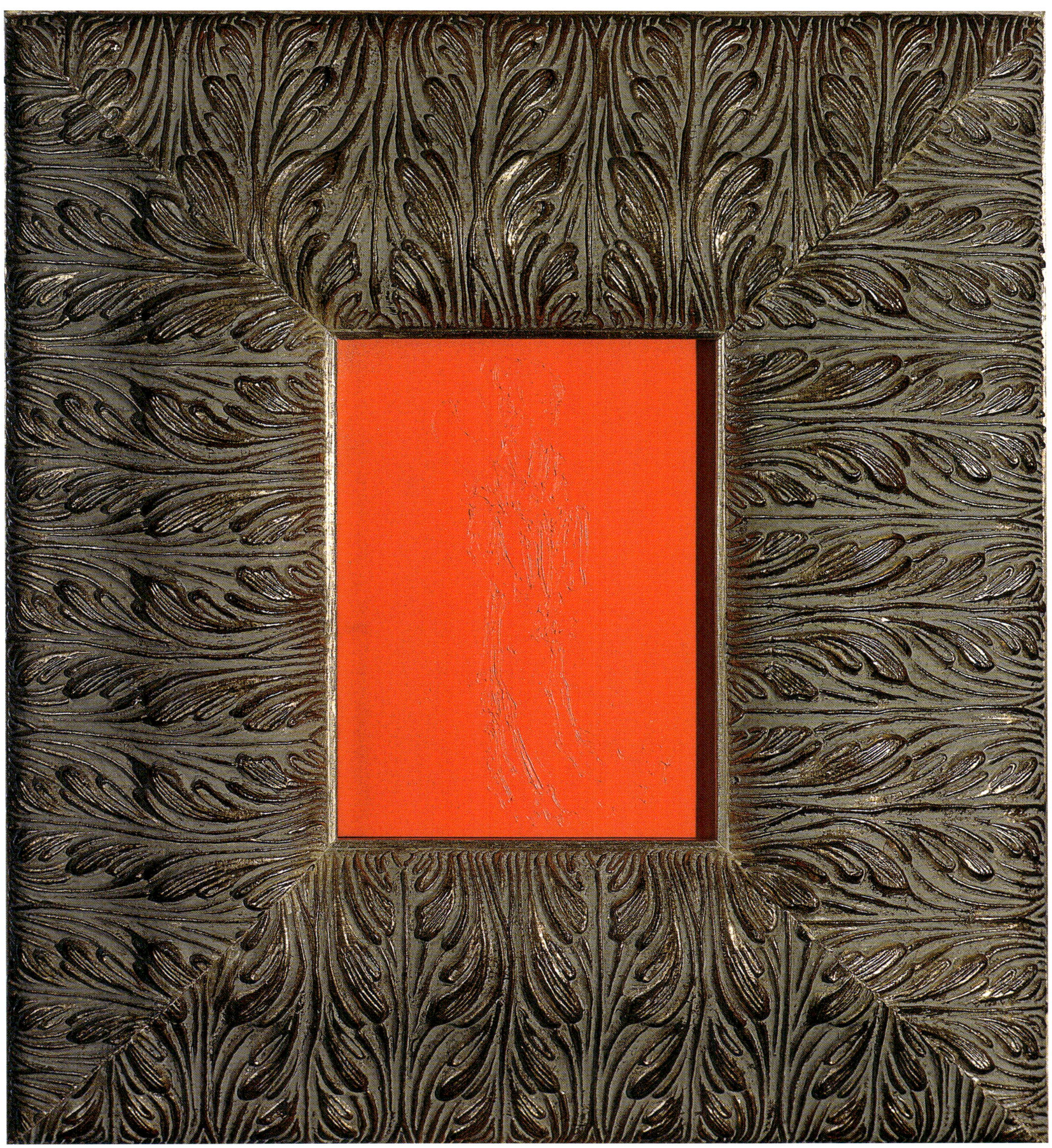

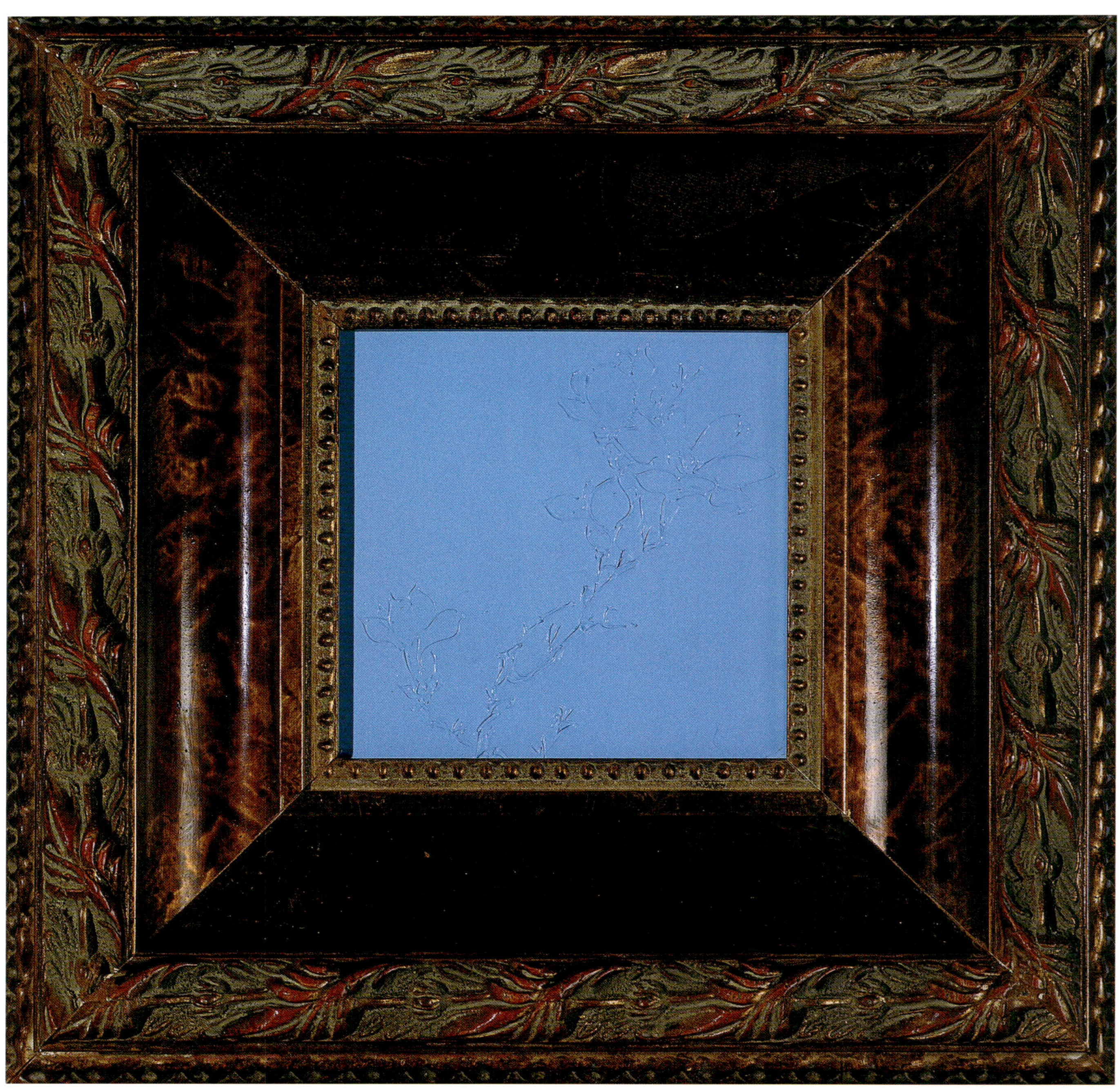

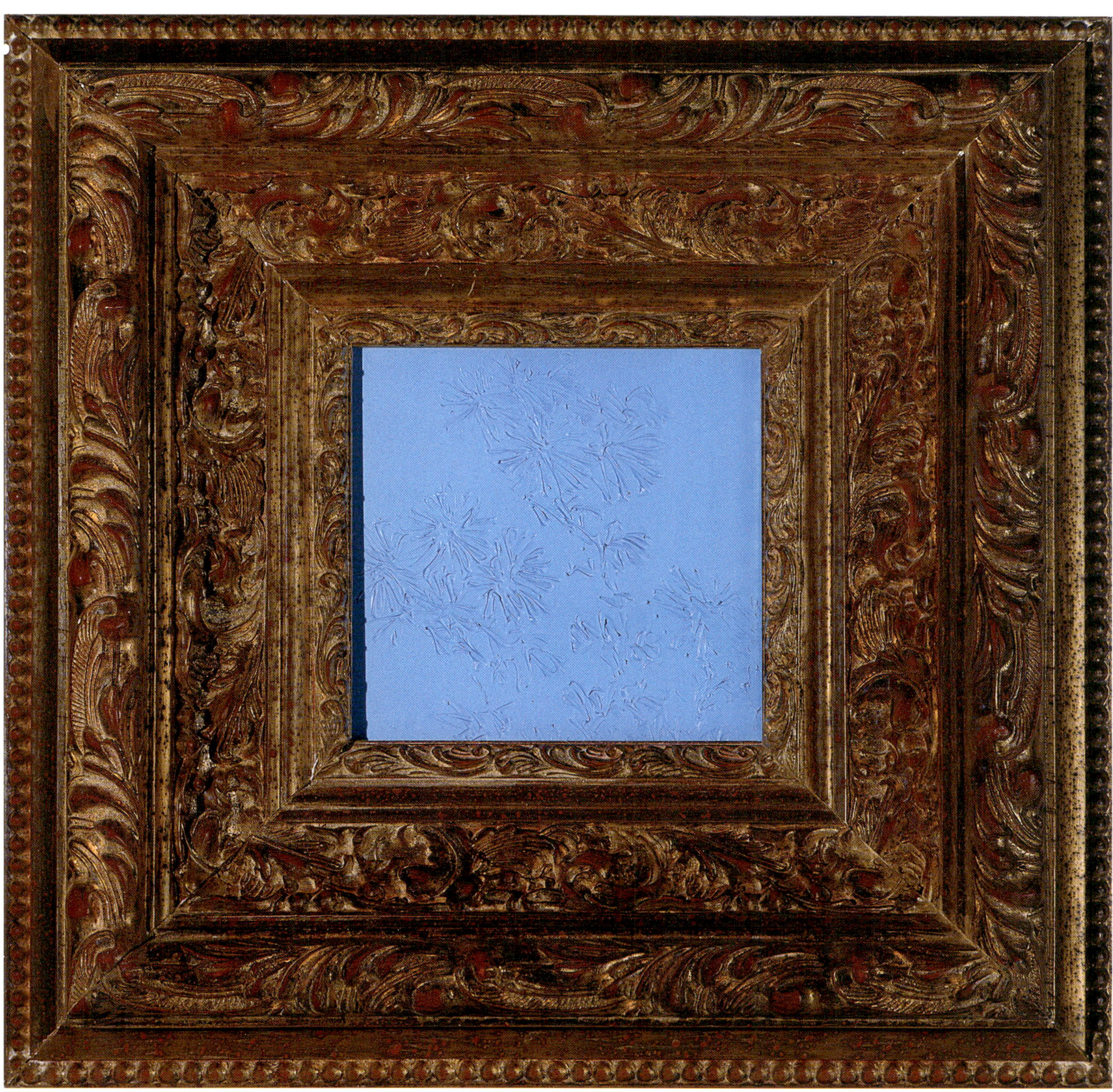

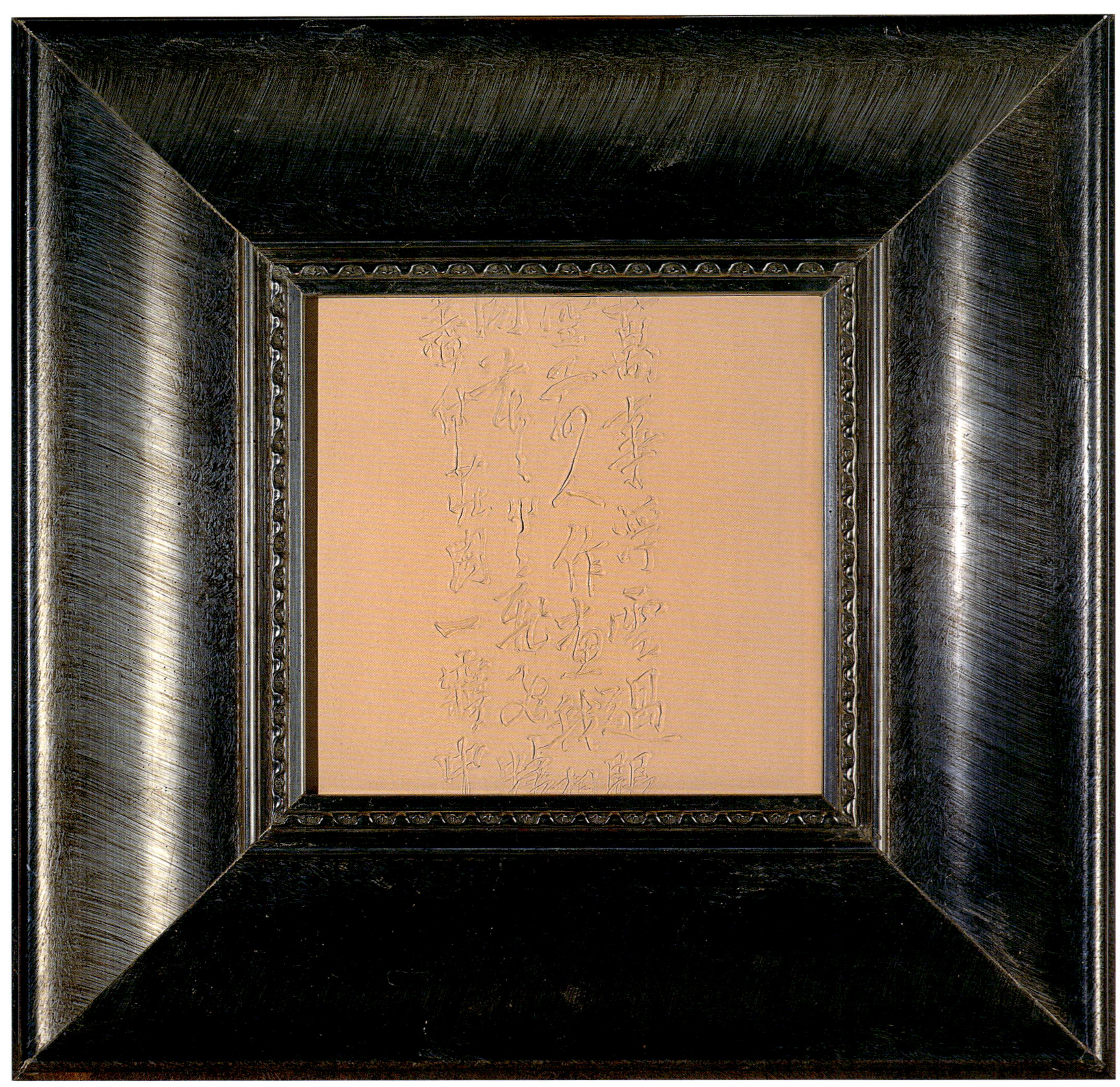

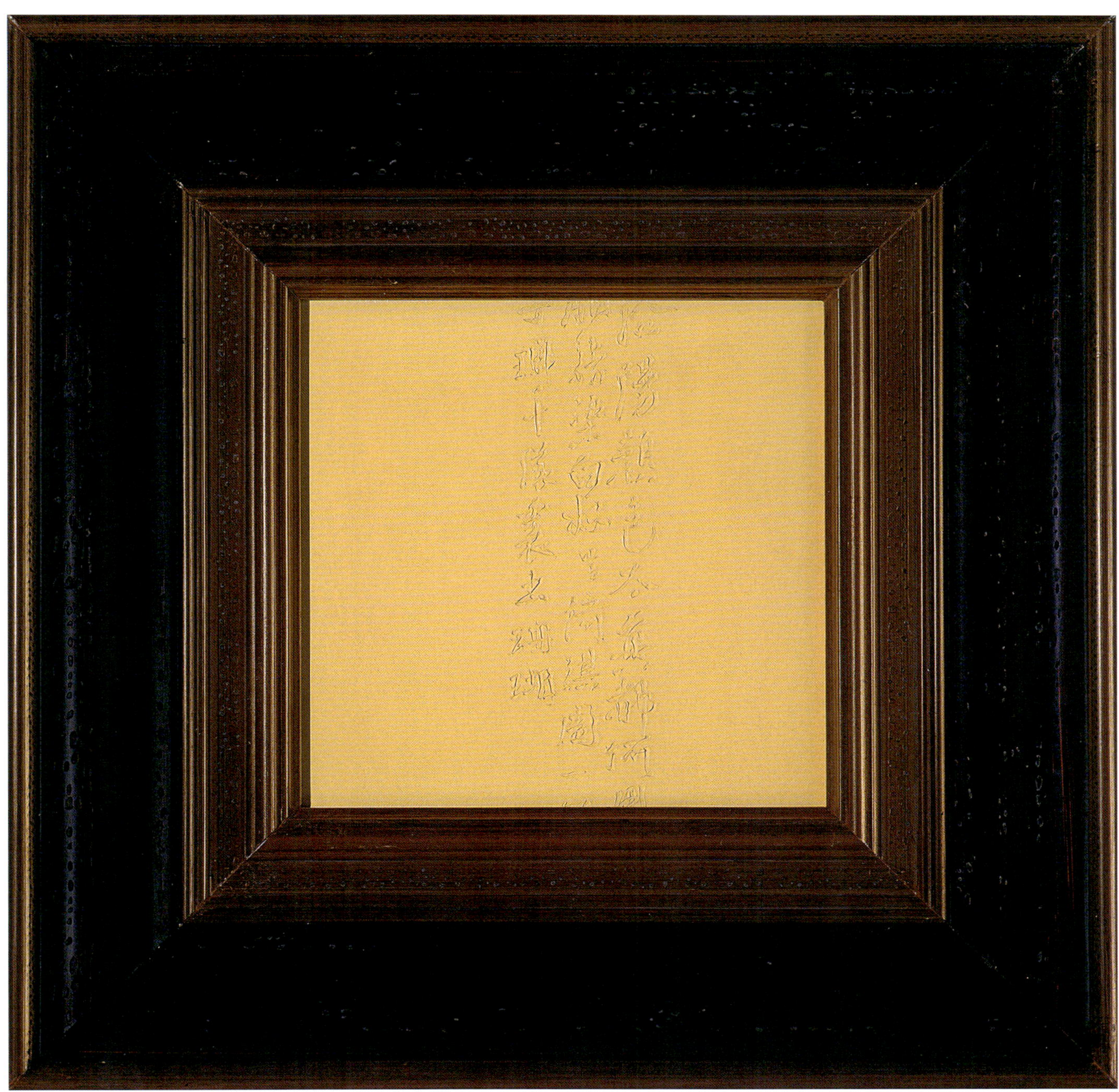

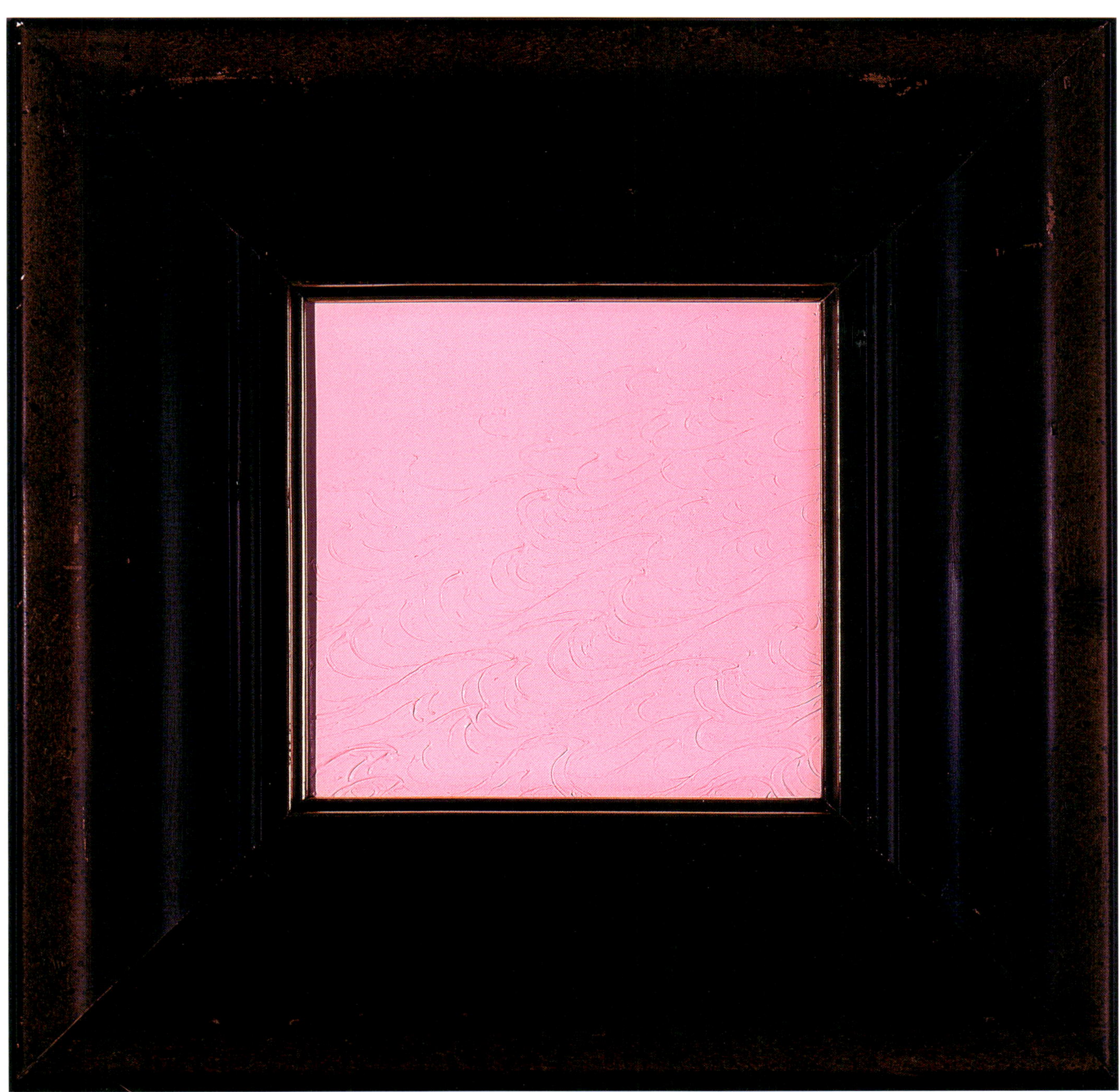

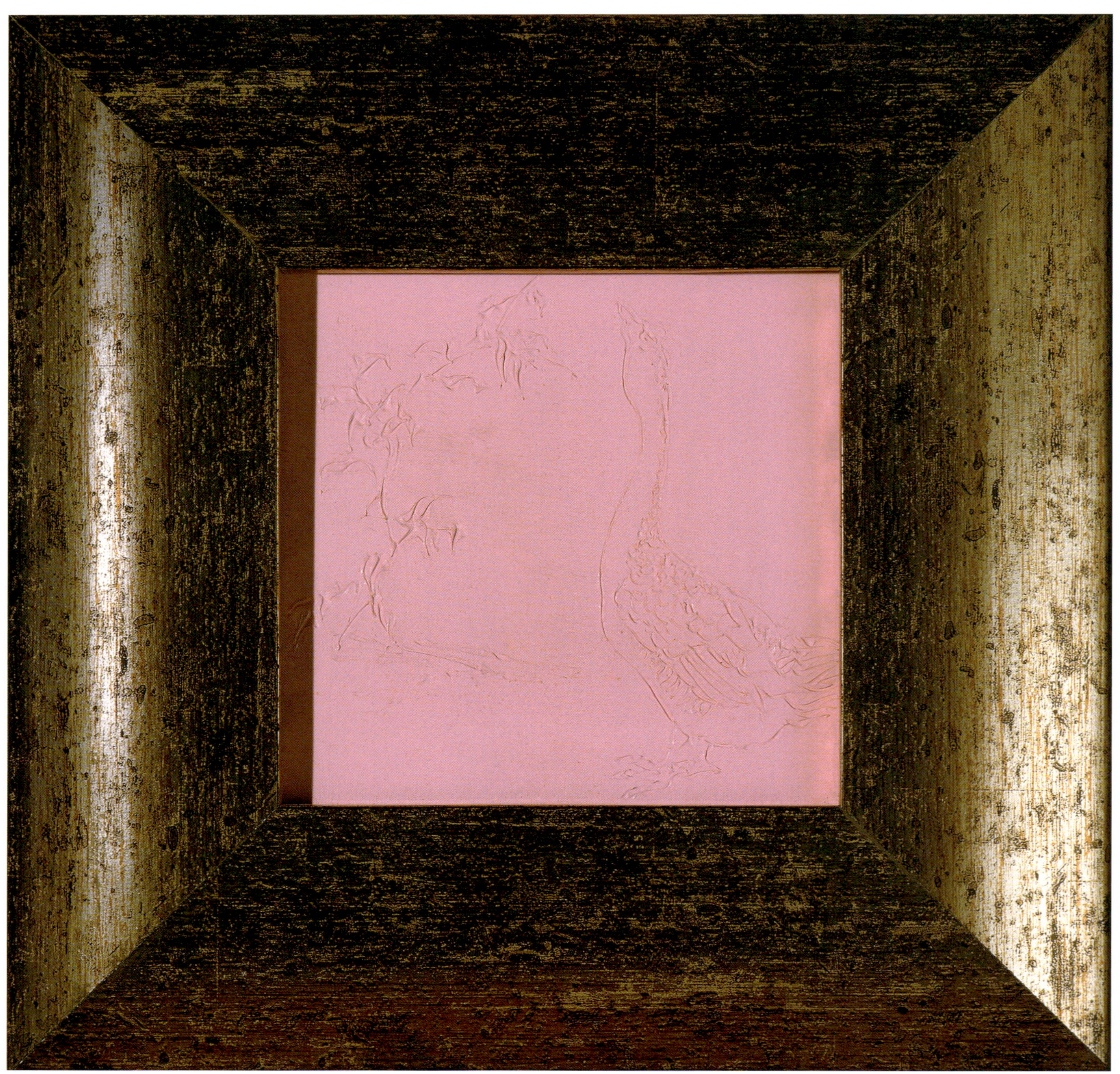

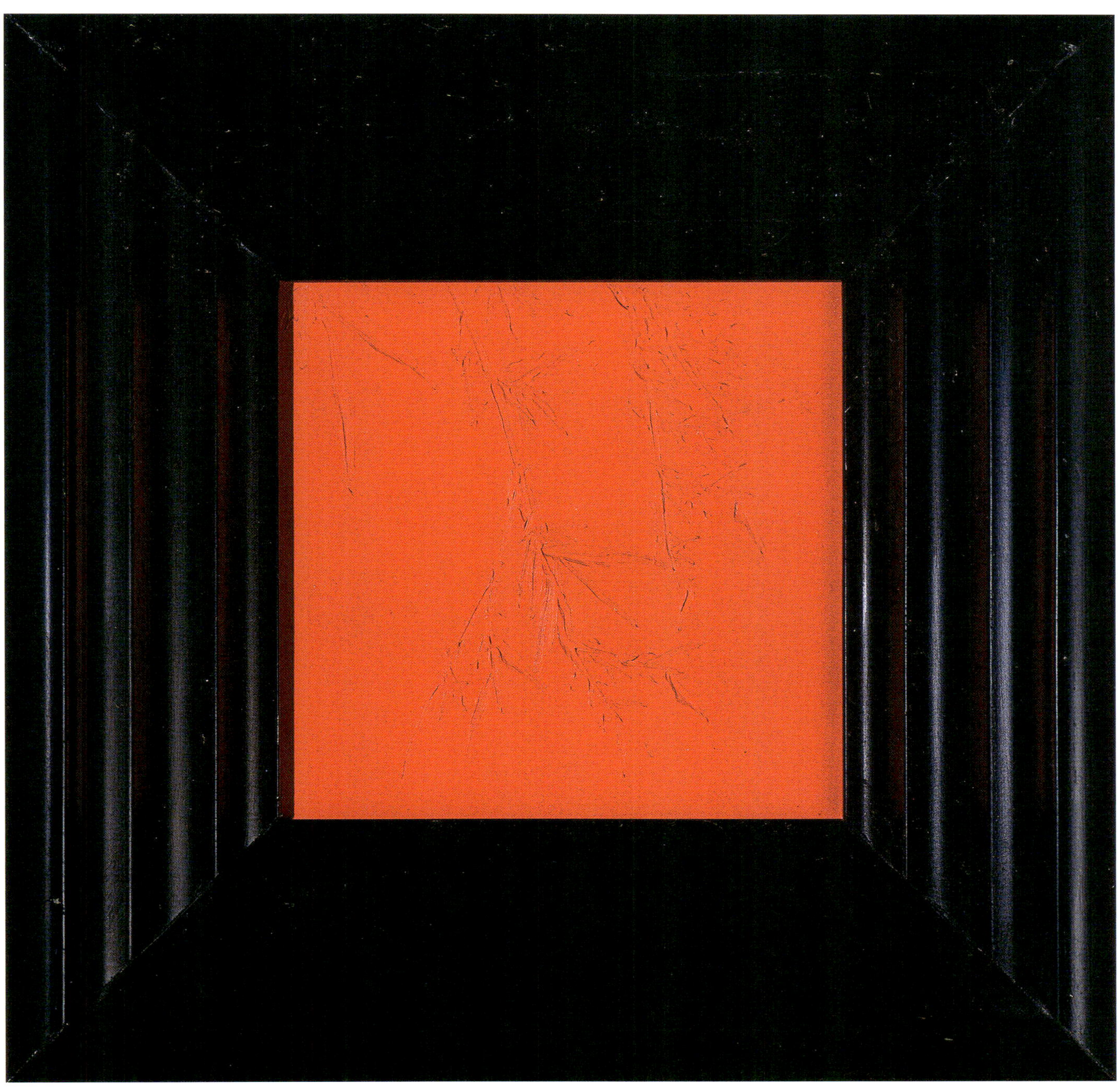

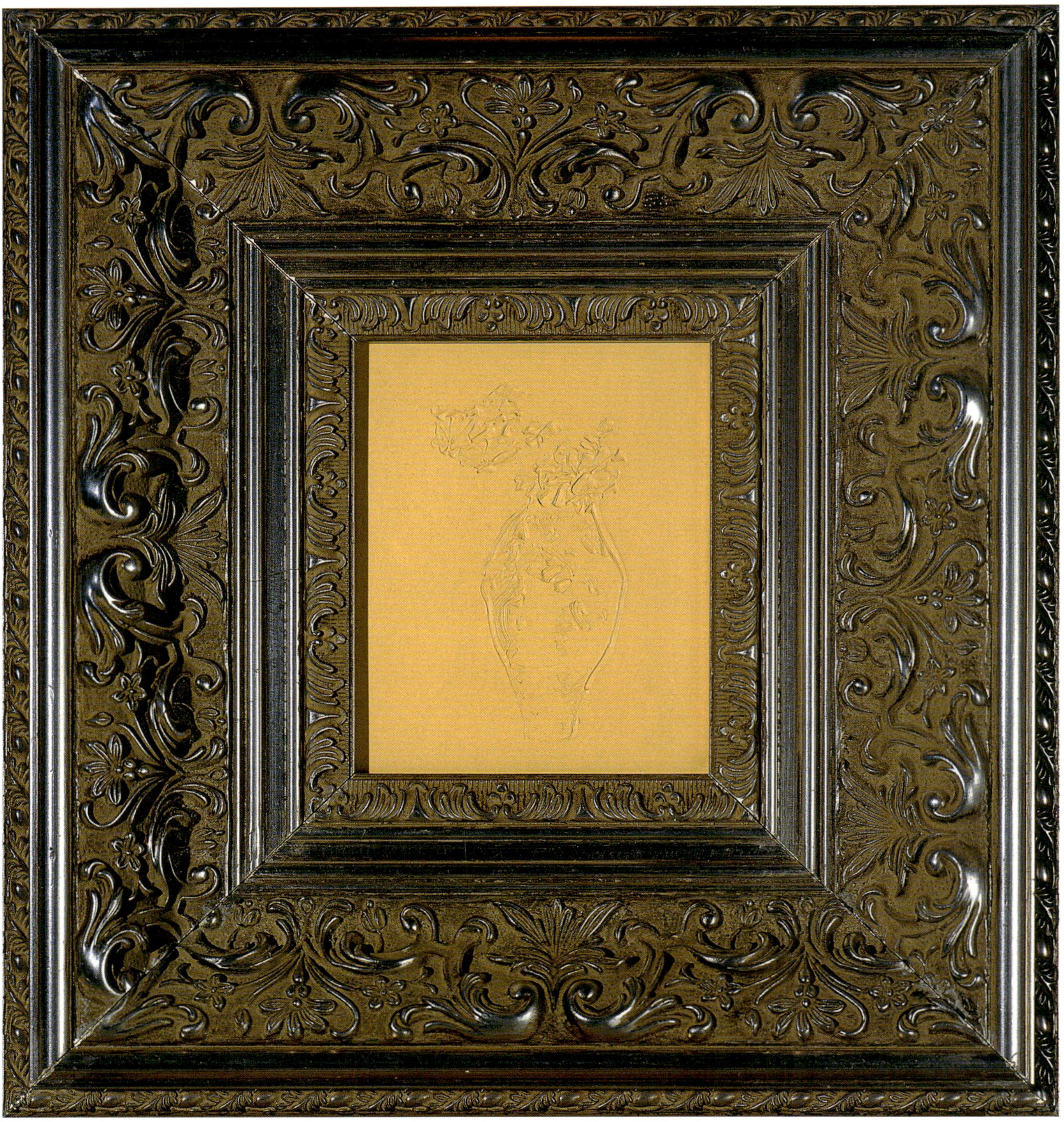

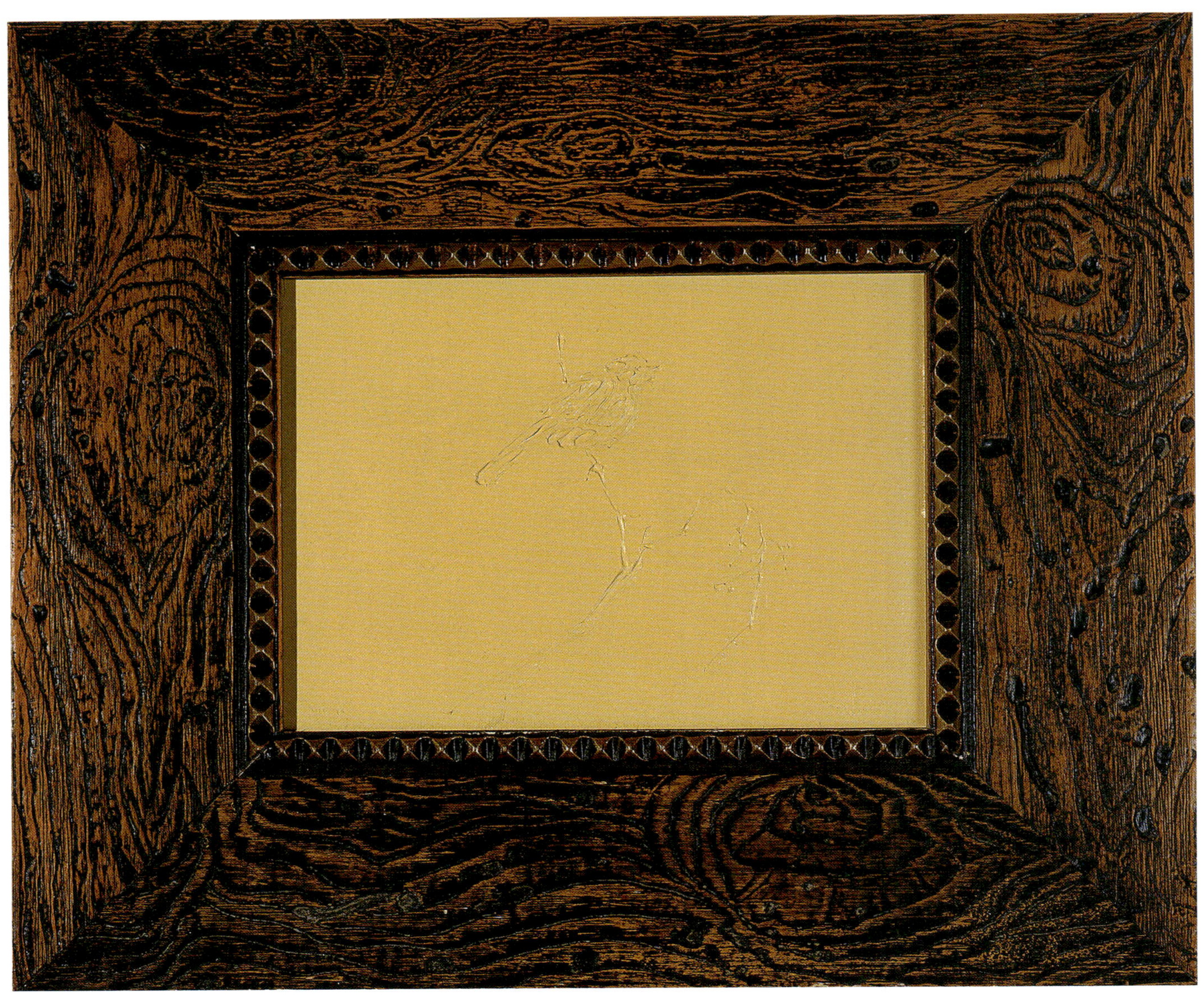

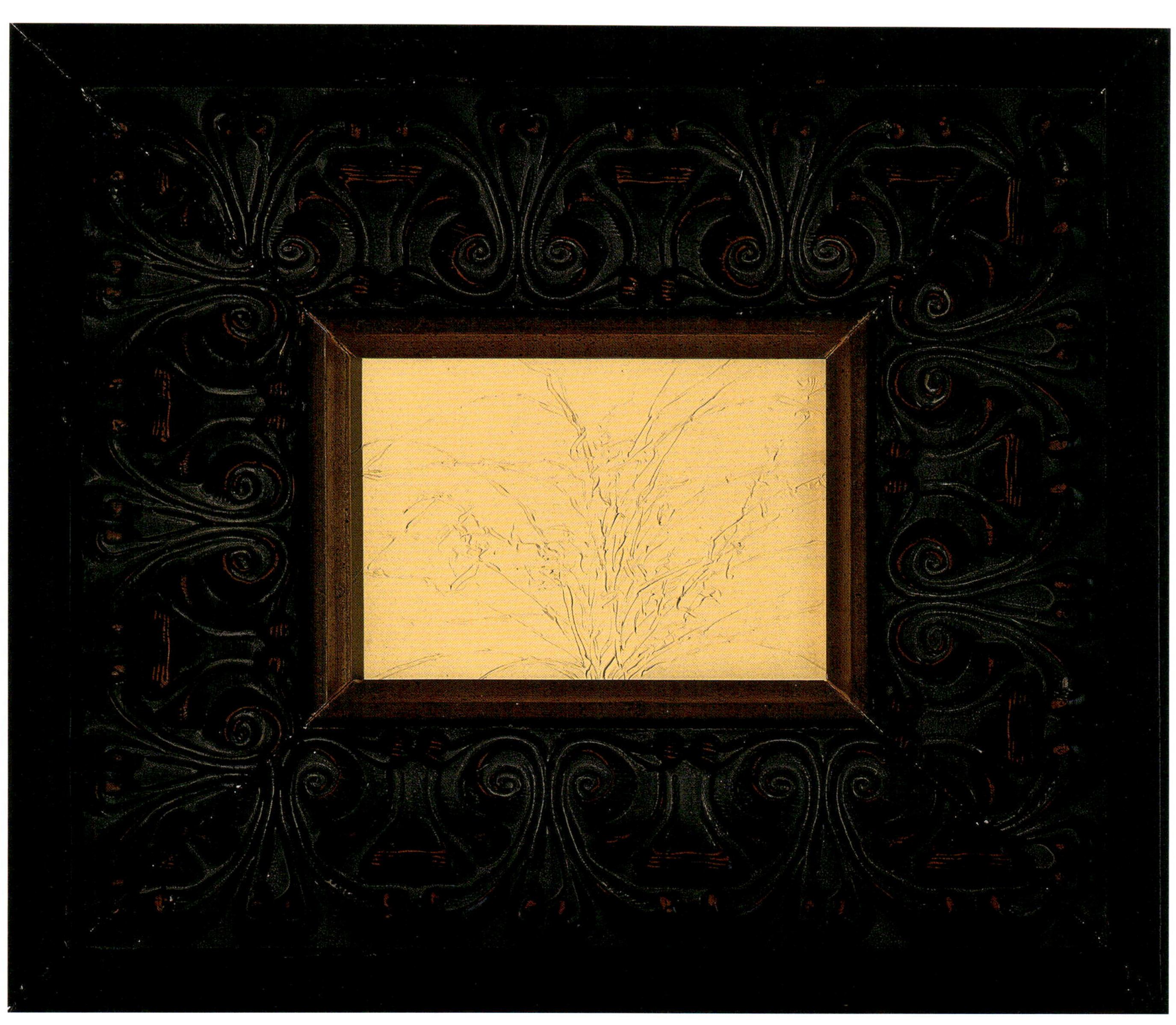

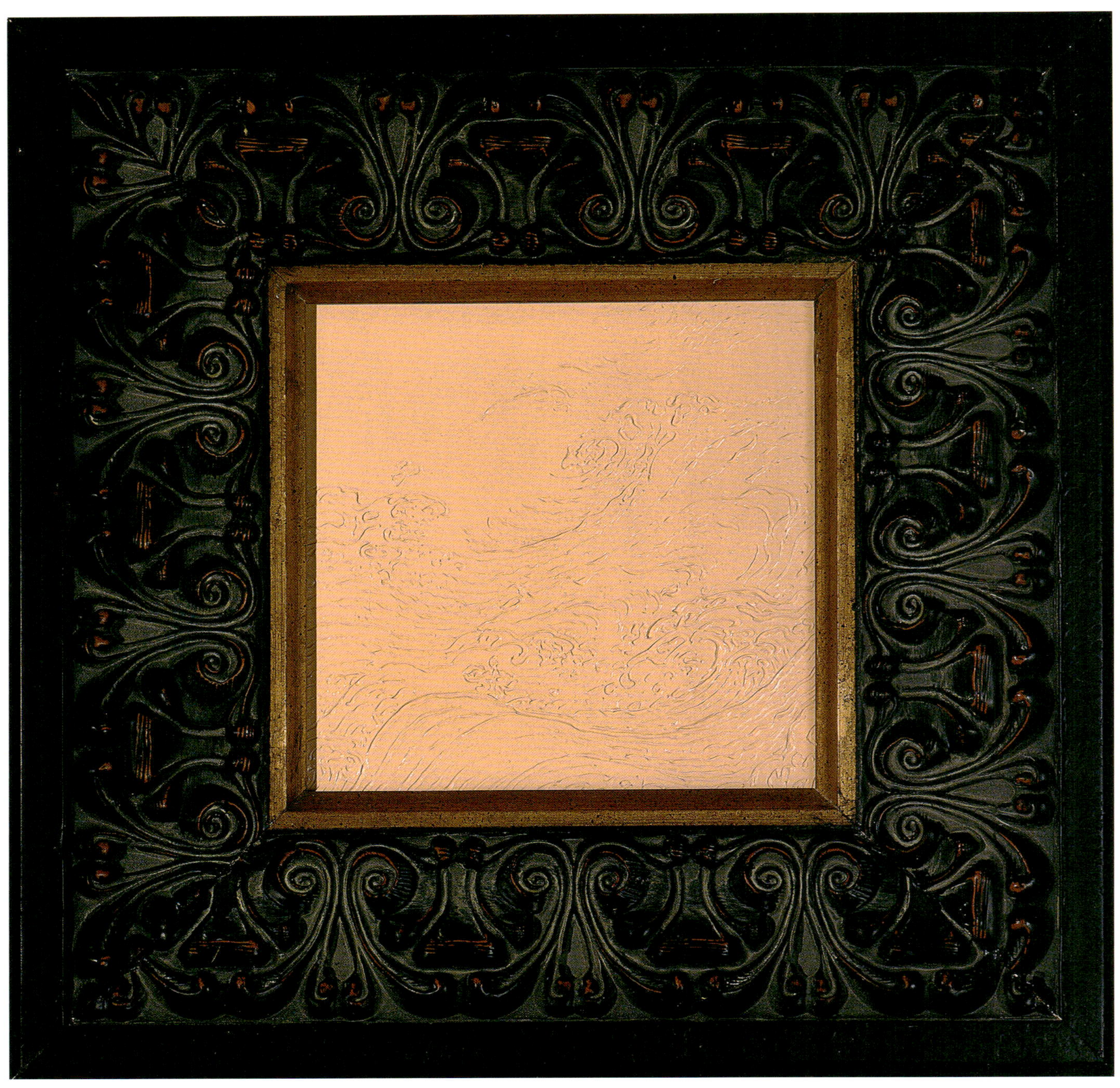

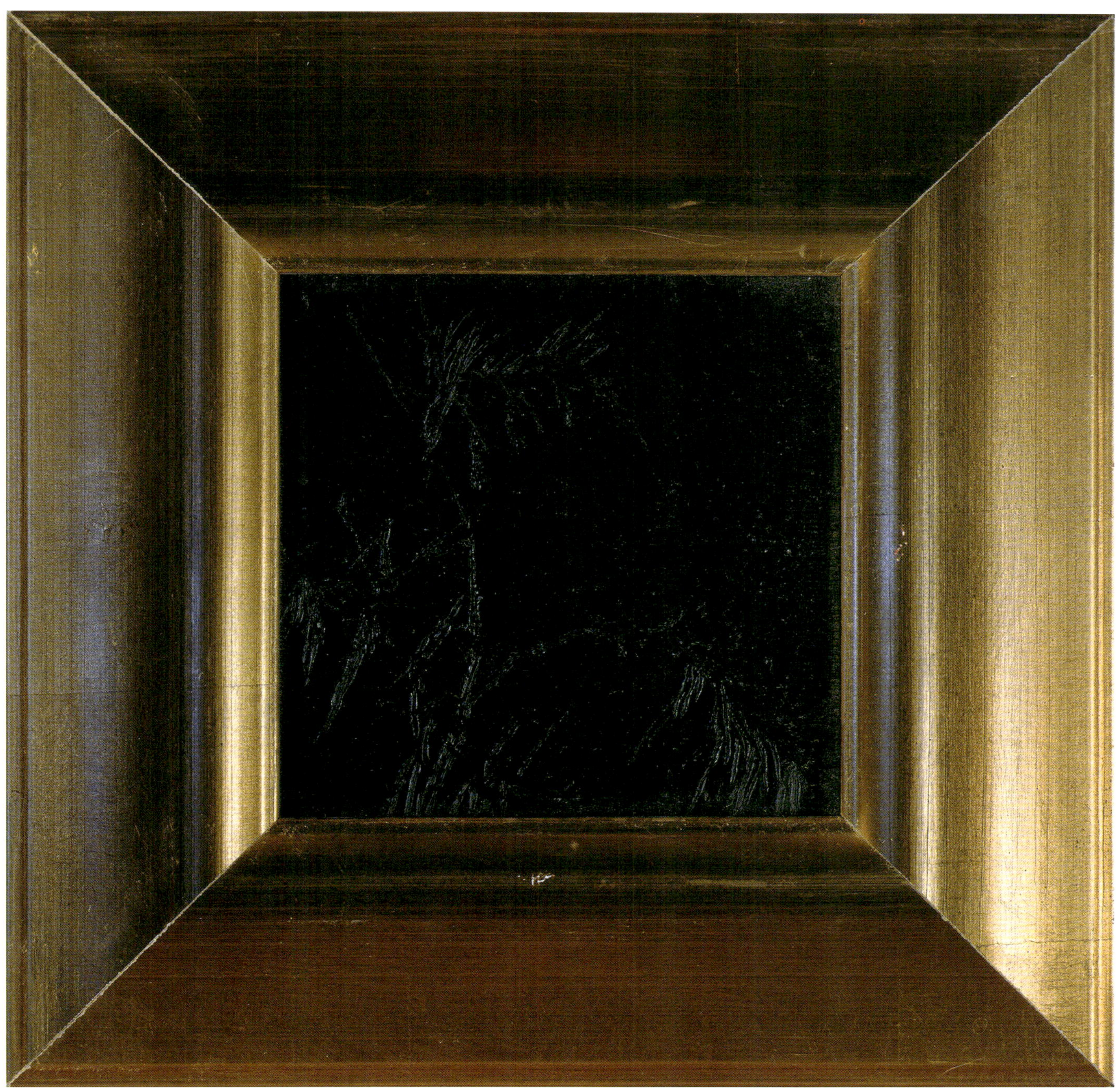

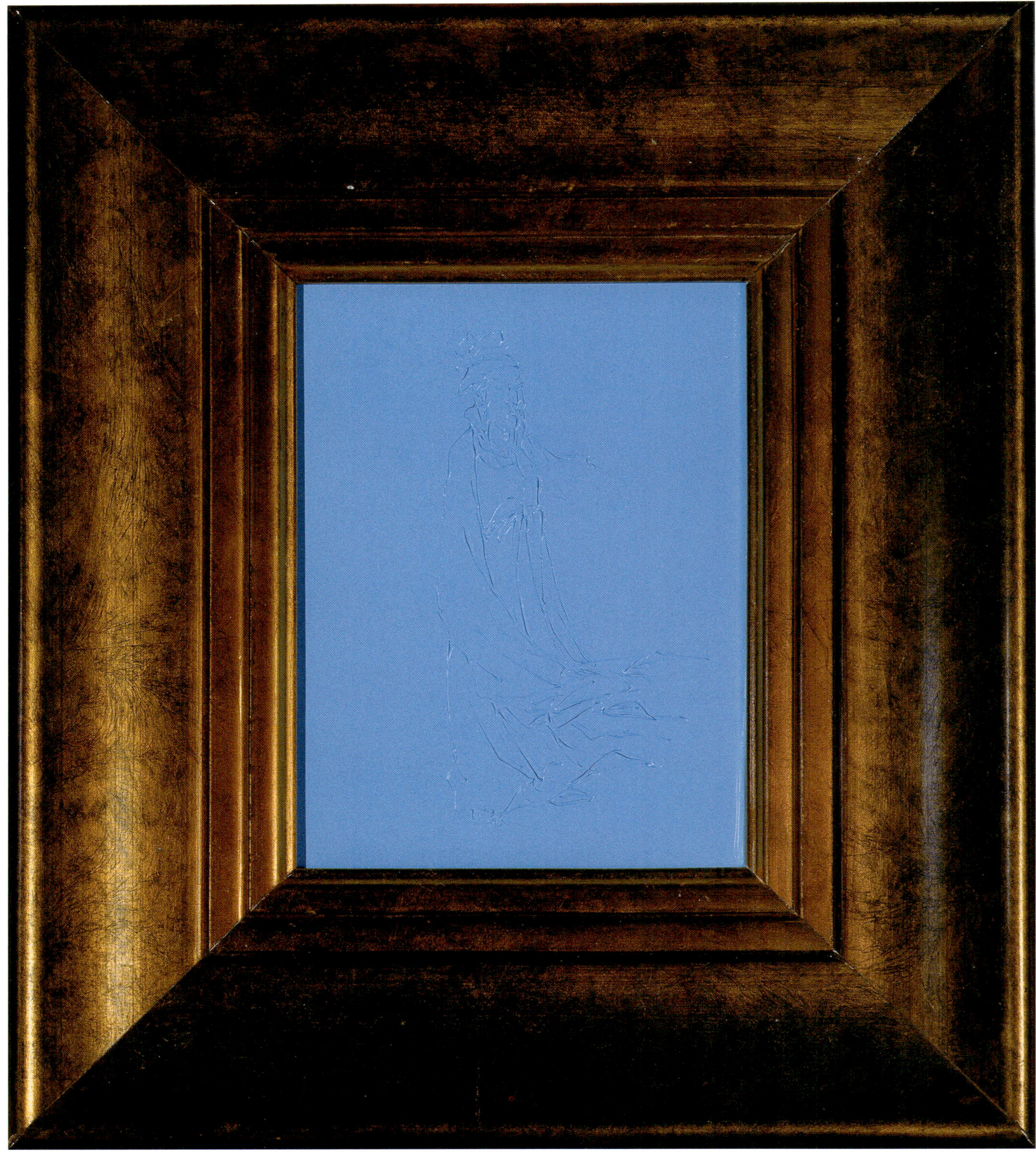

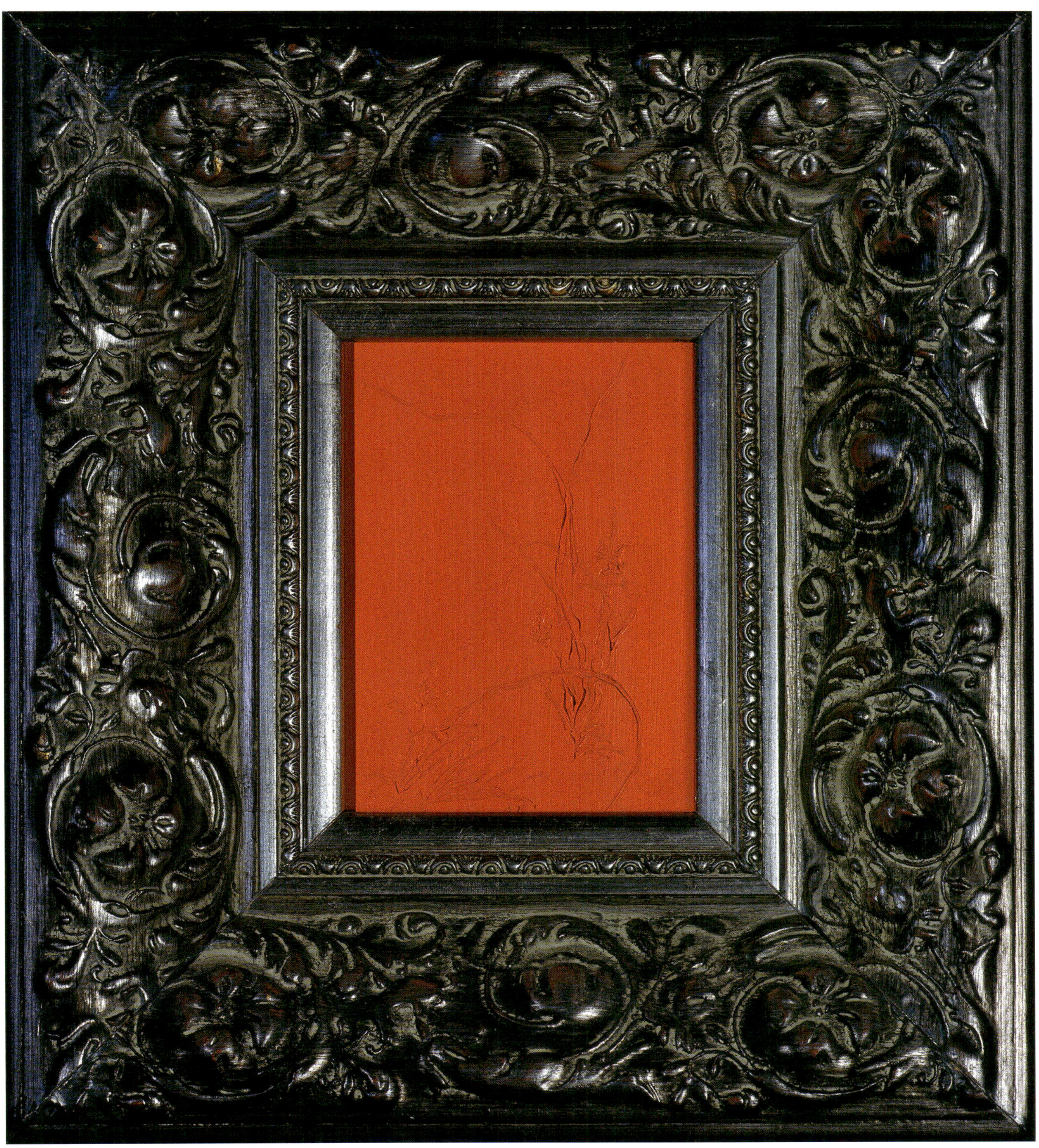

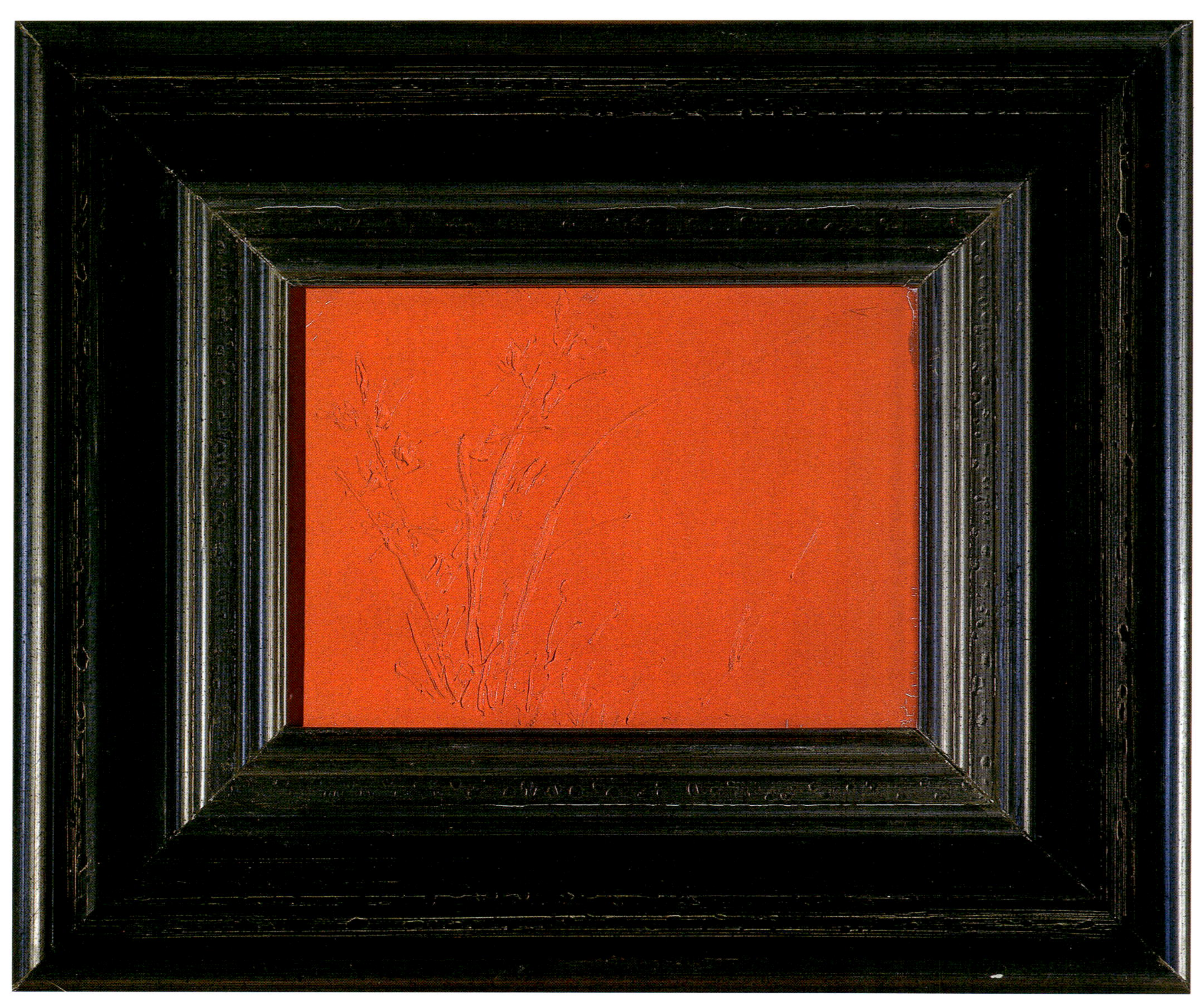

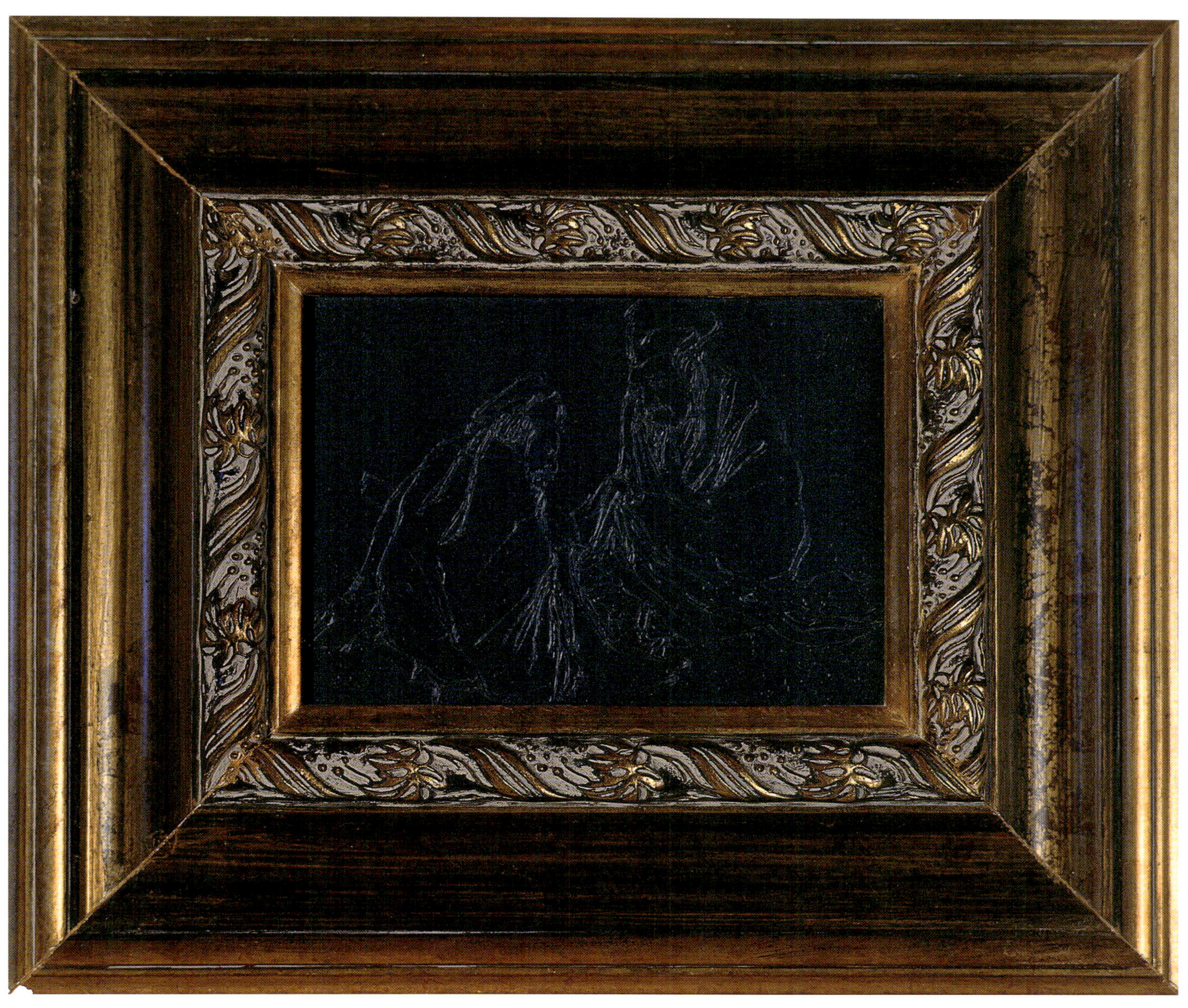

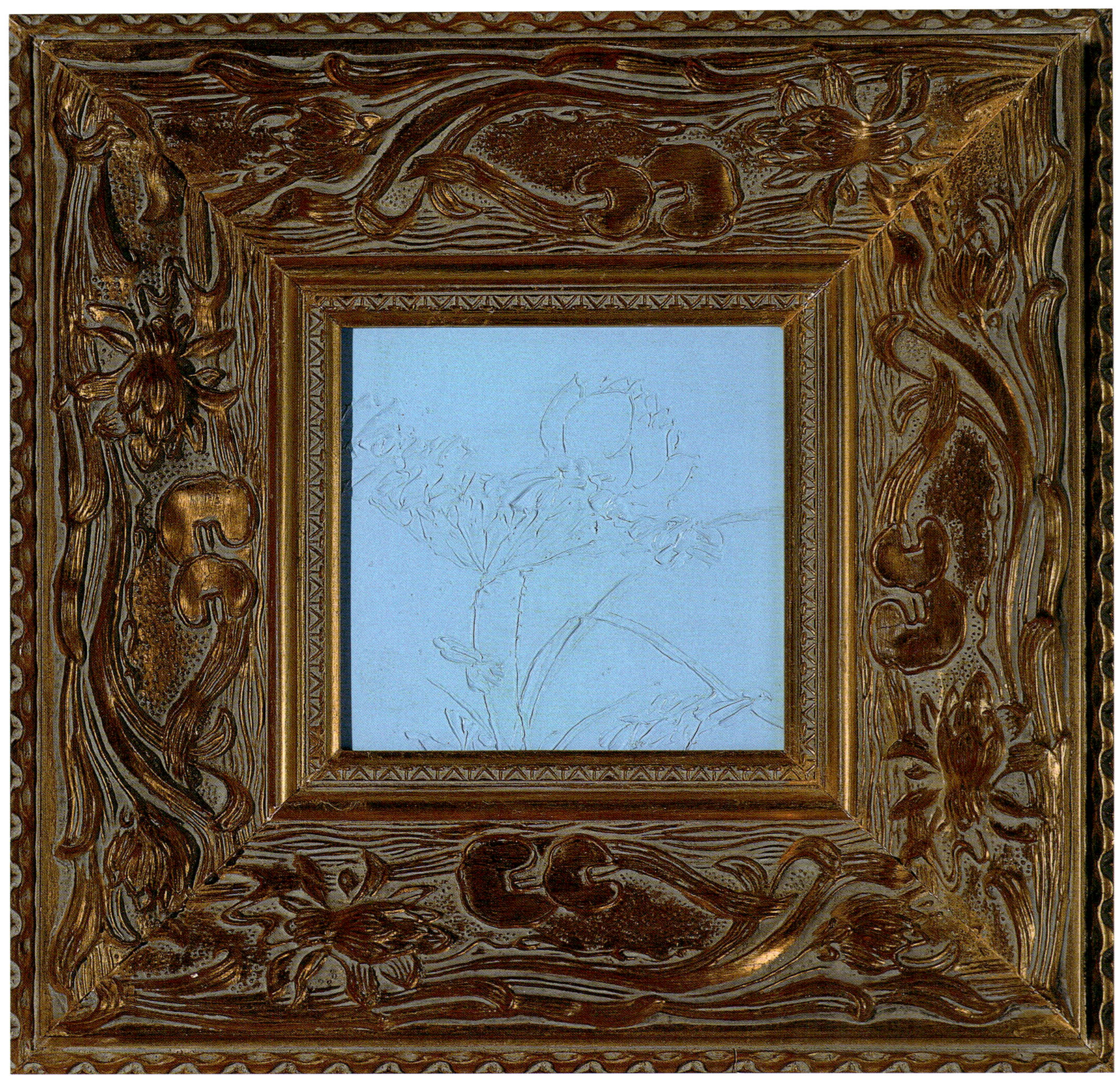

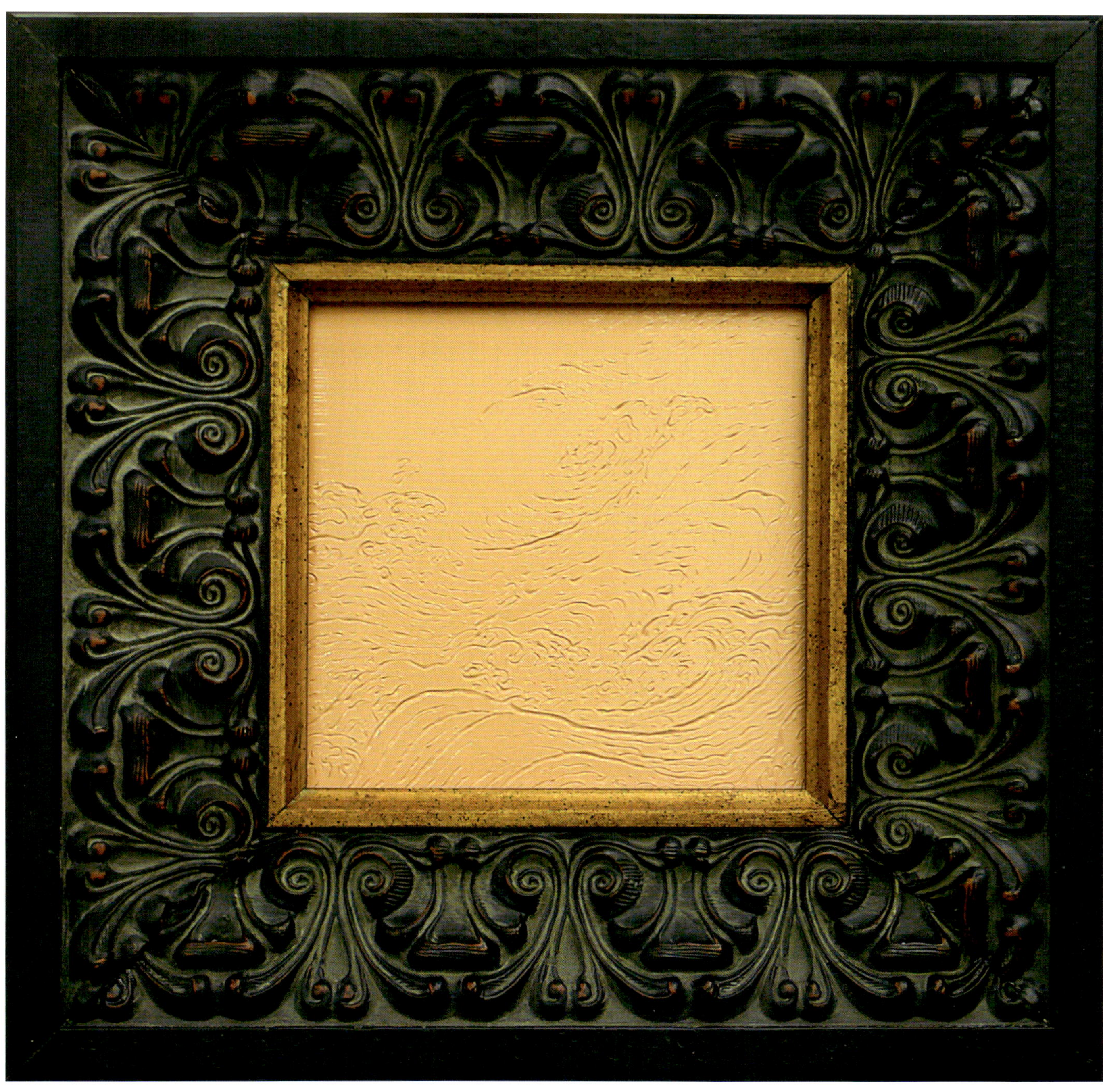

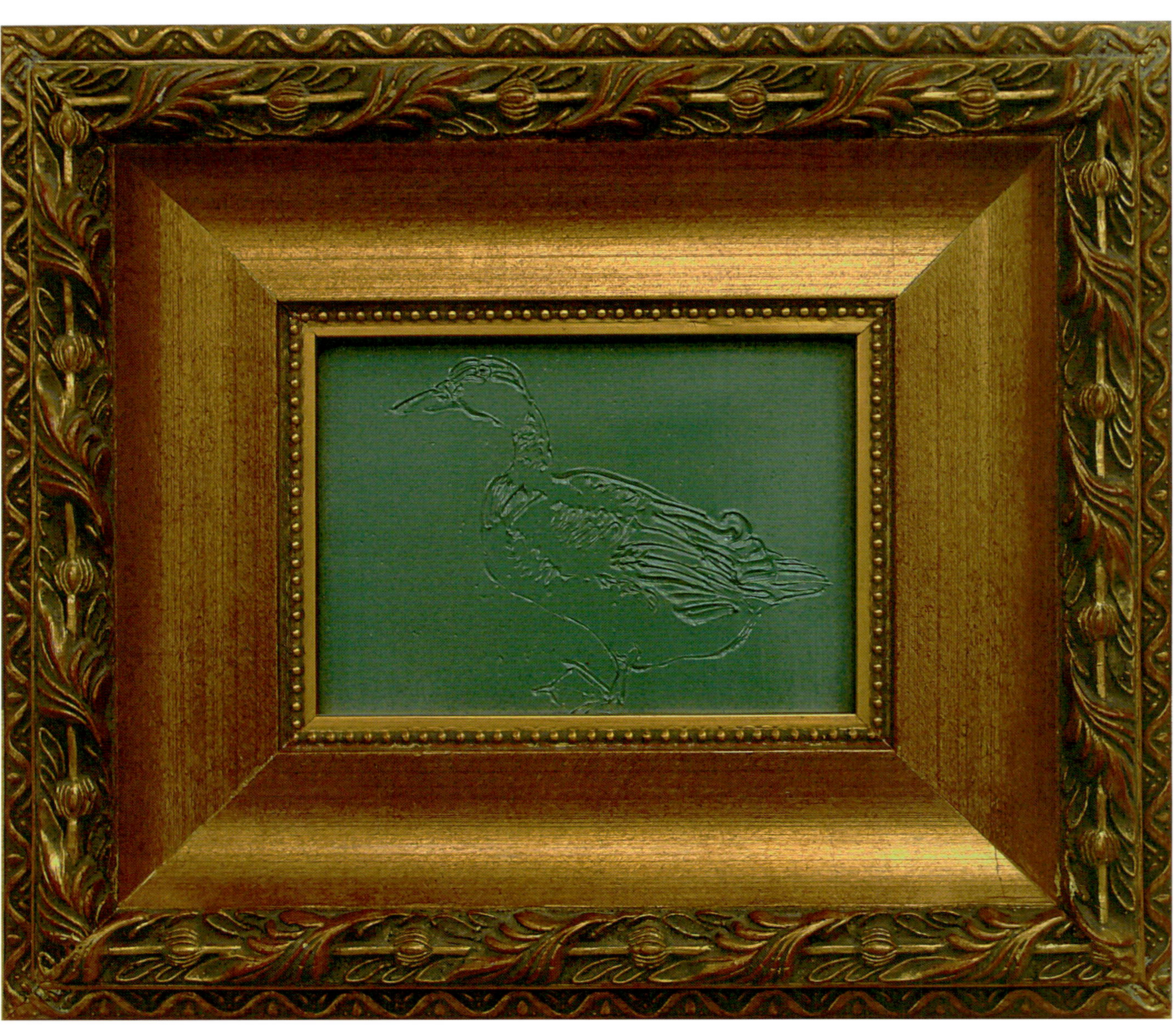

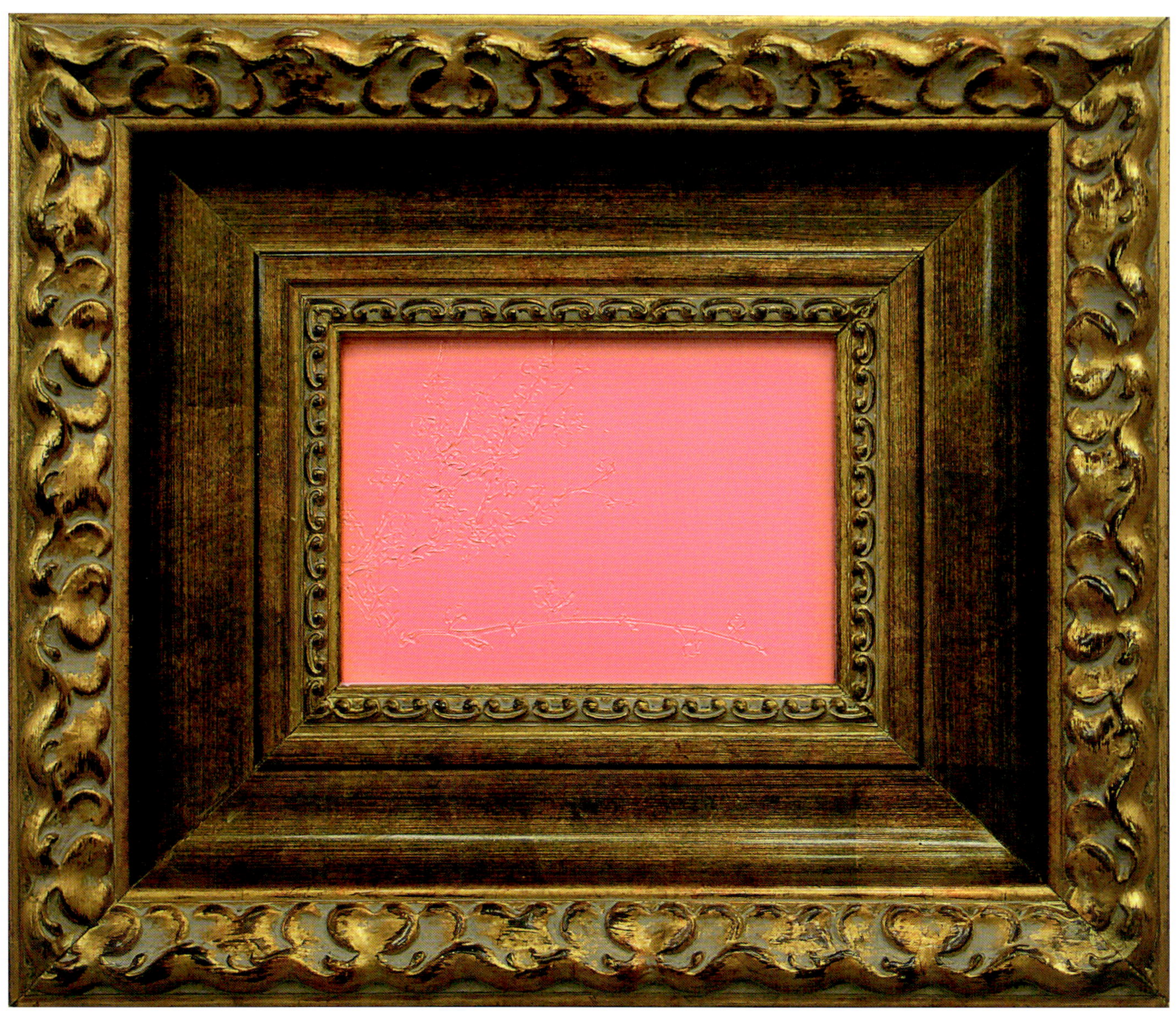

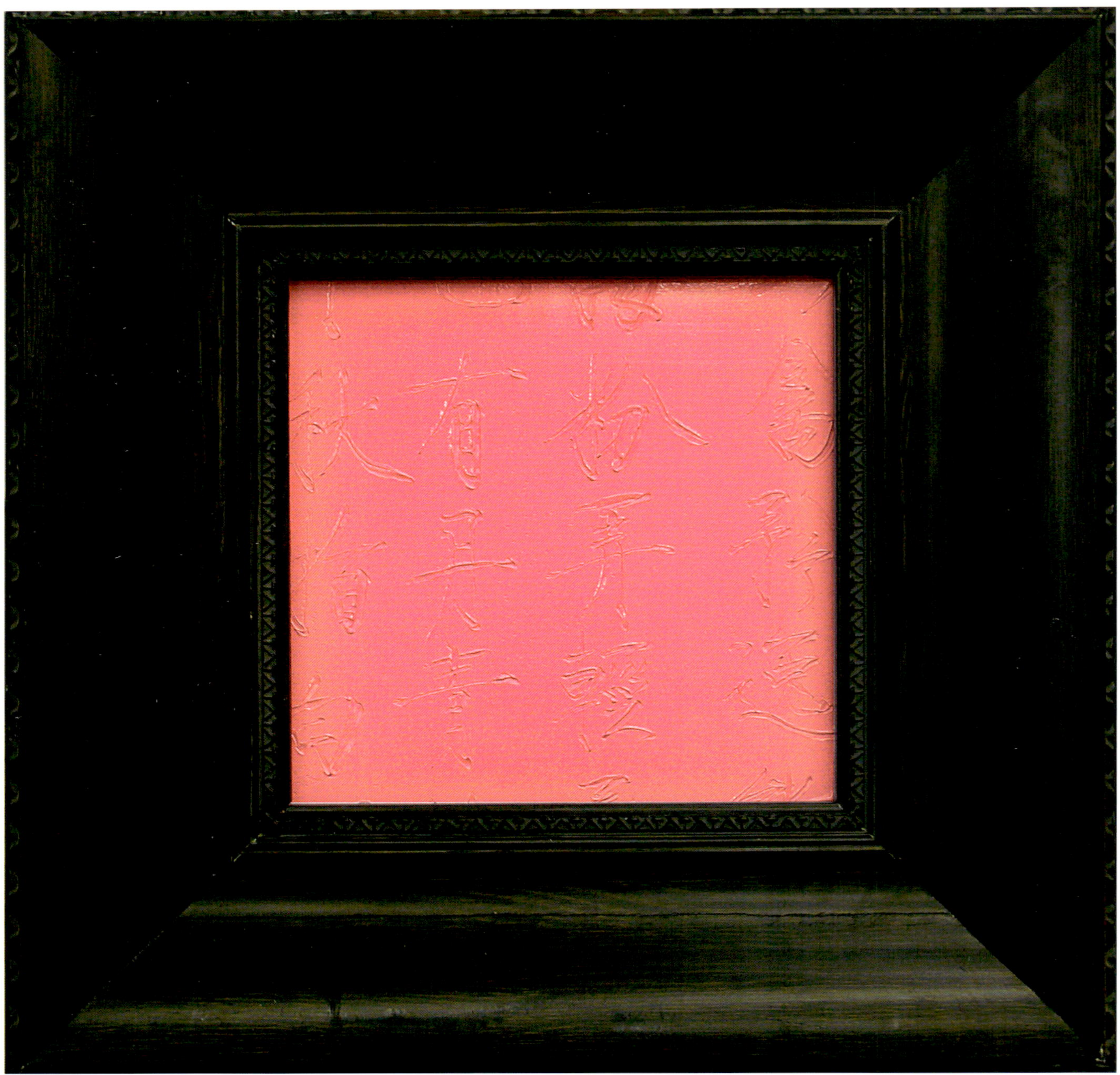

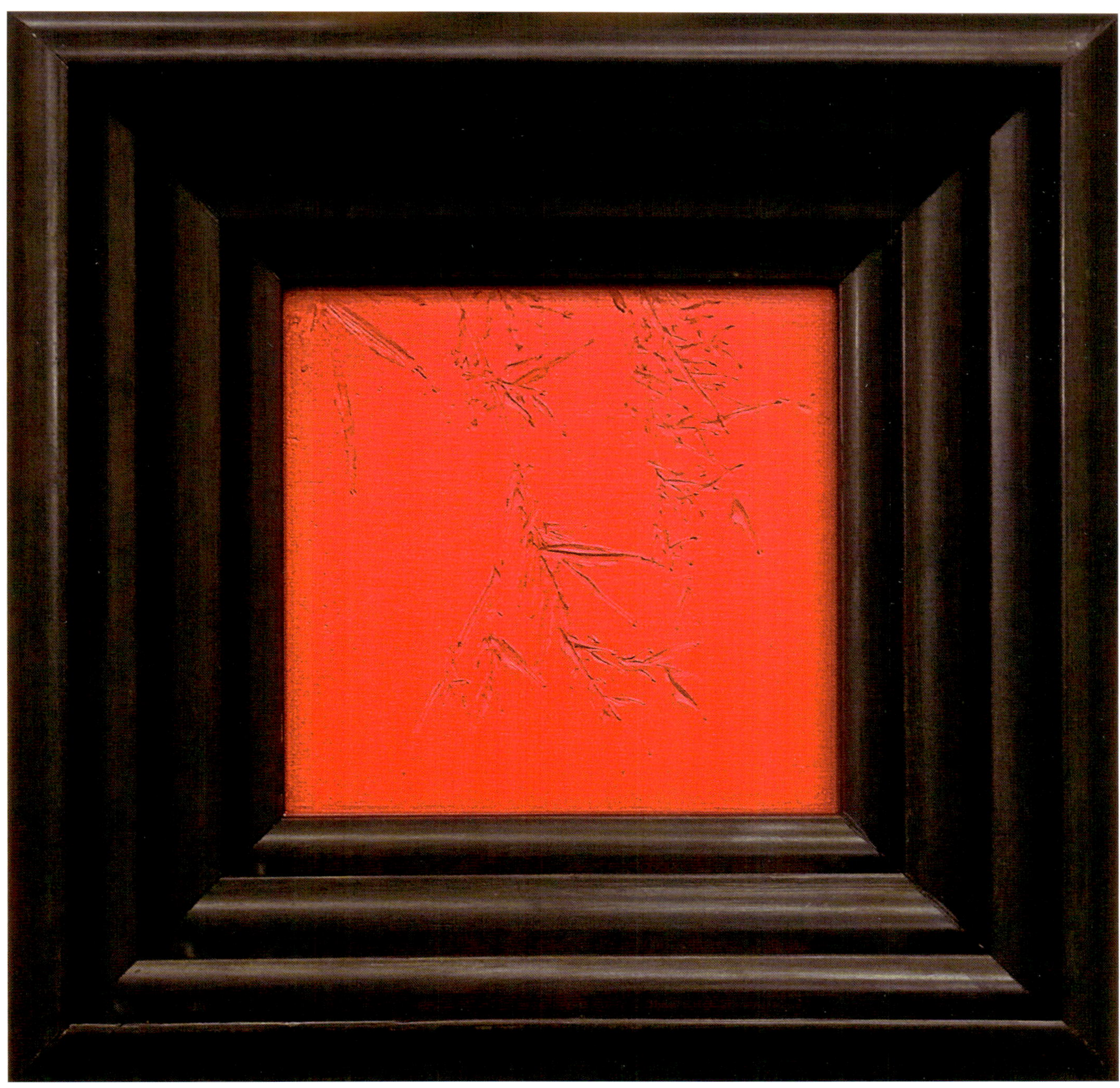

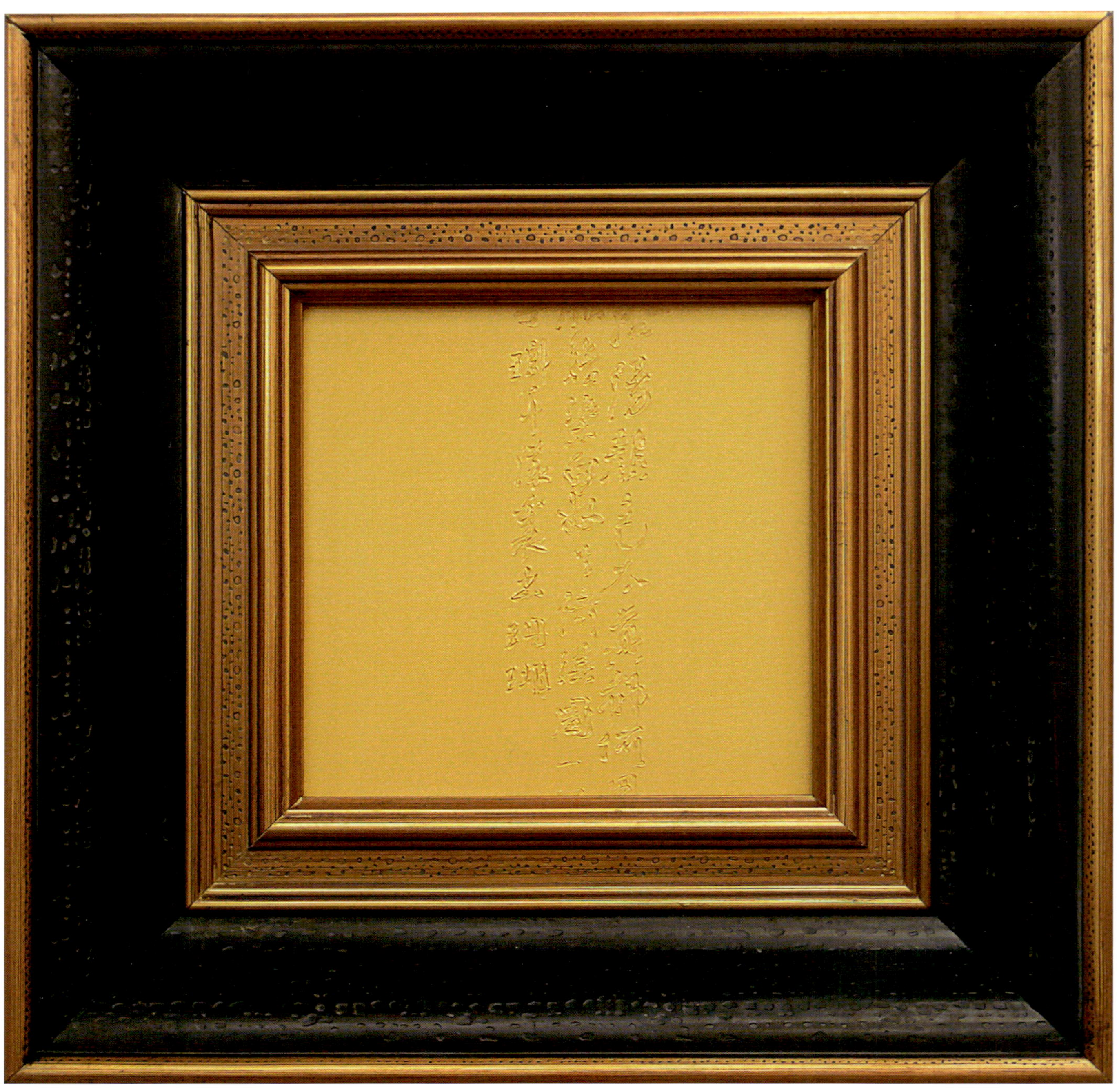

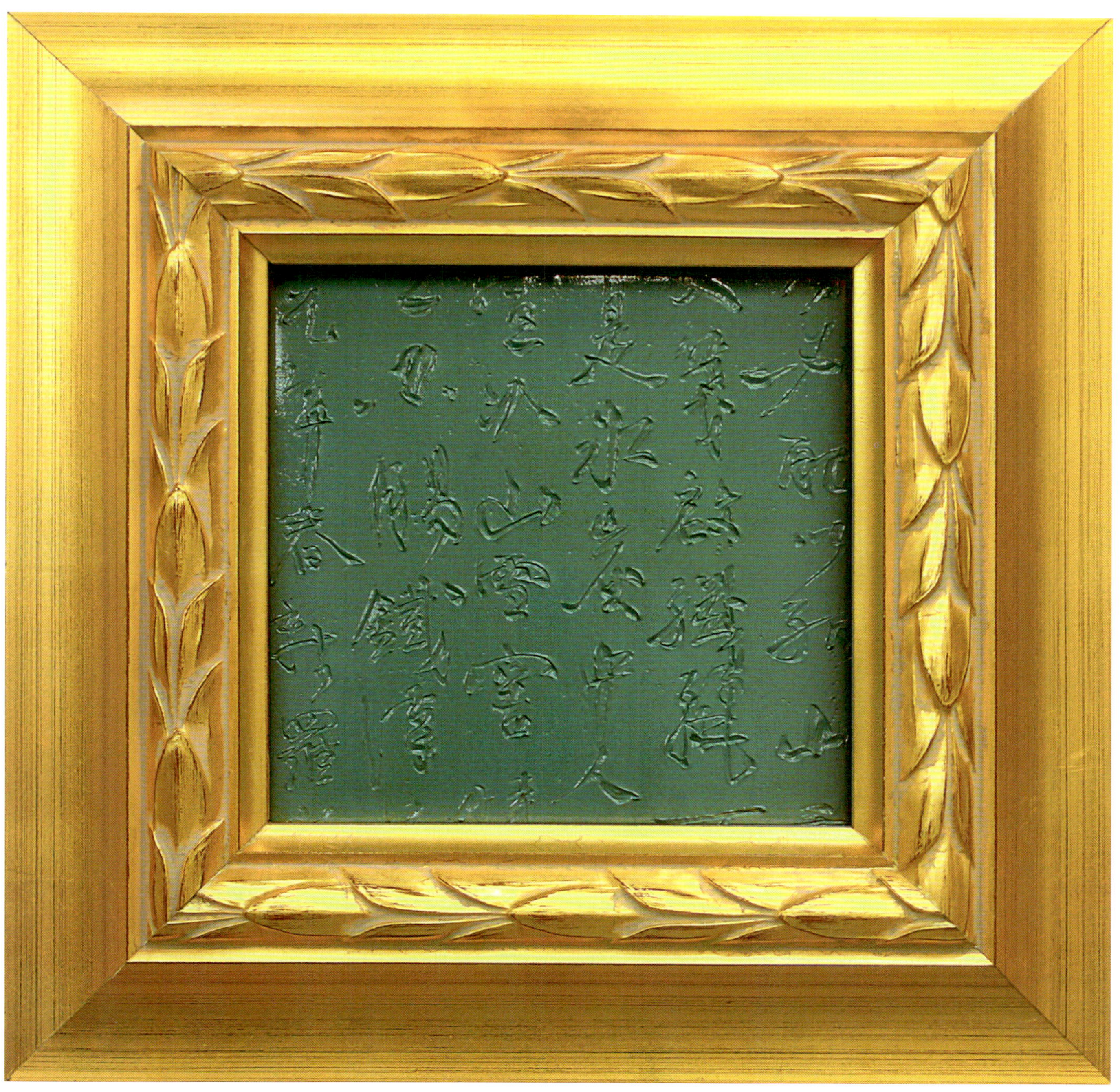

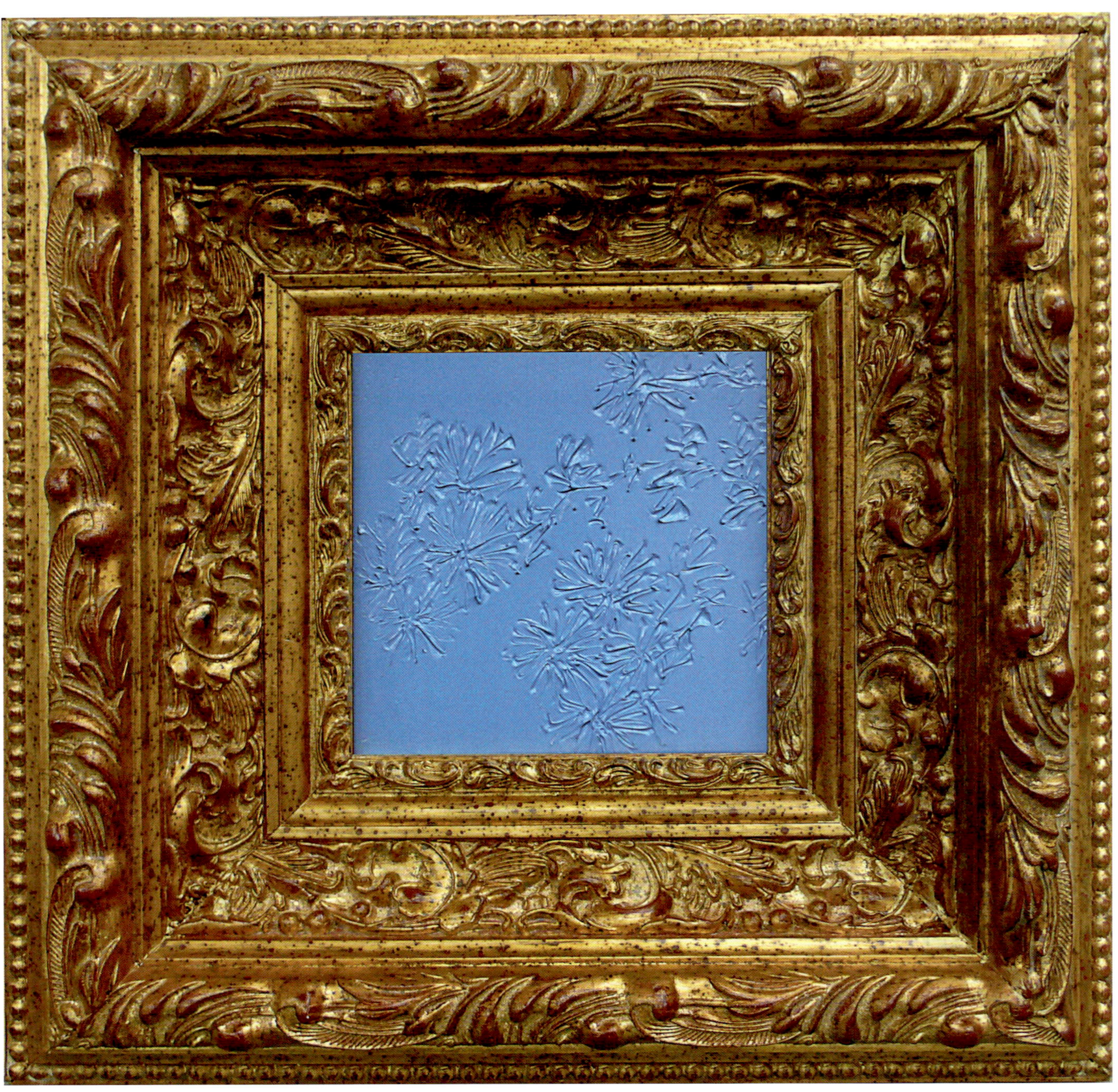

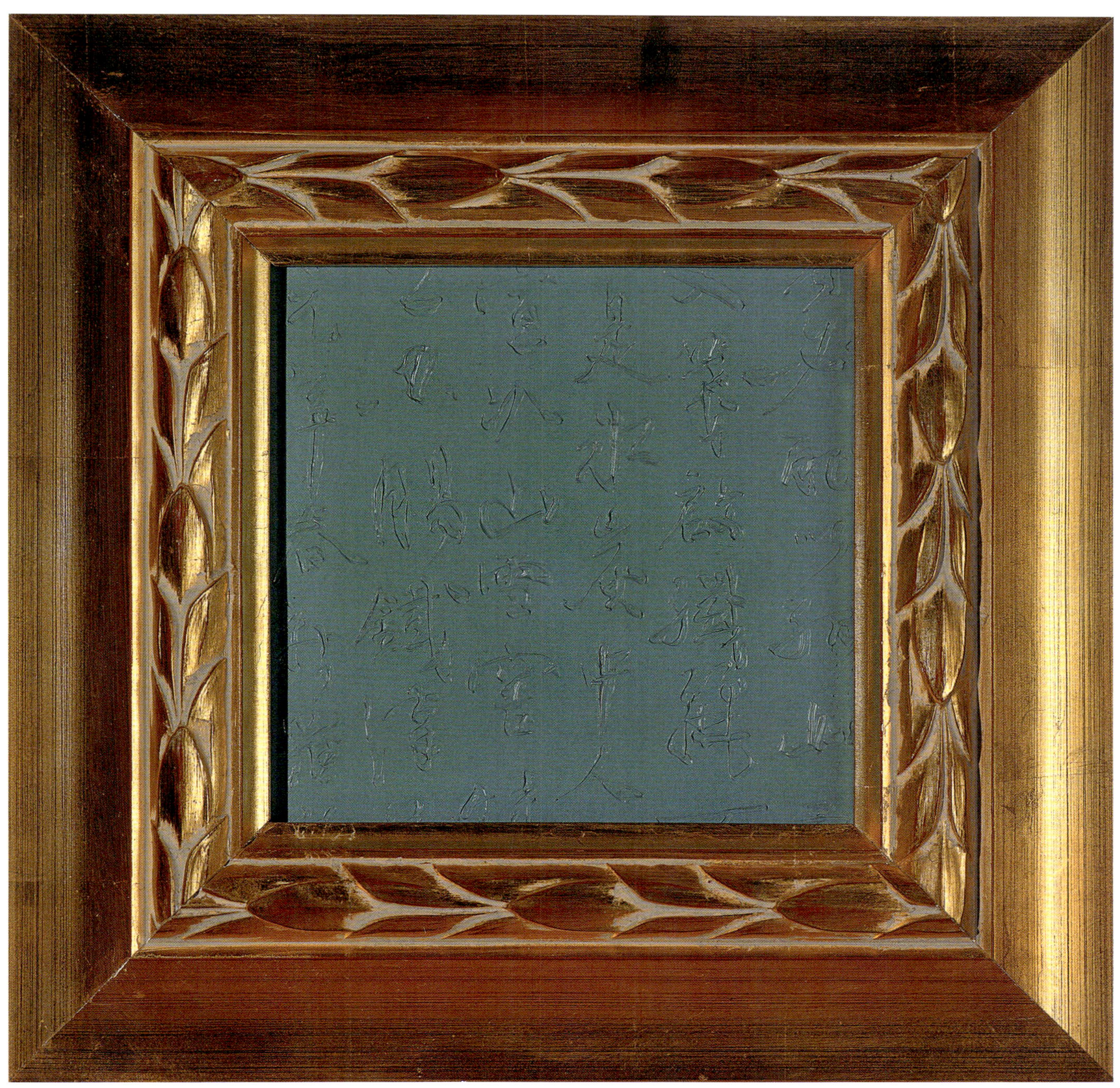

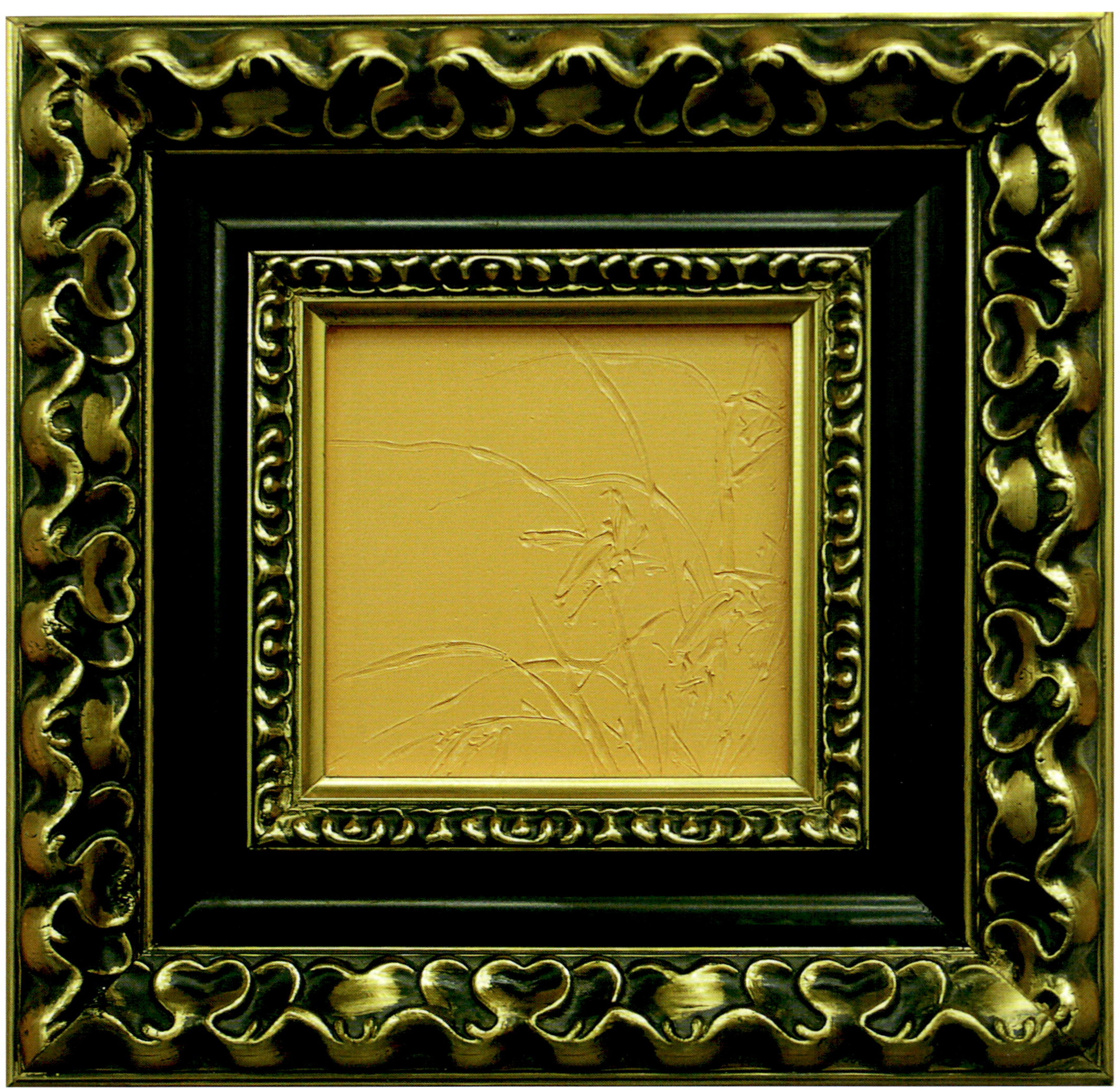

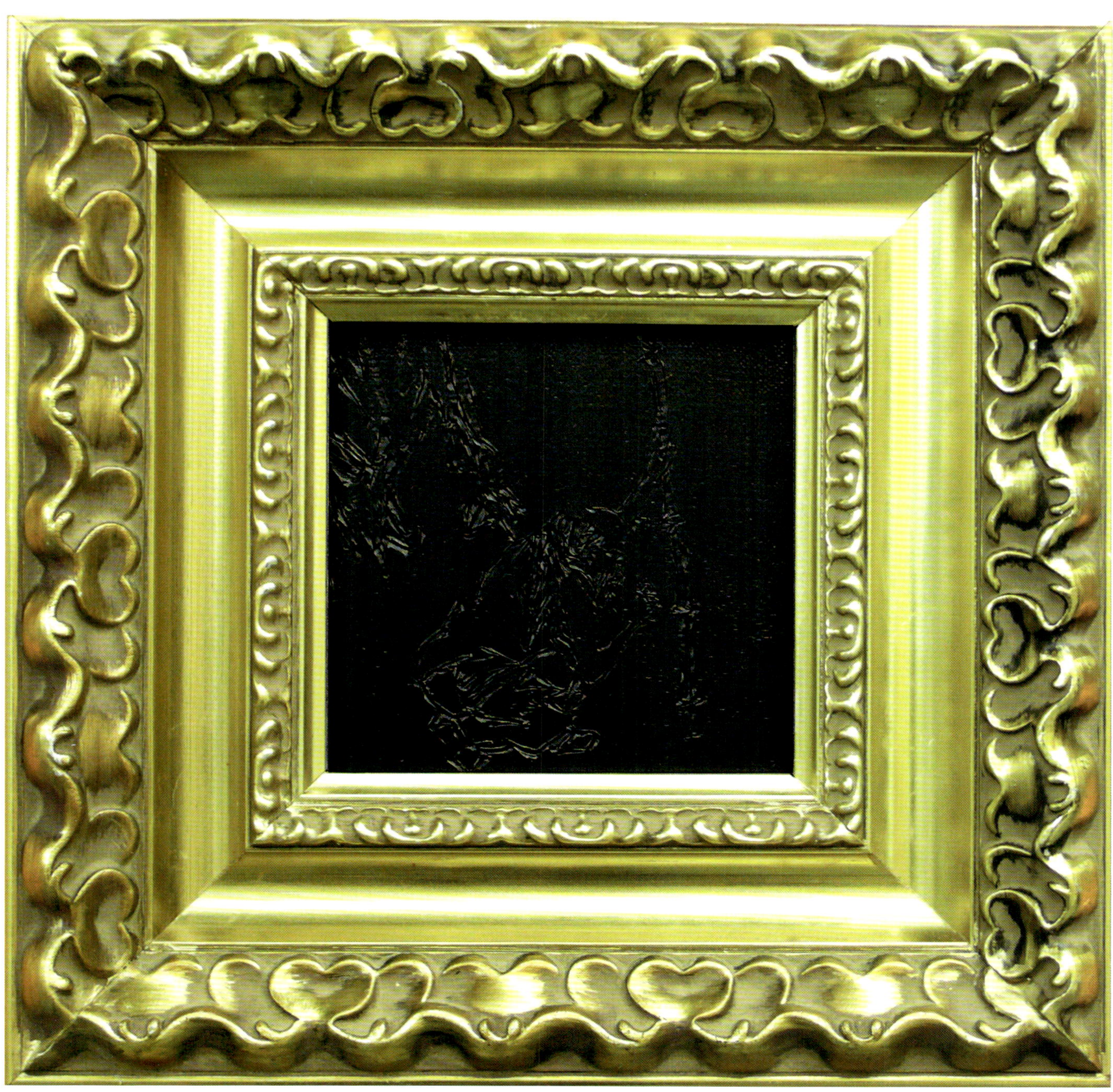

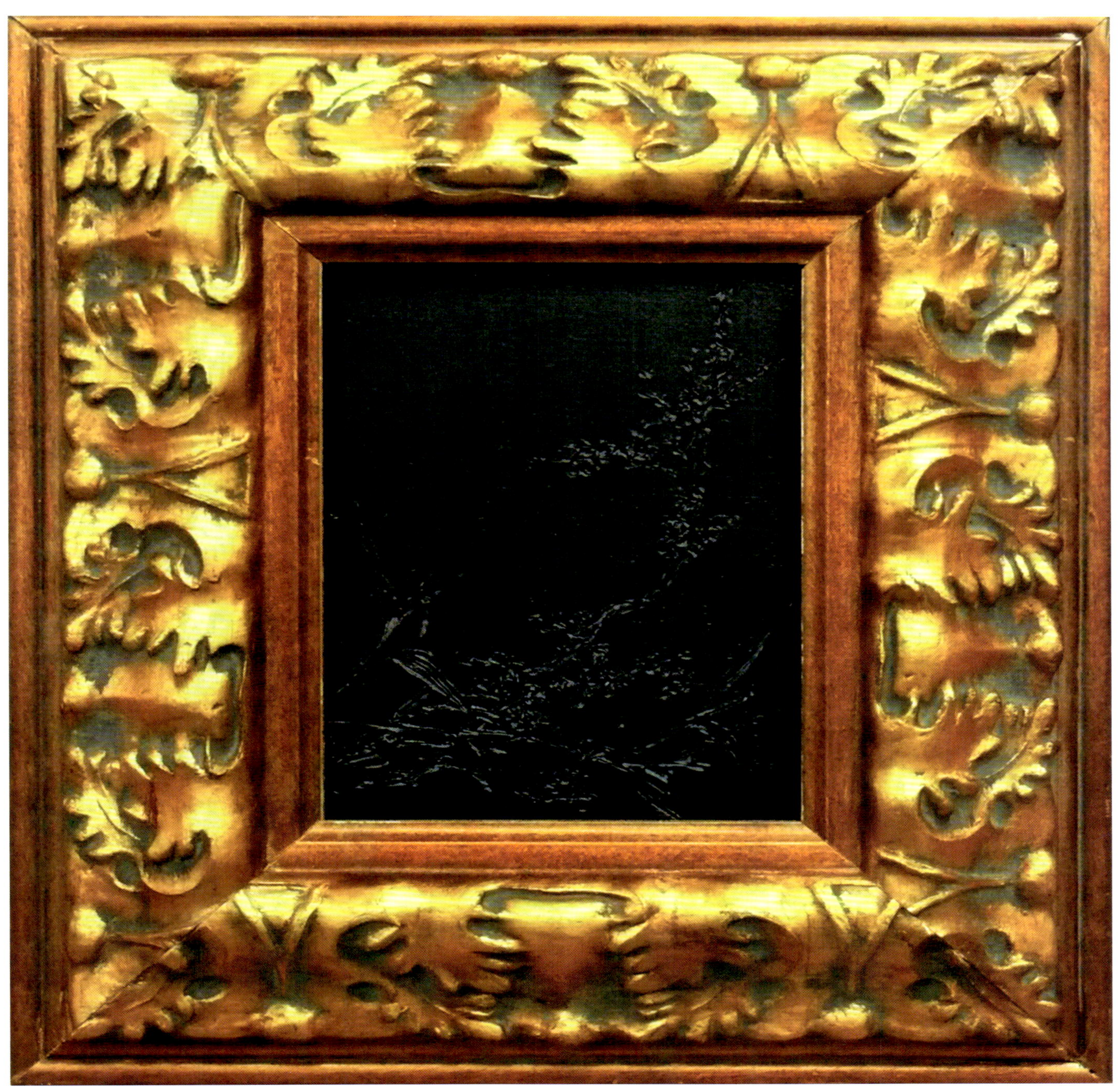

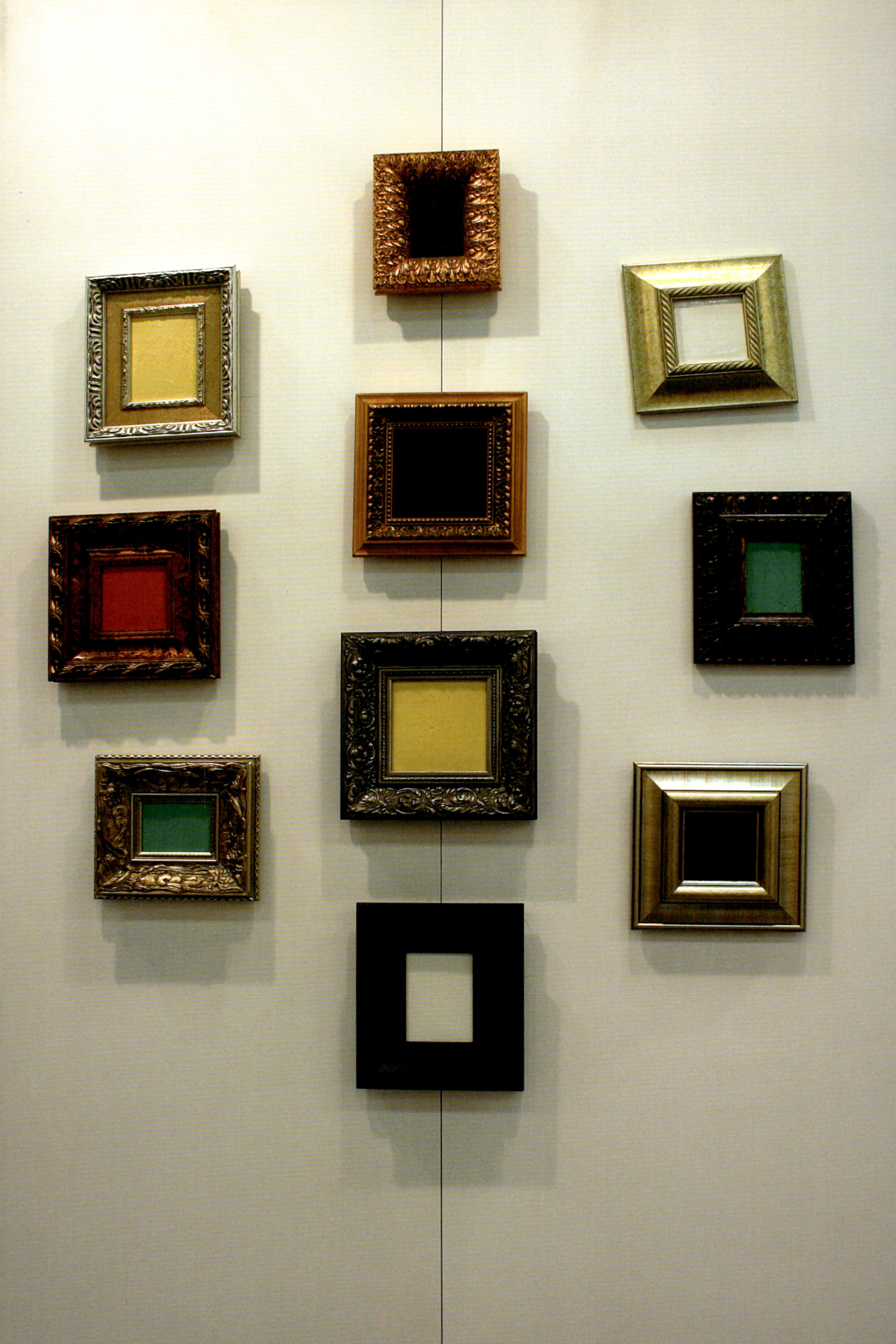

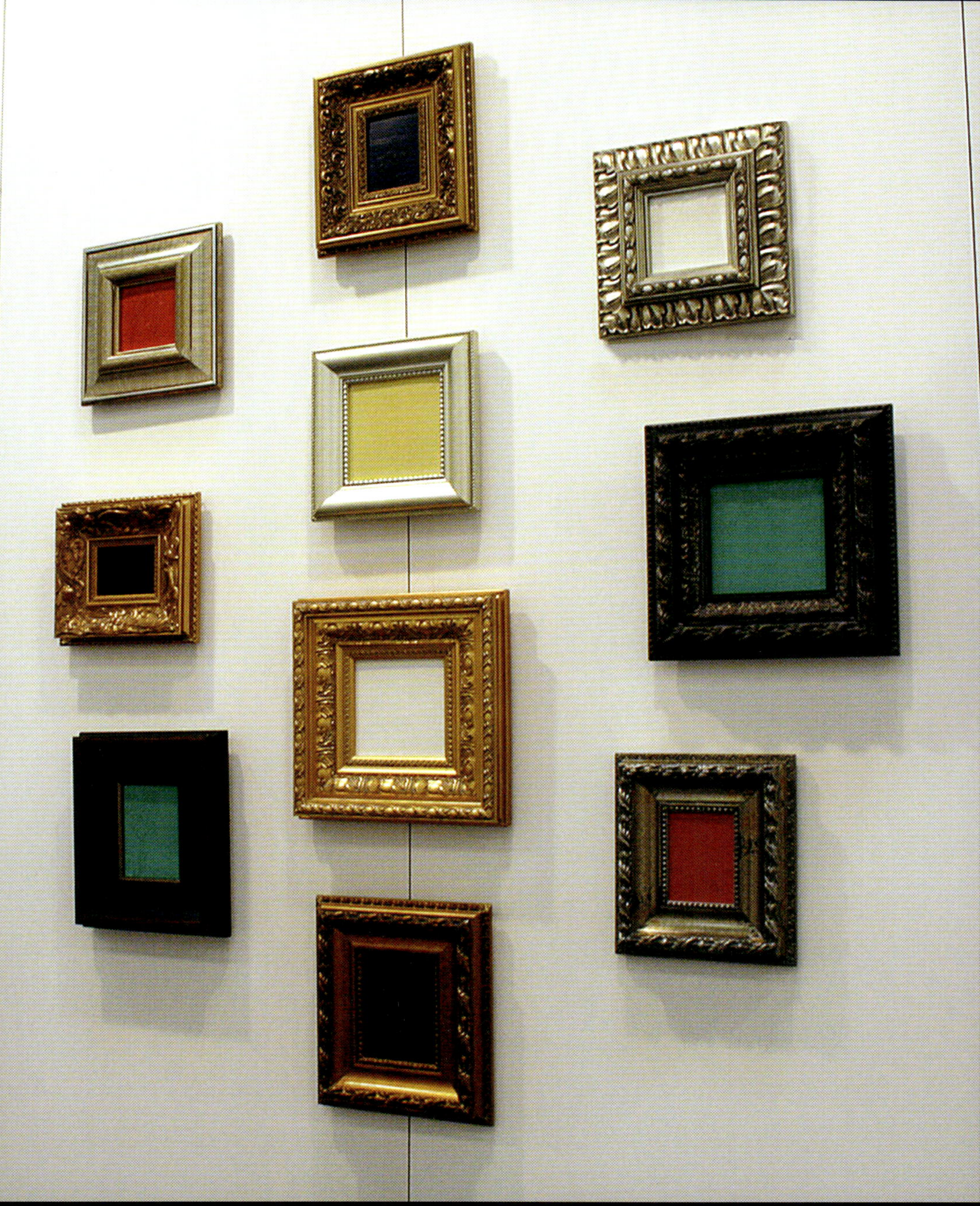

Landscape Series I
paintings
old style frames
variable dimension
2009

Landscape Series II
paintings
old style frames
variable dimension
2009

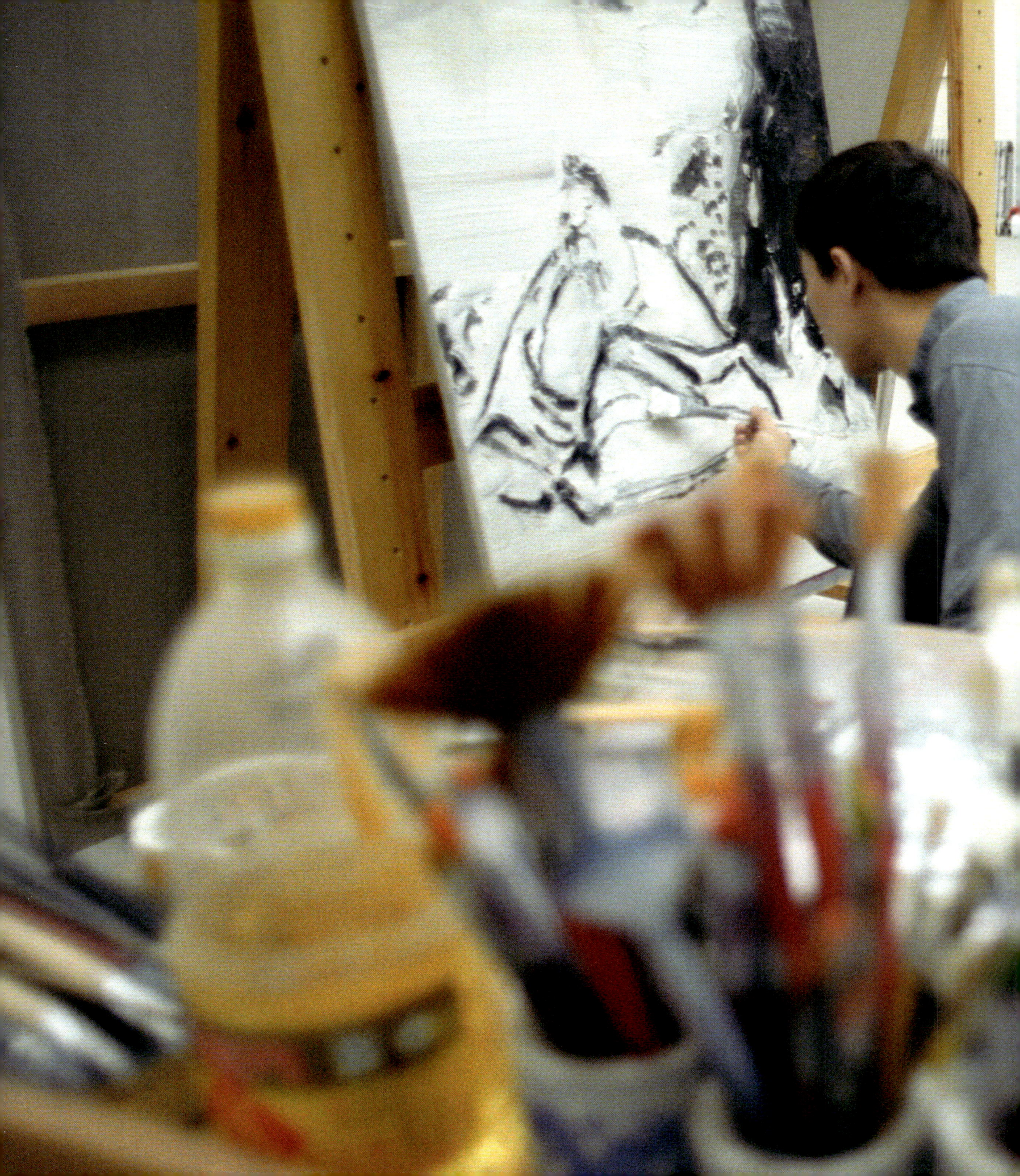

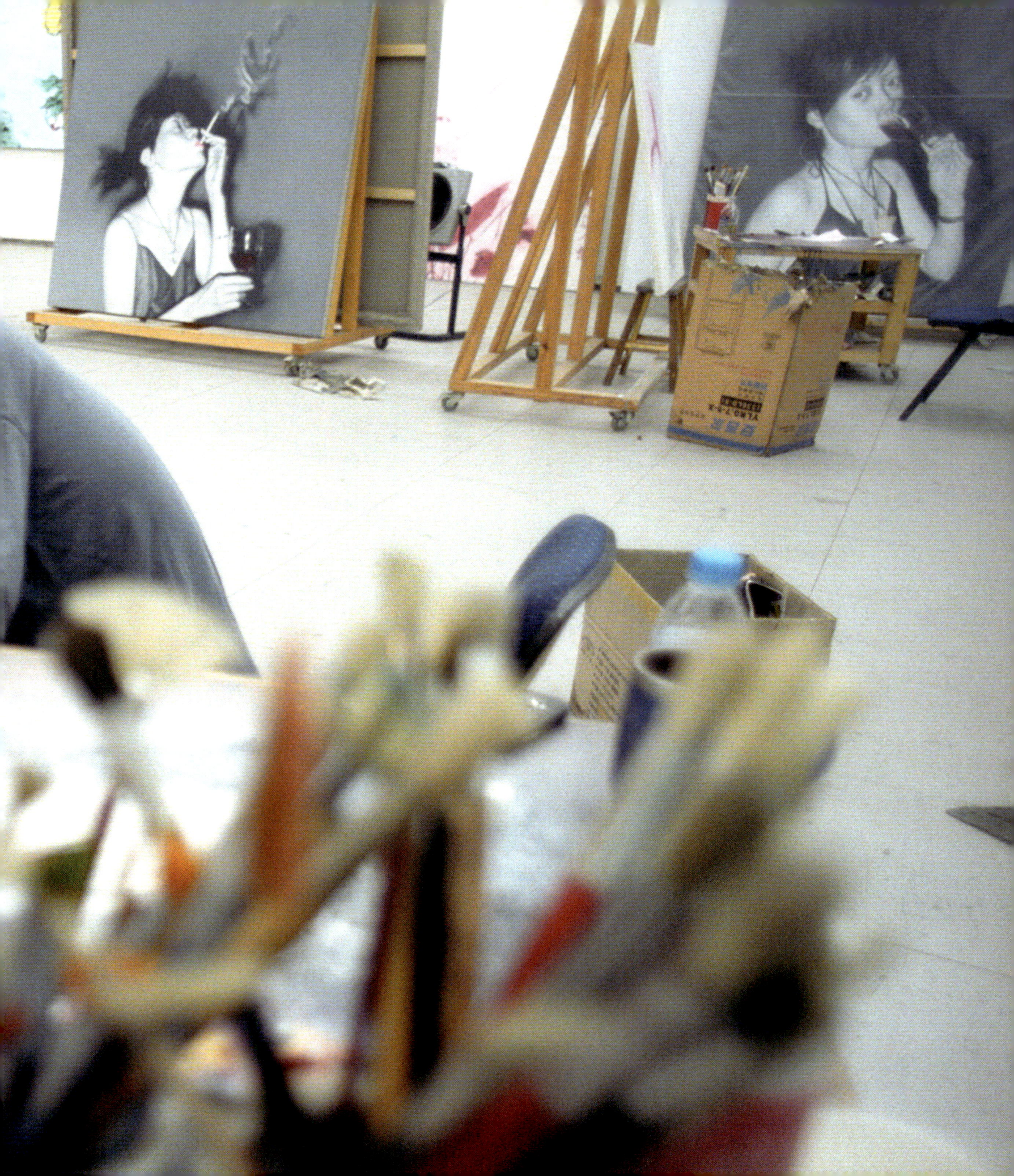

Biography

1968 Born in Yunnan Province
1989 Graduated from the Sichuan Academy of Fine Arts, Dept. of Art Education
Present Professional artist living in Beijing

EXHIBITION
2010 He Sen – Scenari Illusori – Primo Marella Gallery, Milan, Italy

2009-2010 Cina. Rinascita Contemporanea – Palazzo Reale, Milan, Italy

2009 The Second Reality – Chinese Contemporary Art Group Exhibition Meridian International Center, Washington, USA
Senchung – Kukjie Gallery, Seul, Korea
The Outsiders – Marella Gallery, Milan, Italy
Asian Contemporary Art, Rudolf Budja Galerie/ Artmosphere Galerien, Wien, Austria
Venice Biennale, Venice, Italy
Metropolis Now! — A Selection of Chinese Contemporary Art ÐThe Meridian International Center, Washington, D.C.
Best Print Collection of HeSen,A Story Gallery,Busan (SOLO)

2008 Do You Have Time Tonight, Galerie Frank Schlag & Cie, Essen, Germany (solo)
Come Together, Jack Tilton Gallery, New York, USA (solo)
"Rendez-Vous", Marella Gallery, Beijing, China
Beyond Reality, Beyond Art Space, Beijing, China
La Cina e' Vicina, Pan-Palazzo delle Arti di Napoli, Naples, It
Free Zone: China, BSI Art Collection, Lugano, Italy
Artists in Art History, SZ Art Center, Beijing, China
Painting Rebellion, Gallery TN, Beijing, China
86 Steps to Nine Layers Heaven, Beyond Art Space, Beijing, China
Today's China, Belvue Museum, Brussels, Belgium
3rd Nanjing Triennial, The Nanjing Museum, Nanjing, China

2007 Now and Then, Art Now Gallery, Beijing, China (solo)
Remixed & Revisited: New Visions on China, Arndt Partner, Zurich, Switzerland
Starting from the Southwest Exhibition of Contemporary Art in Southwest China 1985-2007 Guangdong Museum of Art, China
Guiyang Biennale, Guiyang Museum, China
Made in China-Contemporary Chinese Art, Louisiana Museum, Copenhagen, Denmark
Simple Immense, Mun Gallery, Beijing, China
From New Figurative Image to New Painting, Tang Contemporary Art, Beijing, China
Black White Grey-A Conscious Cultural Stance, Today Art Museum, Beijing, China

Floating-New Generation of Art in China, National Museum of Contemporary Art, Seoul, Korea
Summer Exhibition, O-Gallery, Beijing, China
On the Yellow Sea, Gallery A Story, Seoul, Korea
A Wakening From A Ten-Year Long Sleep, HJY Art Center, Beijng, China

2006 Vanity Beauties, Marella Gallery, Beijing, China
"Unclear and Clearness", Chinese Contemporary Art Exhibition
ARCO 06, Madrid, Spain
"Made in China", Opera Gallery, London, England
Heyri Art Space, Seoul, Korea
JIANG HU, Tilton Gallery, New York, Los Angeles
Basel Art Fair, Basel, Switzerland
Varied Images, Invitation Exhibition of China's Contemporary Paintings, Shanghai Art Museum, Shanghai, China
The Blossoming of Realism-The Oil Painting of Mainland China since 1978, Taipei Fine Arts Museum, Taipei

2005 Cina. Pittura Contemporanea, Bologna, Padova, Torino
The Second Triennial of Chinese Art, The Nanjing Museum, Nanjing, China
Grounding Reality, Seoul Art Center, Seoul, Korea
Good Girls, Bad Girls, Red Mansion Foundation, London, England
Born in China, Goedhuis Contemporary, New York & London

2004 Post-revolution and New Generation, Chinablue Gallery Beijing, China
China Avant Garde, Vanessa Art House, Jakarta, Indonesia
(11+1) – Crowds and Voids, Art Scene Warehouse, Shanghai, China
China's Photographic Painting, China Art Seasons Gallery, Beijing, China
New Perspectives in Chinese Painting, Marella Art Contemporary, Milan, Italy
The First Nominative Exhibition of Fine Arts Literature, Hubei Academy of Fine Arts Museum, Hubei Province, China
Shadow Shaped, Beijing Art Now Gallery, China
Hua Jia Di, China Art Seasons Gallery, Beijing, China
Wuhan The First Nominative Exhibition of Fine Arts Literature, Hubei Academy of Fine Arts Museum, Wuhan, China
Beijing Chongqing Shanghai-Painting And Photography, Gallery Karin Sachs, Munich, Germany

2003 Girl. Toy. Smoke, Red Gate Gallery, Beijing, China
Out of the Red—China Art Now, Marella Art Contemporary, Milano, Trevi Flash Art Museum, Perugia, Italy

Modernization and Urbanization, Opening Seoul-Asia Art Now Exhibition, Marronnier Art Center, Seoul, Korea
Post-revolution and New Generation, Chinablue Gallery Beijing, China
New York Asia International Art Fair, New York
"Golden Harvest – Chinese Contemporary Art", National Museum of Contemporary, Zagreb, Croatia
"He Sen Solo Exhibition", Piltzer Gallery, Paris, France

2002 He Sen – Marella Gallery, Milan, Italy

2001 "On Boys and Girls", UpRiver Loft, Kunming Soobin Art Gallery, Singapore
"Up Down Left Right", Chengdu Contemporary Arts Museum, Chengdu, China
1st Chengdu Biennale, Chengdu Contemporary Arts Museum, Chengdu, China Berlin Art Fair, Berlin, Germany

2000 „Gate of the Century 1979-1999", Chinese Art Invitation Exhibition, Shanghai, China
„Individual and Society in Art", Guangdong Art Museum, Guangzhou, China
Melbourne Art Fair, Australia
Women's Portraits, Red Gate Gallery, Beijing (SOLO) , China

1999 "Sharp New Sights from Young Artists Born around 1970", Beijing, China
Shanghai Art Fair, Shanghai, China

1997 "The First Academic Exhibition of Chinese Contemporary Art", Beijing/ Hong Kong, China

1995 "The 3rd Annual Exhibition of Chinese Oil Painting", Beijing, China
"Urban Idealist – New Art from Sichuan", Hong Kong, China
Chinese Contemporary Oil Paintings: From Realism to Post Modernism", Theoremes Gallery, Brussels, Belgium

1994 "Sliced", Chongqing, China

1993 "The First Biennial Exhibition of Chinese Oil Painting", Beijing, China

1992 First Annual Exhibition of Chinese Oil Painting, Hong Kong, China
"The First Biennial Art Exhibition", Guangzhou, China
"The Second Documentary Exhibition of Chinese Contemporary Art", Guangzhou, China
Fist Exhibition, Chongqing (SOLO), China

1989 Sichuan Provincial Fine Art Exhibition, Provincial Gallery, Chengdu, China

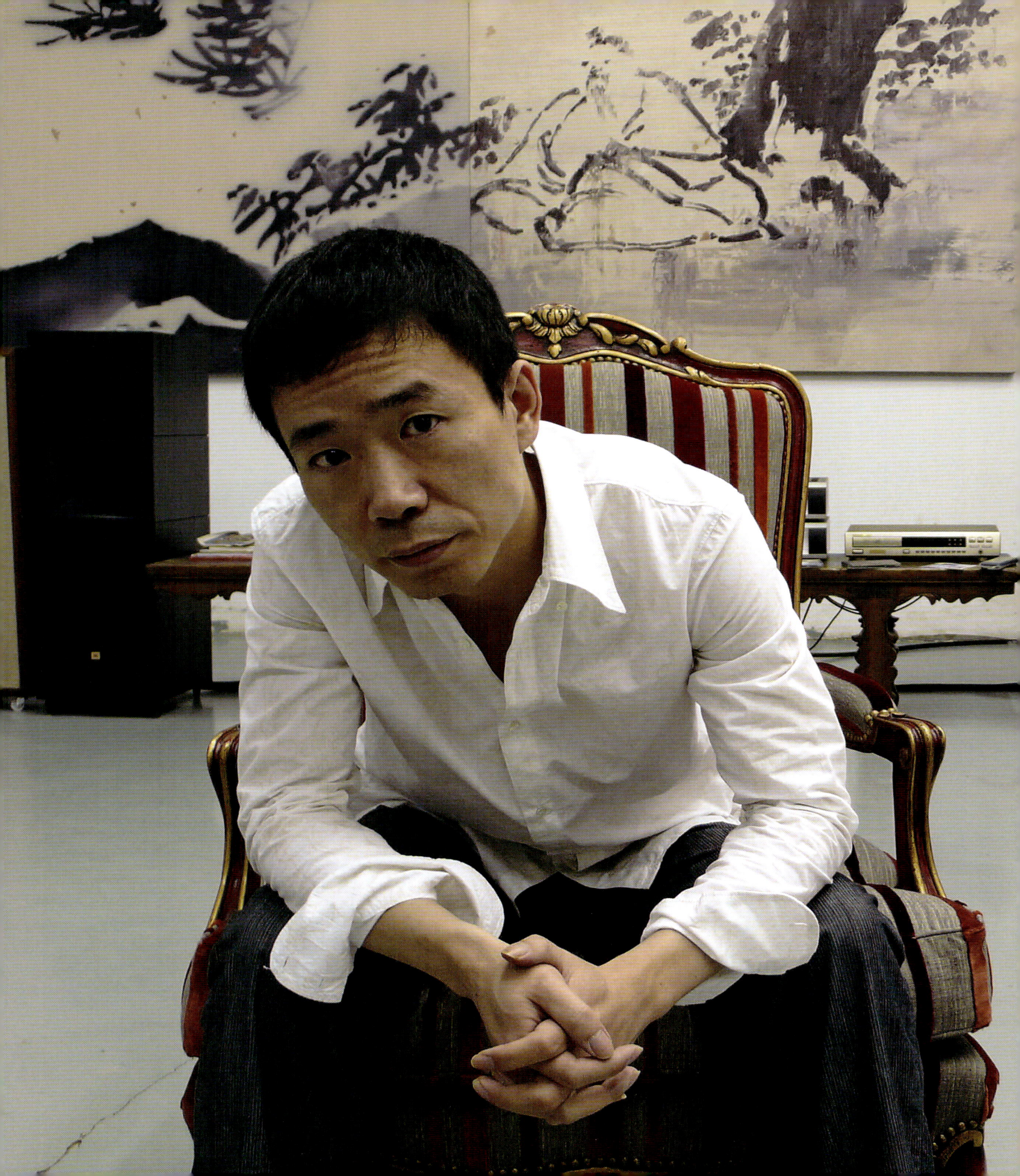

Acknowledgements

Primo Marella Gallery - Milan
Livia Facchetti
Elena Micheletti
Ruggero Ruggieri
Elisa Tumminello

Primo Marella Gallery - Beijing
Eleonora Battiston
Michela Sena

Special thanks to
Logistica Tecnofreight, especially to
Matteo Saponaro, for their precious
collaboration

This book is published on
the occasion of the exhibition:
"He Sen. Scenari illusori"
Primo Marella Gallery, Milan
8th April - 28th May 2010